QUEERING ELEMENTARY EDUCATION

CURRICULUM, CULTURES, AND (HOMO)SEXUALITIES

Edited by James T. Sears

QUEERING
ELEMENTARY EDUCATION

*Advancing the Dialogue
about Sexualities and Schooling*

Edited by
William J. Letts IV
and
James T. Sears

ROWMAN & LITTLEFIELD PUBLISHERS, INC.
Lanham • Boulder • New York • Oxford

ROWMAN & LITTLEFIELD PUBLISHERS, INC.

Published in the United States of America
by Rowman & Littlefield Publishers, Inc.
4720 Boston Way, Lanham, Maryland 20706
http://www.rowmanlittlefield.com

12 Hid's Copse Road
Cumnor Hill, Oxford OX2 9JJ, England

British Library Cataloguing in Publication Information Available

Library of Congress Cataloging-in-Publication Data

Queering elementary education : advancing the dialogue about
    sexualities and schooling / edited by William J. Letts IV and James
    T. Sears
        p.   cm.—(Curriculum, cultures, and (homo)sexualities)
    Includes bibliographical references and index.
    ISBN 0-8476-9368-6 (cloth : alk. paper).—ISBN 0-8476-9369-4
    (pbk. : alk. paper)
    1. Homosexuality and education—United States.   2. Education,
Elementary—Social aspects—United States.   3. Education,
Elementary—United States—Curricula.   4. Sex instruction—United
States.   I. Letts, William J., 1965– .   II. Sears, James T.
(James Thomas), 1951– .   III. Series.
LC192.6.Q85   1999
371'.01'1—dc21   99-23762
                                                           CIP

Printed in the United States of America

♾ ™ The paper used in this publication meets the minimum requirements of
American National Standard for Information Sciences—Permanence of Paper
for Printed Library Materials, ANSI/NISO Z39.48–1992.

CONTENTS

FOREWORD

As I sit at my computer, CNN flickers in the background. The latest horrifying news out of Littleton, Colorado, is being broadcast. Like the commentators, I am shocked. Like my fellow citizens, I am horrified. But unlike most of the people I see on TV, I am not surprised—just as I was not shocked last fall when Matthew Shepard was tied to a Wyoming fence and beaten to death because of his sexual orientation, or last summer when James Byrd was dragged to his death down a Texas roadway because of his race. I wish I could be surprised by acts of hatred and violence, but I'm not.

When I was a first-year teacher in 1985 I went to a workshop where the trainer uttered words I've never forgotten. "Children will live up to the expectations you set for them," he said. This inspired me to challenge my students to believe in their abilities, and to help them achieve more than they (and sometimes even I) often thought was possible at first. It became the driving force of my educational philosophy. In the end I am convinced it's the main reason I was successful during the ten years I spent in the classroom.

It's also why I am not surprised when I learn of acts of violence and hatred, whether they take place in Colorado, Wyoming, Texas, or my own city of New York. Unfortunately, too often we do not set even a basic level of expectation for our students when it comes to respecting others. We remain silent in the face of intolerance. We do little to teach the values of equality and justice. We simply fail to set any kind of expectation at all that these young people must respect each other, even (especially?) when the differences among them are vast and profound.

Nowhere is this failure more evident than when it comes to antigay prejudice, and nowhere is that particular failure more manifest than it is in our elementary schools. Ask any elementary-school teachers you know and—if they're honest—they'll tell you they start hearing it as soon as kindergarten. They hear it on the playgrounds, during recess, at milk time, in the hallways. They hear it when children are playing, when they're socializing, when they think no adults are listening. They hear it all the time. Face it: "That's so gay" has become the mantra of elementary-school children, a mantra invoked whenever a child encounters something or someone they do not like or understand or appreciate. As one third-grader put it plainly when asked by her teacher what "gay" meant: "I don't know. It's just a bad thing."

When eight-year-olds already know that "gay" equals "bad," we shouldn't be surprised if, when they get old enough and mean enough, they act out that message by tying one of their peers to a fence and beating him to death. We'd like to imagine that the people who do such things are aberrations, exceptions to the rule. In part this is true—clearly anyone (even a deeply prejudiced person) who is driven to kill is atypical. But the hatred and attitudes they express are not the exception—they *are* the rule. And we shouldn't be surprised when troubled people vent their rage in murderous fashion on those they have learned it is okay to hate. After all, they're only acting out the lessons they learned in third grade.

I'll admit that, in a world populated by the likes of Jesse Helms and Gary Bauer and Pat Buchanan, we can't blame our schools for all of the prejudice we see visited upon queer people. After all, when the senate majority leader compares us to kleptomaniacs, it's hard to blame bigotry entirely on one's third-grade teacher (although one wonders exactly who Mr. Lott had for *his* teachers, given the profound level of ignorance that pours forth from his mouth). Children learn prejudice from many sources—their families, the media, religious institutions—the list could go on. But the fact remains that schools are the place where children spend more of their time than anywhere else between the ages of five and eighteen, and thus play a seminal role in either confirming prejudice or combating it. It's the first public place our citizenry shares, and as such is the crucible where democratic values are put to the test. It's the place where we either learn to get along or learn to hate. Too often it's the place where prejudice becomes ingrained.

Despite the self-evident need for antiprejudice education and the obvious fact that we must start teaching the lesson of respect as early as possible, we still hear complaints from our opponents that we are foisting some kind of "agenda" on the schools (as if equality and justice were some kind of "special rights" instead of the birthrights of the American people). As the head of the largest organization in the country dedicated to ending antigay bias in K–12 schools, I often find myself confronted with people who attack me for "bringing this issue into the schools." How laughable this statement is, I often think. The reality is that this issue—antigay bigotry—is already in our schools. It's not only in our schools, it's pervasive, it's rampant, it's out of control. Little kids are learning to hate, and they're learning it right now, in elementary schools across America. It's not a question of whether or not we should "bring this issue into our schools." It's a question of whether or not we are going to address an issue that is om- nipresent in our schools. If we mean it when we make students pledge al- legiance to a flag that promises "liberty and justice for all" at the start of each school day, then the choice is clear: We must address antigay bigotry, and we must do it as soon as students start going to school.

In this groundbreaking volume of plainly written, cutting-edge schol- arship, Will Letts and Jim Sears have pointed us down the path to a brighter tomorrow. Here they bring together a diverse range of writers who offer both theoretical constructs and practical advice to those who believe our schools should actively foster the values of justice. *Queering Elementary Ed- ucation* gives us tools we need to move ahead. The sweeping nature of the essays—addressing issues of race, the perspectives of students, parents, and teachers, the challenges of different disciplines, and a host of other mat- ters—offers invaluable breadth and depth. From Davis's challenge to the twin images of the "hypersexualized" black youth / "sissy boy" and Rofes's questioning of the canon that gay teachers make no difference, to the telling narratives of lesbian parenthood by Marinoble and Danish, this far-reach- ing volume throws down the gauntlet. In unison, the contributors have said, "If you want to address antigay bigotry in elementary schools, there's a way." I now challenge you, the readers—and, through you, thousands of schools across the country—to answer this question: Now that Will, Jim, and their contributors have shown us the way, do you have the will?

As the latest report from Colorado fades from my television, I am sad- dened to think that some day soon there will doubtless be a fresh tragedy that will horrify and stun our nation. But I am made hopeful by the work of the educators who have contributed to this volume—scholars often doing this as a labor of love, for their work is too cutting edge to allow them to feed at the fellowship trough that more conventional scholars and teachers feast upon—that a brighter day will dawn soon. Students indeed will live up to the expectations we set for them. Let's start setting the ex- pectation that you must value every human being as a precious gift, that you must respect even those you disagree with, that you must treasure the differences among us, as soon as possible. The sooner we teach those les- sons, the sooner we'll be spared future tragedies, and the sooner we can all turn on our televisions and go to our schools and walk down our streets without fear. It's a day to which I look forward.

Kevin Jennings
Executive Director
The Gay, Lesbian, and Straight
Education Network (GLSEN)

PREFACE

In the summer of 1997 Will Letts and I met at a sidewalk café in West Hollywood. Here, in a community where being queer is not, we talked about how the educational landscape had changed since I and others first challenged the homophobia and heterosexism that permeated this nation's colleges and high schools. Though much still needs to be done (especially in my homeland south of the Mason-Dixon line), great strides have been made for queer youth. However, for those attending or working in elementary schools the heteronormative routine has changed little since my school days with Dick and Jane. On that afternoon *Queering Elementary Education* was conceived.

Queering Elementary Education? More than a few bookstore browsers and even some educators for social justice may take issue with this title. Isn't "queer" a word that dares not speak its name? Why do we have to bring sex into elementary education? Isn't this further evidence of "the homosexual agenda"?

Language has the power to bracket our everyday understandings of our lifeworlds. This volume challenges assumptions about teaching, childhood, race and gender, and families. Collectively, the authors of these twenty-two essays ask simple questions that raise fundamental issues, such as: Are gay and lesbian teachers good? What is a family? Who makes a girl or a boy?

This is the first in a series of books under the general heading, Curriculum, Cultures, and (Homo)Sexualities. Written in an intelligible, thoughtful, and clear manner, each book builds upon a foundation of cultural studies, curriculum studies, and queer theory/gay studies. These books encourage readers to think differently—to think queerly—about schools, sexualities, and cultures. In the process, perhaps, we will become more concerned about children's capacity for caring and wisdom and less obsessed with their vocational portfolios or marital futures.

James T. Sears

ACKNOWLEDGMENTS

First, we wish to acknowledge the "queer" teachers, parents, and students (some gay, others not) who enter elementary and middle schools, making them safer places and their communities less intolerant.

Second, our thanks to our friends at Rowman & Littlefield. Publishers are not immune from pressures to closet long-silenced voices. In championing this book and this series, we acknowledge the vision and support of Jill Rothenberg, editor for education and gender studies, and Dean Birkenkamp, senior editor. This book has also been very well served by other members of the Rowman & Littlefield family: Christine Gatliffe, Dorothy Bradley, Rebecca Hoogs, and Sheila Burnett.

We'd like to acknowledge the work of one person who has especially felt the pressure to bend to conformity, the award-winning director of the groundbreaking documentary *It's Elementary*. Debra Chasnoff's vision to develop this film and her courage to challenge those who would mold us into sexual sameness deserve special commendation.

Additionally, Will thanks James Earl Davis, Kathy Schultz, Julie Schmidt, Zoubeida Dagher, Steve Fifield, Deborah Hicks, Sandra Harding, and especially Nancy Brickhouse for all being such wonderful intellectual mentors, such fine examples of "ways of being" in academia, and such great friends. He would also like to thank Taj Carson and Hope Longwell-Grice for being comrades-in-arms in the struggle to get through graduate school, and for sustaining him with intellectual and emotional friendship. Thanks to Julie Cwikla for her invaluable computer assistance and good humor, and especially for helping him out in his hours and hours of need. Will thanks his family, and especially his parents Carolyn and Bill, for raising him in an environment saturated with love, respect, and the encouragement to dream big dreams. This is the type of childhood that this entire volume is about. Thanks for making it a reality. Will dedicates his work on this book to Andrew, Chlöe, and Conor, and all other youngsters who hold the promise for a more democratic and just future.

Jim acknowledges the skilled assistance of Wayne Smalley, his publicist, who has helped promote this book with the same dedication and enthusiasm he brought to *Lonely Hunters* and *Curriculum, Religion, and Public Education*. For the encouragement to write and speak about issues that really matter, and arousing fundamentalist ire and waging Charleston tongues, Jim thanks his longtime companion, Bob.

MATTHEW'S LULLABY

Perry Brass

I have found a home
of my own and people
who will love me as theirs.
I want you to know
that I share their feelings
and we are brothers and sisters
who know what closeness is.
I will need their love
and strength to guard me
in the darkness up ahead,
and though I lie alone
and in cold and pain,
I will hold their warmth
to me. I will ask them
to hug me against the cold
and hold me close and shield my eyes
from hatred and the razor wire
of its cruelty. I will ask them
for water and bread to nourish me,
for wool and flannel and shoes
for my naked feet. We have
so far to go before the cold night sleeps
and for me to awaken in the arms
of my kind brothers. In loneliness
there may be insight, but alone
I cannot feel your warmth with me.
You must come and take me
and lead me back to my bed
and my room. There I will fall asleep

and dream in your arms. There I will
drift into compassionate sleep.
There will I drift
into sweet, compassionate sleep

Tuesday, October 13, 1998
Bronx, New York
for Matthew Shepard,
21 years old, died October 12, 1998

· Part 1 ·

FOUNDATIONAL ISSUES

How does one go about queering elementary education? Why is sexual diversity a critical issue for elementary schools and educators? What is the relationship between the feminization of elementary education and the prevalence of homophobia in schools? This section begins to answer these questions by challenging widely held foundational assumptions about childhood, sexuality, and pedagogy.

The first chapter suggests five elementary propositions to reconceptualize who, what, how we teach. Drawing from anthropology and biology, as well as popular culture and school practice, James Sears details the multiple meanings of "queering elementary education" and "teaching queerly." The task for "queer" educators, he argues, is "creating classrooms that challenge categorical thinking, promote interpersonal intelligence, and foster critical consciousness."

The next chapter details the importance of including (homo)sexualities in elementary schools. Advocating "risky teaching," Kathy Bickmore asserts that "even preschool children have some capacity to understand and talk through conflicts" and "sensitive issues." Decrying the self-censorship typical in elementary classrooms, this essay explores how honest discussions and age-appropriate knowledge are essential curricular elements within an inclusive classroom. It is in this type of classroom that "children may learn, as developing citizens, to question the categories and rules that have formed them, and to create a new world with more democratic space for all."

The iconic image of an elementary schoolteacher is that of a chaste and nurturing female. Lisa Weems examines how the historical construction of the "categories of sex, gender, and sexuality converge in the notion of 'the pedagogy of love'" feminizes teaching and reinscribes "heteronormative boundaries between the normal and the perverse." The result, as she details in chapter 3, is the policing of sexuality ranging from the dismissal of queer teachers to the enforcement of heterosexual identities.

Collectively, these essayists bracket heteronormative assumptions and interrogate the meanings of queerness. In the process, they ready the reader for a revisioning of pedagogy that is at the heart of *Queering Elementary Education*.

1

· 1 ·

TEACHING QUEERLY:
SOME ELEMENTARY PROPOSITIONS

James T. Sears

I was born in a midwestern farming community that had a checkerboard flatness. My world was clearly divided. Adams always followed Jefferson Street; First Avenue never crossed Second. In my town, as in the black-and-white television world of the Andersons, Cleavers, and Nelsons, there were no shades of gray. There were no long-kept secrets. As a white, middle-class male, I learned through my family, my school, and my church how to dress, what to think, and when to repent. I learned that only girls wore dresses and sported stylish long hair. I learned to write within the broad lines of my ruled paper as I sat beneath an American flag and a scantily clothed, crucified Christ. I learned that God punished sinners but loved the repentant. I learned that homosexuality was sinful; that *I* was a sinner.

It has been ten years since I wrote these opening words to *Growing Up Gay in the South,* chronicling the childhood and adolescent lives of thirty-six lesbians, bisexuals, and gay southerners. Two decades earlier I had graduated from elementary school.

In the span of that generation those who are Queer in America have gained voice and visibility, although we continue to experience harassment and reproof. No longer subject to McCarthy-era witch hunts such as those conducted by Florida's infamous Johns Committee (Sears 1997a), we remain barred from serving openly in our country's military, and sodomy statutes are invoked to justify custody decisions. Although homosexuality is more open in our culture, the timidity of curriculum developers and the lure of the closet mean that today's queer youth still experience the feeling of being "the only one in the world." Although homosexual behavior is no longer outlawed in twenty-nine states, only a few, like Wisconsin and Massachusetts, have enacted protections against discrimination on the basis of sexual orientation and translated these protections into school policies.

However, no more than half of those communities with protective legislation have developed curriculum or offered in-service about sexual orientation—and only a handful do at the elementary level (Rienzo, Button, and Wald 1996).

At the cusp of the millennium we continue to squander valuable resources confronting those who disingenuously tag these protections and provisions as "special rights." Meanwhile, a college student is kidnapped, robbed, burned, beaten, and tied in scarecrow fashion to a wooden ranch post on a windswept Laramie range, abandoned to die alone. His generation—like mine and those before—suffer from the silence, neglect, denial, and reproach in dummy-down elementary curricula that too often are intellectually vacuous, politically sedate, and bureaucratically administered.

During this age of the Internet and Ellen, queer childhood has not substantially changed since my years of playground torments and classroom disregard. Today's homophobic bullies are no less harmful, and supportive teachers are only slightly more visible than they were during the era of *Sputnik* and *Leave It to Beaver*. Across the generations "acting queerly" still brands one with the scarlet (or purple) letter. "Straightening up" dictates gender conformity for sissies and tomboys. "Having an agenda" means challenging school curricula that remain silent about *our* ancestors' contributions to the arts and sciences, military and politics, sports and technology. And "flaunting one's sexuality" is a not so subtle subterfuge for heterosexual privilege and homosexual panic.

SPEAKING THE UNSPOKEN

I use the term *queer* to signify those who have been defined or have chosen to define themselves as sexual outsiders. Human beings who love, or make love to, the same or both genders; individuals who choose to change gender identities by dress, hormones, demeanor, or surgery; persons who elect to behave in gender-discordant manners. I, like many of the contributors in this book, celebrate *queer* because our childhoods were perverted by those who brandished this word in the staccato repartee of classmates, in insults hurled into the radio waves, and in hellfire condemnation from pulpits. I reclaim this word for those heterosexuals who are frigid in expressing tenderness and affection for the same gender, who mask erotic feelings in homophobic jokes, gay-bashing, and heterosexual prowess, or who harbor parental fears or furtive family trees.

Teaching queerly is not teaching sex. It embodies educators who model honesty, civility, authenticity, integrity, fairness, and respect. *Queering*

Elementary Education is not a sinister stratagem in the "gay agenda." As forthcoming chapters detail, it is creating classrooms that challenge categorical thinking, promote interpersonal intelligence, and foster critical consciousness.

Queer elementary classrooms are those where parents and educators care enough about their children to trust the human capacity for understanding, and their educative abilities to foster insight into the human condition. Those who teach queerly refuse to participate in the great sexual sorting machine called schooling wherein diminutive GI Joes and Barbies become star quarterbacks and prom queens, while the Linuses and Tinky Winkys become wallflowers or human doormats.

Queering education means bracketing our simplest classroom activities in which we routinely equate sexual identities with sexual acts, privilege the heterosexual condition, and presume sexual destinies. Queer teachers are those who develop curricula and pedagogy that afford *every* child dignity rooted in self-worth and esteem for others. Queer teachers imagine the world through a child's eyes while seeking to transform it through adult authorship.

In short, queering education happens when we look at schooling upside down and view childhood from the inside out. Teaching queerly demands we explore taken-for-granted assumptions about diversity, identities, childhood, and prejudice. Toward this end I offer five elementary propositions. Although not all contributors or readers will concur on each point or illustration, collectively these challenge us to reconceptualize who, what, and how we teach. It is the raison d'être for *Queering Elementary Education*.

PROPOSITION 1: DIVERSITY IS A HUMAN HALLMARK

From skin color to blood type, from creation myths to family constellations, humans evidence diversity. However, when it comes to sexuality and gender, many educators mold children into curriculum cookie-cutter identities. Students are socialized into this make-believe world of self and the other: male/female (biological sex), heterosexual/homosexual (sexual orientation), man/woman (gender identity), masculine/feminine (gender roles), opposite/same (sexual behavior), straight/gay (sexual identity).

When educators enter classrooms of difference, they bring with them these categorical blinders diminishing the richness of humanity. In fact, diversity exists even within each of these categories—for example, in multiple X and Y chromosomal combinations (Kessler 1998). Furthermore, each of these six categories (more properly regarded as spectrums of difference) is interrelated. Thus, the various intersections of biological sex, sexual orientation, gender identity, gender role, sexual behavior, and sexual identity are best visualized as concentric wheels.

These "Diversity Wheels" convey a more holistic understanding of human beings (Sears 1997b). In one configuration, for example, where someone was born "male" but viewed herself as a woman and acted accordingly, there is the temptation to "align properly" one's biological sex through surgery or hormonal therapy. In traditional Native American culture such an individual would be viewed as possessing "two spirits" and accorded status within the tribe (Blackwood 1984); in our culture we mutilate bodies to correspond to ostensibly objective sexual categories and cripple children's spirits who fail to conform to these.

Those who transgress are subject to derision and reprimand. Jerry Falwell recently accused one of the Teletubby characters on the popular PBS TV children's show of being gay. The purple-colored Tinky Winky carries a red patent-leather handbag and sports a triangular antenna. The founder of the Moral Majority explained on NBC's *Today* that "Christians do not agree with . . . little boys running around with purses and acting effeminate and leaving the idea that the masculine male, the feminine female, is out, and gay is okay." In response one gay newspaper chain ran parody ads satirizing the "Ex-Gay" movement sponsored by Falwell and other Christian Right leaders. Imploring Tinky Winky to "Put Down That Purse— You Can Change," a fictional organization offers support to other suspicious cartoon figures like *Sesame Street*'s Bert and Ernie, Peppermint Patty of *Peanuts*, and Warner Brothers' Elmer Fudd. The publisher, William Waybourn, commented: "Tinky Winky was made that way—purple, happy, and toting a purse. He cannot be expected to change his color, nor should anyone else" (Windowmedia 1999; Mifflin 1999).

A cornerstone of teaching queerly is to deconstruct these sexual and gender binaries (deployed and reified through social text and grammar) that are the linchpins of heteronormativity (Britzman 1995; Bryson and de Castell 1993). Considering the postmodern moment, Pinar (1998) queries: "How can we teach others while reconfiguring ourselves?" (8).

PROPOSITION 2:
(HOMO)SEXUALITIES ARE CONSTRUCTED ESSENCES

Identities grafted onto various sexual behaviors vary across culture and history (Ford and Beach 1951). In some Latin cultures, for example, the sexual position assumed in male-male sexual behavior defines one as *macho* and the other as *maricón* (Murray 1987), whereas "chumming," "Boston-marriages," and other female romantic friendships of the nineteenth century were seen in asexual terms (Faderman 1981). As Jeffrey Weeks (1999) recently observed: "Identities which once seemed categoric are now seen as fluid, relational, hybrid"(17).

Although sexual identity is constructed within a cultural context, the predisposition for sexual behavior is biologically based. The accumulated scientific evidence renders a verdict that sexual orientation is more akin to left- or right-handedness than to an alternative "lifestyle" (Burr 1996; Strickland 1995). Identical twins, for example, have a one-in-two chance of both being gay if one is gay, compared to fraternal twins (one in five) and adopted brothers (one in ten). Furthermore, most identical-twin homosexual brothers have five different patches of genetic material in common (designated the Xq28 chromosome)—a statistical overlap that is highly unlikely (200 to 1) to occur by random (Hamer et al. 1995; Pillard and Bailey 1991; Turner 1995).

The precise biology for the "cause" of homosexuality has not been found (some identical twins were not of the same sexual identity). However, the argument that—absent ironclad evidence—homosexuals choose their "lifestyle" is the "equivalent of saying that since we haven't found the gene that governs left-handedness—and we haven't—then left-handed people choose to be left-handed (or, at a minimum, we can't determine if they do so)" (Burr 1996, 9). Genetic evidence coupled with hormonal research, neurobiological science as well as evidence drawn from anthropology to zoology, overwhelm other etiological explanations.

Thus, the old nature/nurture debate is really two sides of the same coin. Sexual identity is constructed from cultural materials; sexual orientation is conditioned on biological factors. The degree to which this predisposition for (homo)sexual behavior is realized is, in fact, a measure of social coercion and personal resolve. The question, thus, for educators who teach queerly is not what causes homosexuality but what factors contribute to the homophobia and heterosexism that make coping with one's sexual orientation so difficult.

PROPOSITION 3: HOMOPHOBIA AND HETEROSEXISM ARE ACQUIRED

The belief in the superiority of heterosexuality or heterosexuals (heterosexism), and the deep-seated hatred or fear of those who love the same gender (homophobia), are acquired early in life and serve a variety of functions (Herek 1987; Sears 1997c). Expressing antigay attitudes or behaviors, for example, can be a function of peer pressure or the avoidance of personal sexual/gender anxieties.

Homophobic and heterosexist attitudes, feelings, and behaviors are also related to personal beliefs and traits such as religious conservatism, traditional view of gender roles, and level of education (Sears 1997c). Relatively few studies have been conducted with professionals working with elementary or preschool-age children. However, early-childhood teachers appear to have more tolerant attitudes for tomboylike behaviors among girls than for sissified behaviors of boys and are less likely to see girls' behavior evidencing eminent adult homosexuality (Cahill and Adams 1997). Further, elementary teachers are receptive to increasing their knowledge and awareness on gay issues (Marinoble 1997), and preservice elementary teachers express less homophobia than do their secondary counterparts (Sears 1992) while they are generally supportive about queer families (Maney and Cain 1997).

Today the hidden and not-so-hidden costs of homophobia and heterosexism are no longer being borne solely by well-meaning educators or harassed children. School districts confront multimillion-dollar lawsuits. For example, Jamie Nabozny, a Wisconsin middle-school student, was repeatedly kicked unconscious and urinated upon (along with many other lesser torments). The principal lamely warned him to expect such treatment if he chose to be openly gay. A jury found this principal and two other administrators guilty of violating Nabozny's rights; the family received a nine-hundred-thousand-dollar out-of-court settlement.

Heterosexism and homophobia can be reduced through purposive intervention (Sears 1997c). Although most emphasis has been on bias reduction among college students and professionals, we must consider how *not* to instill, foster, or intensify these prejudices in the first place. For example, though there is no evidence that homosexual teachers (or parents) "recruit" children for homosexuality, they "might make children less homophobic and less xenophobic" (Rofes, this volume, 91).

Queering elementary education demands that we confront our prejudices inculcated through decades of heterosocialization. Mulhern and Martinez, in this book, observe insightfully: "Teaching queerly required more than a conviction. Confronted with a lack of knowledge and remnants of the homophobia we had grown up with, we had to peel back layers of fear and discomfort and educate ourselves" (255).

PROPOSITION 4: CHILDHOOD INNOCENCE IS A FICTIVE ABSOLUTE

There has been a growing body of scholarship that challenges our everyday conceptions of childhood. From the groundbreaking work of Philippe Aries (1962) to the postmodern critique of Jonathan Silin

(1995), the construction of childhood parallels the economic and cultural shifts that propelled feudal societies into the industrial age. As urban manufacturers displaced cottage industries, miniature adults were transformed into Dickensesque children. By the late nineteenth century teaching had become a woman's profession and the cult of childhood—coupling notions of childhood innocence and ignorance with adult denial of knowledge and power—emerged.

Perhaps Pestalozzi, as Weems points out in chapter 3, was correct in asserting that social institutions corrupt the innate goodness of the young. Certainly, with the emergence of the schooling industry during this century, desire has been masculinized and innocence institutionalized. Acknowledging children as sexual beings or allowing males (particularly homosexuals) to teach in elementary grades dislodges the classroom from the "safe haven" of heteronormativity. As Silin (1995) points out:

> History links women, children and homosexuals in the same nexus of unfulfilled desires. For it is the emergence of the mental health perspectives that announces the psychological needs of children and the unique abilities of women to fulfill them and at the same time defines the homosexual threat to normal development. The homosexual, embodying everything that the child is not, allows us to see what the child is—innocent and without desire, a blank slate on which we may write at will. (194)

Childhood innocence is a veneer that we as adults impress onto children, enabling us to deny desire comfortably and to silence sexuality. As a third-grader observes in the award-winning educational film *It's Elementary* (Chasnoff and Cohen 1996): "It's amazing how teachers don't notice all the stuff that's going on."

In Cambridge's progressive Fayerweather School, fifth- and sixth-grade students worked on an oral-history project about Anita Bryant's visit. The discussion that followed, recalled their teacher, was one that happens only "when fifth and sixth grade kids are suddenly given permission to talk openly about the idea of being gay or lesbian. . . . The questions that we hear most from kids this age are 'How do you know if you are gay?' and 'Can gay people have babies?'" (Eccles 1998, 8)

Children whose sexual/gender configurations fall outside the heteronormative standard cope daily with yet-unnamed transgressions. There is David, a third-grader described in Marinoble's chapter, who doesn't feel "like the other guys," or the fifth-grader who proudly reads his poem: "My dad is queer and he likes his beer, But I don't care so please don't stare."

Parents of children as young as three years of age, however, are keenly aware of these transgressions. They often question teachers about sexual orientation in the context of their own child's cross-gender behavior (Casper et al. 1996). Those teachers who view such behavior as "normal" (some cannot imagine responding to such an inquiry), dismiss it as transitory. But, as the researchers ask: "If it is normal for a six-year-old boy to dress in clothing of the other gender then he is okay. . . . But, if he continues with this behavior in later years, then when is he no longer okay?" (277).

Seen from the child's perspective—not the adult gaze of the child—teaching queerly means developing "new ways for queers to recollect, confront, and interpret the ways homophobia and the colonization of children worked together to wreak havoc on our early years" (Rofes, 1998, 22).

PROPOSITION 5: FAMILIES ARE FIRST

The gravest threat that the recognition and acceptance of lesbian/gay families in elementary schools pose is the removal of the family as instrument of heterosexual socialization. "Family first" is a euphemism for the uncritical exaltation of *Father Knows Best* households that, in fact, exist only in black-and-white TV reruns. Fewer than one in four students come to school from a home occupied by both biological parents; most come from an array of family configurations (Glick 1988).

The concepts of *family* and *parenthood* have become "unhinged" in this era of postmodernity (Stacey 1999). Although there have always been children born of homosexually inclined mothers or fathers, the advent of biotechnology and movements of liberation have resulted, as Kissen writes in chapter 14, in a veritable "gayby boom." Artificial insemination, in vitro fertilization, single-parent or second-parent adoptions, have rapidly increased queer households from Long Island to Cobb County.

Innumerable scientific studies have concluded that homosexual parents compare favorably to their heterosexual counterparts (Laird 1993; Sears 1999). This research, however, challenges a heterosexist assumption: Heterosexual families are first. "The reigning premise has been that gay and lesbian families are dangerously, and *prima facie*, 'queer' in the pejorative sense, unless proven otherwise" (Stacey 1999, 388). In this heteronormative world lesbian parents are appreciative of what their heterosexual counterparts would likely term expected professional behavior by school officials who "didn't treat them any different from other parents"(Hulsebosch, Koerner, and Ryan, this volume, 185).

Homosexual apologists also claim that having a lesbian or gay parent has *no* impact on the development of children. This negates the very strength that open, honest, caring, and queer-supportive households can have on children of *all* sexual orientations (Costello 1997; Golombok and Tasker 1996). Allowing children freedom to develop their sexual identities, absent guilt or conditional love, is an important attribute of queer households (and classrooms).

As cultural cops of the ancien régime, elementary teachers unmindfully enforce "compulsory heterosexuality" through stories of nuclear animal families and questions about mommies or daddies. In chapter 17 Danish writes of her and her partner's experience with their adoptive three-year-old daughter who returns home to inform them that she had told her teacher and classmates, in response to a question about her father, that he had died. "This experience convinced us that even a school comfortable with us as lesbians did not know *enough* about how to imagine the world for our daughter" (Danish, this volume, 196).

Erasing queer families from the curriculum for the "sake of the child" does not remove them from the day-to-day realities of school life and children's worlds. In 1983 Goodman reviewed twenty-two books of children's literature, published since 1969, with lesbian or gay characters—most with negative messages and stereotypes such as the loneliness and bleakness of homosexual life, or adult characters depicted as homosexual recruiters or predators. By the mid-nineties, however, more than one hundred other children's books had been published, many with gay-positive characters and themes (Lobban and Clyde 1996).

Of course, this does not mean that books like *My Two Uncles* (Vigna 1995) or *Anna Day and the O-Ring* (Wickens 1994) are available to children, as one survey of elementary- and middle-school libraries demonstrated (Rubin 1995). Despite the presence of children with gay families in all ten rural school districts, no district had fiction on the topic. Furthermore, although these books challenge children's images of traditional families, they are "juxtaposed with traditional concepts of childhood. . . . [and] appear intent on consolidating the power of adults within a family unit and rendering children as pure and dependent creatures" (Rofes 1998, 20).

In contrast, Vygotskian and critical pedagogues model alternate approaches for queering elementary education. Rather than teaching about lesbian or gay families, for example, educators encourage children to struggle with the traditional definition of family vis-à-vis their diverse experiences "to enrich their everyday concepts of family" (Casper et al. 1996, 285). Another first-grade teacher, relying on critical pedagogy, reads *Asha's Mums* to her students (Krakow 1998). Here Asha is upset because her teacher tells her that the permission form is incorrectly filled out—she has two moms. Later some of the children who listened to the story chose to write a letter to the district superintendent requesting that their school's form be changed (which the superintendent later recommended). The modernist classroom "strains toward erasing difference" (Seidman 1993, 127), but difference defines diversity. Fairy family tales are an integral curriculum element in queering elementary education.

CONCLUSION

There is growing recognition that sexual-diversity issues are central to multicultural education (Gollnick and Chinn 1994; Grant 1995). Teaching queerly, though, will not likely come about without debate and conflict. Certainly, some educators, as Ellen Varella describes in Kaeser's essay (chapter 15), will be unsettled by the prospect of controversy. Queering elementary education is a refusal to "acquiesce to a scissors and paste mentality of curriculum development in which only the most mundane, least controversial material survives the scrutiny of self-appointed moral vigilantes or the self-censorship of timid school officials" (Sears 1999, 373–74). A curriculum that is the product of the lowest common cultural denominator may offend nobody, but it also serves no one.

REFERENCES

Aries, P. (1962). *Centuries of childhood.* New York: Knopf.

Blackwood, E. (1984). Sexuality and gender in certain Native American tribes. *Signs* 10: 27–42.

Britzman, D. (1995). Is there a queer pedagogy? *Educational Theory* 45(2): 151–65.

Bryson, M., and S. de Castell. (1993). Queer pedagogy make im/perfect. *Canadian Journal of Education* 18(3): 285–305.

Burr, C. (1996). *A separate creation.* New York: Hyperion.

Cahill, B., and E. Adams. (1997). An exploratory study of early childhood teachers' attitudes toward gender roles. *Sex Roles* 36: 517–29.

Casper, V., A. K. Cuffaro, S. Schultz, J. Silin, and E. Wickens. (1996). Toward a most thorough understanding of the world: Sexual orientation and early childhood education. *Harvard Educational Review* 77(2): 271–93.

Chasnoff, D., director/producer, and H. Cohen, producer. (1996). *It's elementary: Talking about gay issues in school.* San Francisco: Women's Educational Media. Film.

Costello, C. (1997). Conceiving identity: Bisexual, lesbian and gay parents consider their children's sexual orientations. *Journal of Sociology and Social Welfare* 34(3): 63–85.

Eccles, I. (1998). The evolution of a gay history project. *The News* (Fayerweather Street School, Cambridge, Mass.), May.

Faderman, L. (1981). *Surpassing the love of men.* New York: Morrow.

Ford, C., and F. Beach. (1951). *Patterns of sexual behavior.* New York: Harper and Row.

Glick, P. (1988). Fifty years of family demography. *Journal of Marriage and the Family* 50(4): 861–73.

Gollnick, D., and P. Chinn. (1994). *Multicultural education in a pluralist society.* New York: Merrill.

Golombok, S., and F. Tasker. (1996). Do parents influence the sexual orientation of their children? *Developmental Psychology* 32(1): 3–11.

Goodman, J. (1983). Out of the closet, but paying the price: Lesbian and gay characters in children's literature. *Interracial Books for Children Bulletin* 14 (3/4): 13–15.

Grant, C., ed. (1995). *Educating for diversity.* Needham Heights, Mass.: Allyn and Bacon.

Hamer, D. H., S. Hu, V. L. Magnuson, N. Hu, and A. M. L. Pattatucci. (1995). A linkage between DNA markers on the X chromosome and male sexual orientation. *Science* 261(July): 321–27.

Herek, G. (1987). Can functions be measured? *Social Psychology Quarterly* 50(4): 451–77.

Kessler, S. (1998). *Lessons from the intersexed.* New Brunswick, N.J.: Rutgers University Press.

Krakow, K. (1998). Talking about children's literature with gay and lesbian themes. Unpublished paper.

Laird, J. (1993). Lesbian and gay families. In *Normal family processes,* ed. F. Walsh. 2d ed. New York: Guildford Press.

Lobban, M., and L. Clyde. (1996). *Out of the closet and into the classroom: Homosexuality in books for young people.* Port Melborne, Australia: Thorpe.

Maney, D., and R. Cain. (1997). Preservice elementary teachers' attitudes toward gay and lesbian parenting. *Journal of School Health* 67(6): 236–41.

Marinoble, M. (1997). Elementary school teachers: Homophobia reduction in a staff development context. In *Overcoming heterosexism and homophobia,* ed. J. Sears and W. Williams. New York: Columbia University Press.

Mifflin, L. (1999). Falwell takes on the Teletubbies. *New York Times.* 15 February.

Murray, S. (1987). *Male homosexuality in Central and South America.* New York: Gay Academic Union.

Pillard R., and J. Bailey. (1991). A genetic study of male sexual orientation. *Archive of General Psychiatry* 48 (December): 1089–96.

Pinar, W. (1998). Introduction. In *Queer theory in education,* ed. W. Pinar. Mahwah, N.J.: Lawrence Erlbaum.

Rienzo, B., J. Button, and K. Wald. (1996). The politics of school-based programs which address sexual orientation. *Journal of School Health* 66(1): 33–40.

Rofes, E. (1998). Innocence, perversion and Heather's two mommies. *Journal of Gay, Lesbian and Bisexual Identity* 3(1): 3–26.

Rubin, S. (1995). Children who grow up with gay or lesbian parents. Master's thesis. University of Wisconsin–Madison.

Sears, J. (1992). Educators, homosexuality, and homosexual students. *Journal of Homosexuality* 22(3/4): 29–79.

———. (1997a). *Lonely hunters*. New York: HarperCollins/Westview.

———. (1997b). Centering culture: Teaching for critical sexual literacy using the sexual diversity wheel. *Journal of Moral Education* 26(3): 273–83.

———. (1997c). Thinking critically/intervening effectively about homophobia and heterosexism. In *Overcoming heterosexism and homophobia*, ed. J. Sears and W. Williams. New York: Columbia University Press.

———. (1999). Challenges for educators: Lesbian, gay, and bisexual Families. In *Contemporary issues in curriculum,* ed. A. Ornstein and L. Behar-Horenstein. 2nd ed. Needham Heights, Mass.: Allyn and Bacon.

Seidman, S. (1993). Identity and politics in a "postmodern" gay culture. In *Fear of a queer planet,* ed. M. Warner. Minneapolis: University of Minnesota Press.

Silin, J. (1995). *Sex, death, and the education of children.* New York: Teachers College Press.

Stacey, J. (1999). Gay and lesbian families are here. In *American families: A multicultural reader,* ed. S. Coontz. New York: Routledge.

Strickland, B. (1995). Research on sexual orientation and human development. *Developmental Psychology* 31(1): 137–40.

Turner, W. (1995). Homosexuality, Type 1: An Xq28 phenomenon. *Archives of Sexual Behavior* 24(2): 109–34.

Vigna, J. (1995). *My two uncles.* Morton Grove, Ill.: Albert Whitman.

Weeks, J. (1999). Myths and fictions in modern sexualities. In *A dangerous knowing: Sexuality, pedagogy, and popular culture,* ed. D. Epstein and J. Sears. London: Cassell.

Wickens, E. (1994). *Anna Day and the O-ring.* Boston: Alyson Press.

Windowmedia. (1999). Can Teletubby Be Saved from Gay "Lifestyle"? Press release, 10 February, Washington D.C.

· 2 ·

WHY DISCUSS SEXUALITY IN ELEMENTARY SCHOOL?

Kathy Bickmore

Elementary schools are places where young people's identities are formed, as individuals and as citizens. As public institutions, schools touch nearly every child and provide powerful sanction for certain knowledge. Elementary teachers have the capacity to help children learn how to share public space with people similar to, and different from, themselves. This chapter discusses why homosexual people should be included in these elementary conversations, then identifies places in the curriculum where teachers might help children to learn such inclusivity.

The first reason to discuss sexuality in elementary school is that it is already present in students' lives. Assumptions about children's "innocence" regarding sexuality are outdated. Given the amount of (mis)information about gender relations and sexuality that flows freely these days in public spaces, media, and peer groups, elementary educators could not prevent children from acquiring sexual information even if we wanted to do so. The recent movie *It's Elementary* (Chasnoff and Cohen 1996), filmed in six U.S. elementary and middle schools, provides evidence that many young children know a lot more about homosexuality and gender questions than adults might predict. Children in actual classrooms were invited to ask questions and to describe what they thought was meant by the words *gay*, *lesbian*, and *homosexual*. Although they are not a representative sample, these children very quickly generated long lists of information, gleaned from the media and from peers—some of it inaccurate and/or negative, some of it relatively neutral, all of it incomplete. All of the children had heard words such as *gay* used as slurs or put-downs, whether or not they knew their definitions. Children also generally knew that families do not all include one mommy and one daddy, and furthermore that they risk being teased and hurt if they are known to live in unusual families (Epstein 1998).

15

Gender identities, including the discomfort associated with violating presumed gender boundaries, are learned early in life. The practice of teasing a playmate by mislabeling his or her gender is common by age three or four (Garvey 1984, 196). By elementary school peer enforcement of narrow gender roles through homophobic harassment and name-calling has become common (Rofes 1995). The AIDS epidemic and the resurgence of religious fundamentalism have brought homophobia to the surface of public consciousness, unleashing a rash of highly visible intolerance and violence (Aronson 1994; Hoffman 1995). By the time they enter middle school, girls and boys have learned that their gender identity is defined in large part by heterosexual behavior: They generally believe, for example, that a girl "must" have (or seek) a boyfriend, and vice versa (Harris and Bliss 1997; Mandel 1996). Clearly students do learn about homosexuality in elementary schools—through their peers, if not through their teachers. Because this knowledge is shared covertly rather than in open lessons, it is particularly vulnerable to inaccuracy and bigotry.

Sexuality is present and visible, although generally unremarked, in the public images experienced by virtually all children in the Western world (Richardson 1998). Public figures, television shows, comic strips, billboard advertising, and so forth present powerful implicit models of what it means to be a valued member of society (Epstein and Johnson 1998). The reason people often don't notice the sexuality in these images is that they assume as "common sense" the dominant and exclusionary view that "our way" is to live in heterosexual, married families.

Curriculum resource materials and teaching strategies employ these value-loaded images, including the supposed normality or inevitability of heterosexuality, long before they admit to talking about sex. Just as politicians or comedians often mirror the identities that they assume are familiar and attractive to their audiences, so do elementary teachers. The estimates that teachers and resource authors make of what will be relevant to their students' values and lives are inevitably biased by the educators' own experiences and fears (Ellsworth 1997; Gordon 1992). In the name of comfort and accessibility for the (imagined) typical young student, standardized and increasingly outdated notions of "family" are reintroduced to children—unheralded—not as topics to question but as quiet corollaries to lessons on mathematics, geography, or literacy. Thus elementary schooling inevitably draws upon and influences the sexual aspects of children's developing citizen identities.

RISKY TEACHING

Gender role socialization, including the accompanying (de)valuation of (homo)sexual identities, is an inevitable element of the ways children are guided to behave by the hidden curriculum of peer interaction and school activities. When brought into the light of the explicit curriculum, these topics are clearly unsafe terrain for teachers: The news carries recurring scandals in which individual teachers are targeted for saying too much about sex, or for even allowing children to read about the existence of homosexual people (EGALE 1998; Garner 1996). Teachers who wish to teach inclusivity "are in a terrible bind—they can either ignore children's often dangerous misinformation, or step in and address it and be censured" (Giese 1998).

Most current public controversies surrounding school censorship in North America involve curriculum and library materials that mention sex, nakedness, or gay/lesbian people, although a range of other topics such as spirituality or race relations are also targeted (Herzog 1994; Miner 1998). At the elementary-school level the troubling truth is that most censorship is self-censorship: Materials often have no chance to be challenged or defended, because they never make it into classrooms in the first place (Hydrick 1994). The assumption that children are too immature and impressionable for certain information, and that adults can and should keep such information away from them, has deep historical roots (Adams 1997). As a result of their own sense of students' prior knowledge and maturity, or in anticipation of parents' possible objections, teachers often manage classroom materials and activities in ways that limit democratic foundations such as free expression and access to information.

Official curriculum guidelines, though not representing students' entire learning experience, shed some light on the murky social and political boundaries within which teachers operate. Often teachers who make independent choices to raise the matter of homosexuality are presumed to be homosexual and are thereby at risk of job loss: Where official guidelines "require" all teachers to cover sexual and homosexual topics, they lower the risk of dealing with such controversial material (Khayatt 1997). A school board equity policy that does not protect sexual preference creates a chilly climate for antihomophobia instruction (Suhanic 1998). On the other hand, human rights legislation that does include sexual orientation, such as the 1992 amendment to Ontario's Education Act, creates a warmer climate for discussions of homosexuality and a safety net for teachers who do so (Giles and Peer 1997).

The affirmation of gay and lesbian people in elementary curricula is roughly analogous to respecting the rights of religious minorities. A Canadian lawyer who has been successful in protecting homosexual rights explains: "I don't compare [the identity of] gays and lesbians to race and ethnicity. I compare it to religion. People argue that you could change your sexual orientation. I argue that you can change your religion, but while you have it it's really important to you. And religion is highly protected" (Mariana Valverde, in Rau 1998, 11).

Substantial risk remains, however, for elementary educators because this precedent in civil rights and economic benefits cases may not extend to freedom of expression in public schools, where religious diversity is not itself well protected. Reading about or discussing any belief or culture has never been shown to cause a child to adopt that way of life (Gutmann and Thompson 1996, 66). However, it is precisely these kinds of deeply held identities, including values and practices involving homosexuality, that are most often censored. Moral precepts are indeed taught in elementary schools, but (by virtue of being implicit and avoiding controversy) they tend to reinforce dominant viewpoints and narrow notions of normalcy, thereby minimizing the possibility of democratic social change.

SEXUALITY IN THE ELEMENTARY CURRICULUM

Sex education curricula are generally intended to provide students with background knowledge and to increase their capacity to make responsible decisions regarding intimate relationships and sexual behavior. There is no evidence that open or explicit sex education leads to increased sexual behavior of any kind: On the contrary, it is widely shown either to have no significant effect or to be associated with safer sexual practices or postponement of sexual activity (Epstein and Johnson 1998, 172; Lenskyj 1990, 219; Reiss 1995, 375). Because the topic is more often censored, similarly robust evidence is not available regarding explicit teaching about homosexuality. However, consequences would logically be analogous. Giving children concepts, vocabulary, and strategies for handling gender role questions and homosexuality is likely to help them to resist homophobic ignorance, to avoid unsafe practices, and to treat themselves and others respectfully (Rofes 1995). Although teachers often are not given much latitude to teach about sexuality, they are certainly held responsible when sex education "fails" to alleviate problems such as the spread of AIDS (Infantry 1998). The assignment of sexuality education to physical/health education, and not to such areas as social studies or literature, may exacerbate the tendency of educators to emphasize abstract clinical information rather than human diversity, social justice, and democratic principles.

Questions of sex, gender, and homosexual identity do fit into the elementary curriculum in a number of places. For example, Ontario's recently approved Health and Physical Education curriculum (grade 1–8) includes a strand called "growth and development . . . [which] focuses on an understanding of sexuality in its broadest context" and a related strand regarding "personal safety . . . [which includes] bullying, peer assault, child abuse, harassment, and violence in relationships . . . [and] living skills such as conflict resolution" (Ontario Ministry of Education and Training 1998a, 10–11). Ontario children, like children in many other locales, are expected to describe animal reproduction by grade 3, to begin identifying human relationship challenges and responsibilities by grade 4, and to discuss puberty and human reproduction biology by grades 5 and 6. Grade 8 emphasizes ethical decision making in relationships and the application of "living skills (for example, decision making, problem solving, and refusal skills)" to sexual matters; it also includes the only mention of HIV and AIDS (19). Because Ontario teachers are not required by elementary health curriculum guidelines to mention homosexuality, teachers who do so may face significant risk. However, there are several places in such a curriculum where discussions of homosexuality could fit into given topic areas (such as puberty or decision making) and would thereby strengthen students' skills and comprehension in those areas.

Gender identity and sexuality are to some degree inescapable in literature and social studies lessons, because the characters in human dramas virtually all have gender identities and intimate relationships. "It is impossible," Reiss has argued, ". . . to teach almost any piece of literature without transgressing onto the field of sex education. . . . Similarly, imagine biology without human reproduction, geography without population studies . . . or religious education without a consideration of the roles of men and women" (1995, 374).

Although sexual identity is at least implied in nearly any story, elementary-level literature used in school generally avoids explicit (or affirmative) mention of homosexuality. For example, homosexual characters (all white and male) appear in one children's picture book out of 97, and one of 144 juvenile literature books, published in Canada in 1994 (Wilson and Green 1995; also Apostol 1998). However, the vast majority of those stories do quietly include sexuality in the form of normalized nuclear family characters and heterosexual relationships. Ironically, heterosexuality is particularly emphasized when the characters are distant from the dominant culture in other ways. Perhaps in order to make literature about culturally dominated groups seem more familiar to mainstream readers, characters who are not middle class and white anglophone are even more consistently portrayed in stereotypically heterosexual families.

Ontario's elementary language curriculum emphasizes skills for interpreting diverse viewpoints, communication with various audiences, and justification of opinions on personal concerns and issues. By grade 7 students are expected to "clarify and develop their own points of view by examining the ideas of others" (Ontario Ministry of Education and Training 1997, 37) and to "respond constructively to alternative ideas or viewpoints"(46). Unfamiliar and controversial writings and ideas, such as literature regarding homosexuality, would be essential for meeting such curriculum outcomes.

Homosexual people are never explicitly mentioned in Ontario's new social studies curriculum, but students' development of "respect, tolerance, and understanding with regard to individuals, groups, and cultures" is given as an overall goal (Ontario Ministry of Education and Training 1998b, 7). In grade 2 students "demonstrate an understanding that communities may be made up of many cultures" (17). In grade 5 students "broaden their understanding of life in a democratic society" and study human rights and the Canadian Charter of Rights (37). Canada's federal legislation does not yet explicitly protect homosexuals, but gay and lesbian rights claims have been made on the basis of both federal and provincial human rights codes. The grade 7 and 8 guidelines emphasize conflict, change, and conflict resolution (47–48, 53–54). As with the health and language curriculum, teachers are not required to deal with homosexuality in Ontario social studies lessons, but they could meet outcomes that are identified in the curriculum guidelines by doing so.

Many teachers' quiet choices to censor homosexual topics are influenced less by fear of political controversy than by the challenge of managing conflict-producing topics efficiently. The increasing pressures of curriculum accountability make some teachers averse to risking deeply meaningful topics, such as human relationships and sexuality, that might open unpredictable avenues for learning and thus not meet narrow short-term objectives. In striving for comfortable classroom environments and high achievement scores, elementary teachers often avoid the vital issues that make social studies, in particular, worth knowing (Houser 1996). As a result, students and teachers often consider such school knowledge to be unimportant and uninteresting; thus they miss out on learning that might help them develop into empowered democratic citizens (Bickmore 1997; Hahn 1996). Discussing sexuality with elementary students is risky—but necessary—because of its very importance to their personal and political lives. "The need for student-centered instruction [on meaningful issues] does not diminish simply because the students' experiences are socially volatile" (Houser 1996, 302).

School safety and conflict management practices, as well as formal curriculum topics, are spaces for teaching the skills and inclinations for participation in inclusive democracy. Efforts to teach children about homosexuality are easier in school contexts that label and limit bullying, gender-based harassment, and heterosexist targeting of teachers and students (Scott 1995). Paradoxically, the opposite is also true: Episodes of extremist violence against homosexuals have inspired social movements for curriculum reform toward inclusivity (Lenskyj 1994). Conflict resolution skills and inclinations against intolerance are by no means sufficient for the development of democracy or the elimination of sexism and homophobia, but they are necessary elements, perhaps even prerequisites (Avery, Sullivan, and Wood 1997; Bickmore 1996).

If we want children to be safe in the long run, and if we want them to learn, then the risky road of facing conflict and sensitive issues must be taken. To develop the capacity for self-preservation, the sense of themselves as a part of the community, and the freedom of thought that are associated with democracy, children need opportunities to practice using the associated concepts and skills (Bickmore 1999). Even preschool children have some capacity to understand and talk through conflicts (Garvey 1984, 143). Children build the autonomy and the confidence for handling difficult questions, attending to contrasting viewpoints, and making decisions, by *doing* so, in the protected but pluralistic space of the public school (Kamii 1991; Lewis 1996). Carefully designed education about sexuality, including homosexuality, can provide such an opportunity. Otherwise, we abdicate responsibility for children's safety and their inclusion in democratic society, leaving them to sort through unreliable sources of information on their own.

CONCLUSION: CENSORSHIP AND CITIZENSHIP

Debates about sexuality-related education in elementary schools tend to hinge on the problem of children's vulnerability, their need for protection. Sexuality, and homosexuality in particular, is generally seen to be unsafe content for young children's classrooms. This assumption misjudges what many children already know about themselves and their world, and also misses the point of what helps an "innocent" develop into a self-sustaining "citizen." Children's relatively small size and power, and their relative *lack* of knowledge, is what makes them vulnerable. As they grow up, children gain the power to protect themselves by learning to acquire and evaluate knowledge, not by being denied information. Young people's self-determination as citizens depends on their opportunities to learn, to correct their misunderstandings, and to get along with diverse others in their communities.

The tragedy of censorship is not only for children whose own experience with gay and lesbian friends or families is rendered invisible or invalid, but also for their classmates. The stories to which children are exposed inform their understandings of what their world can be like. Depriving children of a broad range of ideas limits their capacity to reimagine their social world. "[T]he imagination can be seen as the basis of all experience in the young child. It is out of the spectrum of the possible presented by stories that tease the imagination that the child selects and constructs the 'real'" (Kohl 1995, 65). If we hope that the new generation will recreate a social world that includes less sexism, homophobia, and bigotry, then we need to expose them to stories that suggest such a need, and such a possibility.

It is important to recognize the social systemic nature of bigotries such as heterosexism: It is not the "abnormal" individuals being targeted who need fixing, but rather the others in their groups who must learn to include them as citizens. The group must become *un*accustomed to excluding certain individuals from shared space.

> [An elementary classroom is the child's] first real exposure to the public arena. Children are required to share materials and teachers in a space that belongs to everyone. Within this public space a new concept of open access can develop if we choose to make this a goal. Here will be found not only the strong ties of intimate friendship but, in addition, the habit of full and equal participation, upon request. . . . In general, the approach has been to help the outsiders develop the characteristics that will make them more acceptable to the insiders. I am suggesting something different: the *group* must change its attitudes and expectations toward those who, for whatever reason, are not yet part of the system. (Paley 1992, 21, 33)

The minisociety of an elementary classroom becomes more inclusive when *all* of its members practice respectfully interacting with diverse individuals and unfamiliar ideas. Instead of trying vainly to protect young children from the discomforts of learning, teachers can gently "invite [students] into the ongoing predicament" of a world that includes troubles such as homophobia (Ellsworth 1997, 24). By confronting conflict in an open and caring manner, elementary teachers can create social spaces in which a wide range of children (and ideas) are accepted, and thus enabled to contribute their gifts to the community. Thus the children may learn, as developing citizens, to question the categories and rules that have formed them, and to create a new world with more democratic space for all.

References

Adams, M. L. (1997). *The trouble with normal: Postwar youth and the making of heterosexuality.* Toronto: University of Toronto Press.

Apostol, C. (1998). Sexuality in children's literature. *Ontario Public School Teachers Federation News* 12(2): 24–26.

Aronson, D. (1994). In the schoolyard at twilight: Children with AIDS struggle for acceptance. *Teaching Tolerance* (Fall): 59–61.

Avery, P., J. Sullivan, and S. Wood. (1997). Teaching for tolerance of diverse beliefs. *Theory into Practice* 36(1): 32–38.

Bickmore, K.(1996). Women in the world, women in the classroom: Gender equity in the social studies. *High School Journal* 79(3): 231–41.

———. (1997). Preparation for pluralism: Curricular and extra-curricular practice with conflict resolution. *Theory into Practice* 36(1): 3–10.

———. (1999). Teaching conflict and conflict resolution in school: (Extra-) curricular considerations. In *How children understand war and peace,* ed. A. Raviv, L. Oppenheimer, and D. Bar-Tal. San Francisco: Jossey-Bass.

Chasnoff, D. (Director/Producer), and Cohen, H.(Producer). (1996). *It's elementary: Talking about gay issues in school* [Film]. San Francisco: Women's Educational Media.

EGALE (Equality for Gays and Lesbians Everywhere). (1998). Bigots ban books. <http://www.egale.ca>.

Ellsworth, E. (1997). *Teaching positions.* New York: Teachers College Press.

Epstein, D., and R. Johnson. (1998). *Schooling sexualities.* Buckingham, UK: Open University Press.

Epstein, R. (1998). Parents' night will never be the same. *Our Schools/Our Selves* 9(1): 92–117.

Garner, H. (1996). Why does the women get all the pain? In *True stories,* ed. H. Garner. Melbourne: Text Publishing.

Garvey, C. (1984). *Children's talk.* Cambridge, Mass.: Harvard University Press.

Giese, R. (1998). Teach kids about sex now or suffer consequences later. *Toronto Star,* 11 May.

Giles, J., and A. Peer. (1997). Staff development: A journey of patience and persistence. *The Rainbow Classroom* 2(2): 1, 8–9.

Gordon, T. (1992). Citizens and others: Gender, democracy and education. *International Studies in Sociology of Education* 2(1): 43–56.

Gutmann, A., and D. Thompson. (1996). *Democracy and disagreement.* Cambridge, Mass.: Belknap Press.

Hahn, C. (1996). Research on issues-centered social studies. In *Handbook on teaching social issues,* ed. R. Evans and D. Saxe, Bulletin #93. Washington, D.C.: National Council for the Social Studies.

Harris, M., and G. Bliss. (1997). Coming out in a school setting: Former students' experiences and opinions about disclosure. In *School experiences of gay and lesbian youth: The invisible minority,* ed. M. Harris. New York: Haworth Press.

Herzog, M. J. R. (1994). Teachers' stories about their school censorship experiences. *Democracy and Education* 9(2): 25–28.

Hoffman, L. (1995). Safe and supportive schools for gay, lesbian, and bisexual students: An idea whose time has come. *The Fourth R* 56: 5, 13, 25.

Houser, N. (1996). Negotiating dissonance and safety for the common good: Social education in the elementary classroom. *Theory and Research in Social Education* 24(3): 294–312.

Hydrick, C. J. (1994). The elementary school: Censorship within and without. In *Censorship: A threat to reading, learning, thinking,* ed. J. Simmons. Newark, Del.: International Reading Association.

Infantry, A. (1998). Schools get failing grade in AIDS. *Toronto Star*, editorial, 24 November.

Kamii, C. (1991). Toward autonomy: The importance of critical thinking and choice making. *School Psychology Review* 20(3): 382–88.

Khayatt, D. (1997). Sex and the teacher: Should we come out in class? *Harvard Educational Review* 67(1): 126–43.

Kohl, H. (1995). *Should we burn Babar? Essays on children's literature and the power of stories.* New York: New Press.

Lenskyj, H. (1990). Beyond plumbing and prevention: Feminist approaches to sex education. *Gender and Education* 2(2): 217–30.

———. (1994). Going too far? Sexual orientation(s) in the sex education curriculum. In *Sociology of education in Canada,* ed. L. Erwin and D. MacLennan. Toronto: Copp Clark Longman.

Lewis, C. (1996). Beyond conflict resolution skills: How do children develop the will to solve conflicts at school? *New Directions for Child Development* 73: 91–106.

Mandel, L. (1996). Adolescent gender identity and heterosexism in junior high school. Paper presented at Research on Women in Education conference, San Jose, California, 24 October.

Miner, B. (1998). Reading, writing, and censorship. *Rethinking Schools* 12(3): 4–7.

Ontario Ministry of Education and Training. (1997). *The Ontario curriculum, grades 1–8: Language, 1997.* Ottawa: Queen's Printer.

———. (1998a). *The Ontario curriculum, grades 1–8: Health and physical education, 1998.* Ottawa: Queen's Printer.

———.(1998b). *The Ontario curriculum: Social studies, grades 1–6: History and geography, Grades 7 and 8, 1998.* Ottawa: Queen's Printer.

Paley, V. G. (1992). *You can't say you can't play.* Cambridge, Mass.: Harvard University Press.

Rau, K. (1998). Egghead's arguments win gay rights cases. *Xtra* (Toronto), 5 November.

Reiss, M. (1995). Conflicting philosophies of school sex education. *Journal of Moral Education* 24(4): 371–82.

Richardson, D. (1998). Sexuality and citizenship. *Sociology* 32(1): 83–100.

Rofes, E. (1995). Making schools safe for sissies. *Rethinking Schools* 9(3): 8–9.

Scott, K. (1995). Seventy-five years later: Gender-based harassment in schools. *Social Education* 59(5): 293–97.

Suhanic, G. (1998). Worst fears are realized: School board ignores homos in new equity policy. *Xtra* (Toronto), 5 November.

Wilson, J., and K. Green. (1995). *Canadian children's literature 1994.* Toronto: Canadian Book Review Annual.

· 3 ·

PESTALOZZI, PERVERSITY, AND THE PEDAGOGY OF LOVE

Lisa Weems

This chapter provides a historical and theoretical framework for analyzing sex, gender, and sexuality in early-childhood education. By trac-
ing the historical construction of the field of elementary education, I investigate how the categories of sex, gender, and sexuality converge in the
notion of "the pedagogy of love"(Gutek 1968). I explore the historical invention of primary schoolteachers as an idealized position of mothering
and illustrate the effects of such an invention in the history of U.S. primary
schooling. Specifically, I argue that the pedagogy of love historically situ-
ates the work of primary educators as "feminine," and I explore the ways
in which the pedagogy of love positions some feminine subjects as "natural" mothers/teachers and others as "perverts"/"savages."[1]

WHAT COUNTS AS THE PEDAGOGY OF LOVE?

Periodically, I teach a course in the history of modern education in the
United States. In the course we spend a lot of time talking about the work
of Horace Mann and his efforts in the Common School movement
(1830–1850s). Troubled by the rise of industrialization, immigration, and
urbanization, Mann was convinced that fragmentation (religious, economic, cultural, and so on) posed a serious threat to American society
(Tyack and Hansot 1982). Mann believed that the key to national social
unity lay in mass education or, more accurately, in a common moral training. As one of the most well-educated and persuasive proponents of common schools, Mann traveled across the country to solicit public support
and funding for his vision of the Common School. The ideology and politics of the Common School movement emphasized the necessity of moral
education for the masses.[2] In addition to implementing a moral curricu-

lum that stressed unity and consensus, the Common School movement proposed the standardization of teacher training in terms of academic, moral, and pedagogical elements. Thus, Horace Mann and the Common School advocates needed a stable, inexpensive, and moral teaching force. Enter women, and the pedagogy of love.

There is little disagreement that education is considered a gendered occupation. Much of the work of feminist historians of education has been to document how the profession became gendered through the feminization of teaching during the nineteenth century (Martin 1998).[3] Educational historians branded the instructional model of the Common School the "pedagogy of love" due to its emphasis on love as the basis for, and intended outcome of, elementary education.

The progenitor of the pedagogy of love was Johann Heinrich Pestalozzi (1747–1827). Pestalozzi was a Swiss educationalist concerned with "race regeneration" and education for the masses. Directly influenced by Rousseau's natural philosophy, Pestalozzi thought that children were innately good and that social institutions served to corrupt individuals.[4] Pestalozzi believed that elementary education should recover the innate benevolence of children, which must be nurtured and protected from corruptive social forces. For Pestalozzi social contaminants were a product of industrialization that occurred during his lifetime in his native Switzerland. Pestalozzi believed that industrialism was particularly detrimental to the family in that it took whole families out of the "home" into the public realm (Gutek 1968). The idea of "home" is crucial for Pestalozzi; he believed that primary schools should be modeled after a well-ordered home rather than after an intellectual academy (Silber 1960).

Consistent with social and educational reformists of his time, Pestalozzi viewed education as a vehicle for improving one's social condition as well as larger social problems. Pestalozzi's main concern, however, was with the psychological well-being of children. Elementary education was to intervene in the processes of alienation from self and others brought on by industrialism, which Pestalozzi believed was especially evident in homes of the poor. Pestalozzi's vision of elementary education was that of an idealized maternal education in that the ideal teacher of young students resembled "the good mother": open-hearted, nurturing, and gentle. Pestalozzi believed that the teacher-student relationship should model relations between mother and child. Pestalozzi's "good mother" provides "loving care with complete unselfishness" (Gutek 1968, 62). Gutek notes: "This love relationship between mother and child was a moral relationship in which the mother accepted a set of responsibilities and duties toward the child." A complete selflessness and obligation structured Pestalozzi's idealization of "maternal love." From this relationship between the child and the mother grows the "germ of human love or brotherly love" (Pestalozzi 1931, 88). Pestalozzi writes:

> Obedience and love, gratitude and trust united, develop the first germ of conscience, the first faint shadow of the feeling that it is not right to rage against the loving mother; the first faint shadow of the feeling that the mother is not in the world altogether for his sake; and with it is germinated the feeling that he himself is not in the world for his sake only. The first shadow of duty and right is in the germ.
>   These are the first principles of moral self-development, which are unfolded by the natural relations between mother and child. (89)

For Pestalozzi the relationship between a mother and child is the basis of moral development whereby "maternal love" constitutes relations that are both "natural" and bound by duty.[5] It is interesting to note the paradox in Pestalozzi's theorizing with regards to the mother-child relationship as both natural, yet bound by social and ethical dimensions. If the idealized relationship between mother and child were merely natural, it would not be necessary to formulate, propagate, and legitimate the essential role of women in education.

Even more significant is the fact that Pestalozzi's model of maternal education, Gertrude, was a fictional character rather than a living model educator.[6] Remember that in Pestalozzi's world the majority of teachers were men rather than women. Thus, Pestalozzi's creation of Gertrude, and more important, Horace Mann's adoption of Pestalozzi's model, signals an aspirational shift in the fundamental nature and role of elementary education. The belief that individuals must "cooperate" with the duties of their social location links the Pestalozzian notion of maternal love and a pedagogy of love to a desire for and maintenance of social order.

The pedagogy of love was the missing piece in the legitimization of mass public education and the role of women within it. Although a continent and fifty years divided Pestalozzi's and Mann's movements, Pestalozzi's insistence that women are "natural" teachers mapped onto its American ideological counterpart "republican motherhood."[7] Republican motherhood is a metaphor (made popular by Catherine Beecher) used to describe the relations between women's domestic responsibilities and larger moral, political, and cultural roles. During the early nineteenth century Horace Mann appropriated Beecher's arguments of woman's natural role as culture bearer, coupled with Pestalozzi's pedagogy of love, to argue effectively for women as the "natural" candidates for the profession of teaching.

Central to its implementation was the way in which Common Schools solidified an educational family. The educational family included the schoolmarm and male administrator as the loving parents to the innocent and socially fragile children as students (Spring 1997).

Thus far I have rehearsed the familiar story of the feminization of teaching, which reinscribes the family as a model for education. It is a story that is accepted by educational historians across political orientations (Tyack and Hansot 1982; Spring 1997). Even cultural feminists (Sklar 1976; Martin 1998) tend to valorize women's role as nurturers within both real and imagined families. This story however, reifies the heteronormative family as a model for educational contexts, as well as for national unity. By heteronormativity, I mean that the story reinscribes assumptions of biological essentialism (woman as feminine, and femininity as woman), gender polarity (masculinity and femininity as two opposing yet complementary forces of human nature), and reproduction as a central trope for theorizing educational contexts. What would it look like to read history against these heteronormative assumptions? How can we begin to interrogate the "unsaid" in educational discourses on sex, gender, and sexuality at work in the pedagogy of love?

PERVERSITY AND DESIRE IN ELEMENTARY EDUCATION

Joseph Tobin (1997) refers to desire as the missing discourse in elementary education. This is not to say, however, that desire is absent from our ways of talking and thinking about education. Precisely, discourses on sexuality serve to police the boundaries between the acceptable and the unacceptable forces of desire. As Foucault (1990) notes, analyzing discourse requires attention to that which is unsaid as much as that which is said. If we trace the historicity of categories like love and perversity, we find that they are two sides of the same coin that is the discourse on sexuality within educational scenes. In this section I explore how the pedagogy of love historically has operated to reinscribe heteronormative boundaries between the normal and the perverse within educational scenes.

Simply put, love is permissible, desire is not. Love is equated with order, normality, and civilization (Carter 1997). Love has been linked, philosophically, to Eros, the life and creative force, which forms the natural bonds between mother and child, teacher and student. Similarly, for Pestalozzi love is the basis of morality. Love, defined as the "natural" relationship between mother and child, has the power to develop the "innate germ of benevolence" in the child (Gutek 1968, 66). Hence, the "pedagogy of love" signifies one of the higher forms of virtue, which by definition stems from the reproductive mother.

In contrast, desire represents nature: the undisciplined wants and needs of children and the uncivilized (Pestalozzi 1931). Pestalozzi viewed desire as a primitive yet essential dynamic that forms the bonds of obligation between mother and child. For Pestalozzi *passionate desire* was precisely the force that initiates the child's learning from sensory observation and activity (Gutek 1968; Silber 1960). Concerned with order, Pestalozzi's pedagogy of love sought to build from desire but to discipline a primitive drive into civilized relations of "brotherly love." Nevertheless, for Pestalozzi desire maintained a certain ambivalence theoretically—neither wholly positive nor negative.

I return to the notion of the "unsaid" in discourses on sexuality. Like Foucault (1990) I argue that, since the Victorian period, sexuality is far from repressed in public discourse. To the contrary, prohibitions to speak about sexuality actually work to incite discourses on sexuality in both public and private realms. In fact Foucault notes that one effect of the progressive-era research is the *proliferation* of talk about sexuality within educational and other public contexts. He notes that sexuality is regulated through multiple systems of classification in which particular identities are normalized and others labeled pathological. Furthermore, Foucault argues that the normal is constituted by the pathological and that the invention of homosexuality and the homosexual serves to identify the boundaries of the normal, the natural, the unmarked category—the heteronormative family as constructed in the pedagogy of love. Using Foucault's ideas, we can turn our lens both forward and backward to consider perversity and desire as the categories that both exceed and define the heteronormative educational family.

The pedagogy of love puts into place a cast of characters: the good mother who is naturally nurturing; the innocent but socially susceptible child; the distant yet paternalistic father. Similarly, each of these images works on/against/through implicit assumptions and explicit expressions of an "Other"—a pathological counterpart to the normal. In Pestalozzi's time the good mother is one who transcends the alienating forces of industrialism, who recognizes her duty as a mother to protect and nurture the child, who rescues poor children from a "culturally deprived" home life (Gutek 1968, 31). For Mann the schoolmarm becomes the manager of virtue amid the social chaos of cultural diversity (Tyack and Hansot 1982). And in our own times the "good mother" becomes the one who provides "care" for "at-risk" students—the corrective for the presumed lack of care of "low-income" students.[8]

As the pedagogy of love traveled to the United States, the construction of desire dramatically shifted from a potentially positive to a fundamentally negative force in teaching and learning. Heteronormativity, through the views of elementary teachers as "managers of virtue," attempted to relegate sexuality outside the classroom. For example, administrative policies from 1840 to 1940 required young female teachers to remain unwed. Virtue, in some ways, was defined as abstinence from sexual activity.

It would be up to progressive educators at the turn of the twentieth century to bring desire to the forefront in discussions of elementary education. A key difference, however, is the altered perception of desire as a positive force in the dynamics of teaching and learning to that of a dangerous pathology that must be regulated within all individuals, and that is contagious upon contact with sexual deviants. The work of the sexologists and progressive educators generated new labels to monitor and maintain the boundaries of normality in education (Foucault 1990).

Similarly, we can trace how assumptions about children within the pedagogy of love shifted as educational theory traveled from Europe to the United States. In Pestalozzi's writing, innocent children had only the corruptive force of industrialism from which to be protected. During the Common School era, diversity and fragmentation were the primary threats to unity and consensus. After the turn of the twentieth century "desire" became the villain—the pathological counterpart to the "natural" bonds of heteronormativity. As Jonathan Silin notes, "popular and professional discourses frame sexuality as a dangerous force that must be vigilantly monitored and barred from children's lives" (1997, 214). No longer is "desire" an ambivalent force that operates within and between all individuals. Rather, as desire comes to be considered pathological, it is an attribute that gets projected onto the bodies of children, savages, and perverts (Carter 1997).

What this has meant in educational contexts is that discourses on sexuality render certain bodies and identities natural and good and others deviant and suspect. In the early elementary-education classroom sexuality gets "ordered" in the following way: Only the relations between a (feminine) woman and child can pass as the heteronormative mother, and others become suspect and sometimes labeled perverse. *Perversity* is the term that is used to describe the relations of desire in elementary classrooms that exceed the boundaries of heteronormativity.

Regulating sexuality in elementary education takes many forms, such as the contemporary witch-hunts to rid schools of "perverts" by either firing or forcing to resign those who fall outside the bounds of heteronormativity. Fueled by slippery yet seductive "moral panic," the persecution of lesbians and gay men (especially) occurs in educational contexts under the guise of "protecting" innocent children from sex-obsessed child molesters (Silin 1997, 219). This image prevails despite the statistics on child abuse that repudiate such stereotypes.[9]

Male elementary-education teachers (regardless of their sexual orientation and marital status) particularly feel the effects of moral panic. Many are presumed to be gay, given the heteronormative assumption that gender deviance equals homosexuality. By historical definition, attributes of elementary educators include gentleness, nurturing, and a strong penchant for order. These characteristics, considered markers of femininity and woman's "true nature," make male primary educators suspect as good role models.

Moreover, openly gay male elementary teachers are considered suspect on multiple counts. Discourses on sexuality preclude the possibility of viewing openly gay men as "good" elementary teachers. As King (1997) notes, the assumptions about elementary teaching and gay men are at odds: "First, elementary teachers are constructed as selfless and gay men as self-indulgent. Second, elementary teachers are seen as virginal and gay men as promiscuous and sybaritic. Third, elementary teachers are seen as nurturing and gay men as predatory" (245).

King concludes that gay men are "at risk" for providing care. Consistent with the pedagogy of love, the notion of care locates caring within femininity, femininity within females (at least middle-class Anglo females), and females as the natural and good teachers of young children. In fact, Silin (1997) contends that the homosexual and the child are the most salient pairing in representations of sexuality in elementary education. He argues that representations of gay men as "predatory pedophiles" and children as sexually innocent and fragile perpetuate heteronormativity in education.

Charged with children's moral development, elementary teachers are policed in terms of their lifestyles, activities, and identities as extensions of their character. The problem, it should be obvious, is that gender deviance, sexual orientation, and sex identity (male/female) are not barometers for determining nurturing teachers. The general issue is to recognize how, theoretically and historically, gender, race, class—and especially sexuality— socially construct the model of "good teaching." To liken our constructions of elementary teaching as the work of loving mothers restricts the available role models for all children.

The pedagogy of love marks an entire economy of sex, gender, and sexuality that reinforces the hegemony of the reproductive family as a model for education. Women are charged with the role of protecting children from the sexual dangers of the natural and social realms. Whether the danger is construed as the child's own passionate desire or the perverse desire of the predatory adult, the educational family—taken for granted in historical constructions—offers the pedagogy of love as a safe haven, a corrective and a civilizing force. It is not so much that I am arguing that we do away with the pedagogy of love. Rather, my point is that we might do well to consider how the pedagogy of love is inscribed in discourses of sexuality that treat desires as a force to be contained. Heteronormativity operates to police the boundaries between normal and pathological forms of desire. Discourses of sexuality in education have operated historically to position some sexual positions as natural (the good mother who disciplines desire into love), and others as perverted (the predatory pedophile who cannot control his own desire). In elementary education the sexuality of children is considered underdeveloped and fragile. Defining the work of elementary education as a project of morality has led to the vigilant regulation of sexuality of elementary-educational contexts. It is time to redefine the project.

NOTES

1. The method of this chapter follows the genealogical approach by investigating the descent of discourses rather than the origin of ideas (Foucault 1990). In other words, rather than searching for the "true" or original pedagogy of love, my analysis traces how the pedagogy of love has been constructed and deployed across various historical times and places.

2. For a more in-depth discussion of the Common School movement see Lawrence Cremin (1951), *The American Common School,* and David Tyack (1974), *The One Best System.*

3. The feminization of teaching refers to two dynamics of the field: (1) the majority of teachers are female, and (2) femininity is a valued characteristic of primary schoolteachers (Spring 1997). Tyack and Hansot (1982) discuss the role of women in the Common School movement as the new "managers of virtue."

4. Pestalozzi's vision exemplifies his belief that moral education is the foundation of all forms of education, including physical, vocational, and intellectual. What Pestalozzi means by *foundational* is that moral reasoning precedes all other forms of learning. This point, that learning is incremental and cumulative, has come to signal the radical influence of psychological or developmental models of learning within the field of education. Furthermore, Pestalozzi argued that education must meet the learner on his/her own psychological or emotional terms, and build or develop the child's germinal sense of morality.

5. The paradoxical structure of "nature" is a reoccurring theme in the natural philosophy of social contract theorists such as Jean Jacques Rousseau. See Moyer (1998) for an insightful discussion of this tension in Rousseau's *Emile.*

6. Although the novel *Leonard and Gertrude* is considered by some as Pestalozzi's "best writing," *How Gertrude Teaches Her Children* contains the most in-depth ar-

ticulation of Pestalozzi's theories of Anschauung, self-activity, and the role of maternal love in elementary education. It is crucial to note, however, that Gertrude was a fictional character constructed by Pestalozzi to convey his theory of the "natural" bonds between mother and child. This point is often overlooked, as is the fact that Pestalozzi's attempt to offer a male protagonist as the "good teacher" failed, as written in the 1774 *How Father Pestalozzi Instructed His Three and a Half Year Old Son* (Gutek 1968, 33). To my knowledge the latter text remains untranslated, a sign of its relative failure to appeal to educational leaders.

7. The biography of Catherine Beecher written by Kathryn Kish Sklar (1976) gives a good discussion of the significance of republican motherhood and the education of women.

8. Gloria Ladson-Billings (1994) challenges the hegemony of the "cultural deficit model" in contemporary discussions of urban education. Similarly, Mary Odem (1995) analyzes the ways in which "delinquency" has been constructed historically as a characteristic of working-class and immigrant youth. These authors, although in slightly different terms, express how cultural difference and notions of deficiency get projected onto the bodies of both real and imagined populations.

9. Consider these facts: An adult who is familiar to the child perpetrates 93 percent of reported incidents of abuse. In fact, most abuse takes place in the home, with fewer than 1 percent of the reported cases involving school personnel (Laumann et al., 1994). Jenny, Roesler, and Poyer (1994) found that 82 percent of accused abusers are in a heterosexual relationship with a female relative of the abused child.

REFERENCES

Carter, J. (1997). Normality, whiteness, authorship: Evolutionary sexology and the primitive pervert. In *Science and homosexualities,* ed. V. A. Rosario. New York: Routledge.

Cremin, L. (1951). *The American common school: An historic conception.* New York: Teachers College Press.

Foucault, M. (1990). *The history of sexuality: An introduction, vol. 1,* trans. R. Hurley. Paris: Editions Gallimard, 1976. Reprint, New York: Vintage.

Gutek, G. L. (1968). *Pestalozzi and education.* New York: Random House.

Jenny, C., T. A. Roesler, and K. L. Poyer. (1994). Are children at risk for sexual abuse by homosexuals? *Pediatrics* 94 (1): 41–44.

King, J. A. (1997). Keeping it quiet: Gay teachers in the primary grades. In *Making a place for pleasure in early childhood education,* ed. J. J. Tobin. New Haven: Yale University Press.

Ladson-Billings, G. (1994). *The dreamkeepers: Successful teachers of African American children.* San Francisco: Jossey-Bass.

Laumann, E. O., J. H. Gagnon, R. T. Michael, and S. Michaels, ed. (1994). *The social organization of sexuality: Sexual practices in the United States.* Chicago: University of Chicago Press.

36   *Lisa Weems*

Martin, J. R. (1998). Excluding women from the educational realm. In *Minding women: Reshaping the educational realm*, ed. C.A. Woyshner and H.S. Gelfond. Cambridge, Mass.: Harvard Educational Review.

Moyer, D. (1998). Swaddling difference: Women and the state in *Emile*. Paper presented at the Annual Meeting of the American Educational Research Association, April, San Diego, California.

Odem, M. (1995). *Delinquent daughters: Protecting and policing adolescent female sexuality in the United States, 1885–1920*. Chapel Hill: University of North Carolina Press.

Pestalozzi, J. H. (1931). *How Gertrude teaches her children*. Translated by L. E. Holland and F. C. Turner. 1801. Reprint, in *Pestalozzi*, by L. F. Anderson. New York: McGraw-Hill.

———. *Leonard and Gertrude*. Translated by E. Channing. 1898. Reprint, New York: Gordon Press.

Silber, K. (1960). *Pestalozzi: The man and his work*. New York: Schocken Books.

Silin, J. G. (1997). The pervert in the classroom. In *Making a place for pleasure in early childhood education*, ed. J. J. Tobin. New Haven: Yale University Press.

Sklar, K. K. (1976). *Catherine Beecher: A study in American domesticity*. New York: W. W. Norton.

Spring, J. (1997). *The American school: 1642–1996*. 4th ed. New York: McGraw-Hill.

Tobin, J. J. (1997). The missing discourse of pleasure and desire. In *Making a place for pleasure in early childhood education*, ed. J. J. Tobin. New Haven: Yale University Press.

Tyack, D. (1974). *The one best system: A history of American urban education*. Cambridge, Mass.: Harvard University Press.

Tyack, D., and E. Hansot. (1982). *Managers of virtue: Public school leadership in America, 1820–1980*. New York: Basic Books.

• *Part 2* •

CHILDREN'S SEXUAL AND SOCIAL DEVELOPMENT

"Queer issues do not belong in elementary education. Children are not capable of understanding such issues. And they certainly aren't sexually aware!" Assertions such as these are the hallmark of heterodoxy that leads one in nodding agreement with Mark Twain's dictum, "I never let schooling interfere with my education."

In chapter 4 two early-childhood educators—one lesbian, one heterosexual—provide an overview of child social and sexual development. Betsy Cahill and Rachel Theilheimer document children's capacity to understand difference and awareness of their sexuality as well as the responsiblity of the educator to instill wisdom and reduce bias. In the process they provide specific examples, sources, and guidelines that "affirm children's experiences and help children advocate for themselves and a fair society."

Queering Elementary Education, though, is not simply inserting a textbook illustration comparable to Rosa Parks's refusal to relinquish her bus seat or including nontraditional families in children's books. Queer issues intersect with race, ethnicity, and gender in an array of public and private ways that are far more complex than those who view categories of difference as an additive algorithm (for example, black gays are doubly oppressed). The next three chapters unravel some of these complexities.

James Earl Davis explores the complex intersections of race and sexuality among middle-school black males. Data gleaned from his case studies detail how the image of "hypersexualized" black males, coupled with antifeminist and misogynist programs to strengthen academic and social development, create unsafe space for those who transgress codes of masculinity and blackness. The construction of the black sissy-boy "does not necessarily correspond to a boy's sexual orientation, identity, or experience, but rather reflects a boy's marginalized cultural status and value." Thus, the challenge for educators is to create safe space and to "explore and engage in nontraditional gender projects."

Kevin Kumashiro, who grew up within an Asian American context wherein by "U.S. standards" he lacked "the dominant or hegemonic form of masculinity," personalizes a reversed image of this sissy-boy construction. Chapter 6 explores several "reading strategies" through culturally distinct lenses that make sense of these differing images. What follows are insightful and useful observations of how "educators can help challenge oppression by helping to change traditional reading practices."

How one "queerly raised" child negotiates her identity is the subject of Maria Pallotta-Chiarolli's essay. Here we hear the words of Steph, a seven-year-old "third generation Italian Australian." We listen to stories of her "moving days," from attending Sydney's gay Mardi Gras and sharing it in "Show and Tell," to confronting prejudice among her classmates as her "uncles" suffer from AIDS. These stories "exemplify children's great potential to demonstrate and transcend categorical limitations."

The ability of children to grapple with "adult issues" is centerpiece in this section's final chapter. Since the advent of gay liberation, most advocates (reacting to accusations of "recruitment") have argued that gay teachers do not differ from their heterosexual counterparts. Eric Rofes follows up with some of his middle-school students who were "exposed" to his "lifestyle" during the late seventies. While further supporting research that gay educators don't "turn kids gay," he challenges the notion that teachers, "Like Socrates, Plato, and Me," have no impact and that preteen kids cannot cope with issues of sexual diversity.

Each of these chapters brings an unconventional (queer) reading to how we understand and act on children's social and sexual development. From preschool to middle school the response these contributors uniformly raise to questions rooted in heterodoxy is the Graham Nash lyric, "Children, teach your parents well."

· 4 ·

STONEWALL IN THE HOUSEKEEPING AREA: GAY AND LESBIAN ISSUES IN THE EARLY CHILDHOOD CLASSROOM

Betsy J. Cahill and Rachel Theilheimer

The kindergarten class is learning about Rosa Parks. The children have transformed the housekeeping area into a bus. As they play, read, and talk, they became indignant. "Do you mean we wouldn't be friends? We couldn't even sit together on the bus?" asks Ashanti and John, an African American and European American pair of best friends. The children are learning firsthand about prejudice and inequity and how to fight it.

Picture another scene. Instead of a bus, the housekeeping area is now a street outside a bar. Children have made a banner that says "Stonewall Inn." As in the first reenactment, children look at materials together, including a book about Stonewall that one of their teachers has made for them. The teachers learn what children know about the night in June 1969 that gay people fought back at the Stonewall bar in Greenwich Village and discover that one family had just attended a Gay Pride march. The teachers add information, for example, they tell children about the sign on the bar's door—"They invaded our rights" (Miller 1995)—and the children decide to make one, too.

Is it harder to imagine children playing Stonewall instead of enacting the Montgomery bus incident? Both are major events in the history of Civil Rights in the United States. Maybe a fight outside a bar recreated in an early-childhood classroom is incongruent, even inappropriate. We suspect, though, that the fight and bar are not the only stumbling blocks. Prejudice against gays and lesbians is simply not confronted as curriculum in most classrooms.

In this essay we talk about why gay and lesbian issues belong in classrooms. As two early-childhood educators, one lesbian and one straight, we write about elementary classrooms for the youngest children, from pre-K through third grade. These are the years that lay the foundation for chil-

39

dren's later understandings of themselves and others. We talk about what is known and assumed about children's sexual development: what children are like, what they know, and how they come to know their world. Then we discuss some of the gay and lesbian issues that arise in classrooms. Finally, we envision classrooms where all children—those developing homosexual and heterosexual orientations—are comfortable and learn to fight prejudice against gays and lesbians as well as other kinds of bias.

WHY GAY AND LESBIAN ISSUES BELONG IN CLASSROOMS

Although some people believe young children lack the developmental readiness to deal with gay and lesbian issues, our assumption throughout this chapter is that children are capable of understanding "difference." Research on children's early concepts of race, gender, and physical difference indicates that by age four most children are aware of color, racial, and gender differences, and that awareness is affectively laden (Aboud 1988; Katz 1987; Ramsey 1986). We believe that children have the cognitive capacity also to understand "difference" in family configurations and affectional preferences. Indeed, to wait until a child is in middle or secondary school may be too late, as stereotypes and biases develop in the early years (Baker and Fishbein 1993).

Children want to know about their world, and gays and lesbians are and have always been part of society. As children enjoy stories, for example, they learn about their favorite authors. But if an author such as Hans Christian Andersen was gay, and teachers and children do not know that, they miss the opportunity to see a gay man as a contributing member of society. If children who are developing same-sex affectional and sexual orientations do not know that gays and lesbians are among those they look to as role models, their sense of being alone is further reinforced.

What children could know about being gay or lesbian is related to their present and future families. Every child is part of a multigenerational family, in which elders, the child her- or himself, and/or the child's future offspring may be gay or lesbian. Imagine Sally. As a child, she may have a gay or lesbian parent. Or when she grows up, Sally may be a lesbian and live with a partner, and together they might rear a child who grows up to be straight. Or Sally might marry a man and raise a son who grows up to be a gay man. Maybe Sally's sister is a lesbian and Sally is straight. These are only some of Sally's putative family configurations that include gay or lesbian family members. Letting a five-year-old Sally and her classmates know that gays and lesbians are part of our world will help her understand her current and later experiences with people in her family, and beyond it.

Children's feelings about homosexuality cannot be taken lightly. Children who develop into gay or lesbian young people with negative perceptions about being gay are at "high risk for physical and psychosocial dysfunction" (Besner and Spungin 1995, 47). This includes a disproportionately high rate of suicide. Gay and lesbian youths have a greater likelihood of running away from home because of family conflicts, and half of gay youth who have run away engage in prostitution to support themselves (Besner and Spungin 1995).

Homophobia affects children who grow up to be straight or gay. It results in discrimination, both subtle and overt. Homophobia restricts interactions between men, between women, and between men and women. Homophobia can lead to harassment and, possibly, violence, such as the fatal attack on Matthew Shepard. Schools can change all this by affirming children's experiences and helping children become activists for a fair society.

WHAT CHILDREN ARE LIKE, WHAT THEY KNOW, AND HOW THEY COME TO KNOW

As a society, we create definitions of the nature of children, and our expectations of them follow from these definitions (Cannella 1997). A common belief in the innocence of children results in the belief that children have no sexuality. Many in Western cultures feel a simultaneous repugnance for and attraction to sex. These feelings make them doubly uneasy about thinking of naive children as sexual beings. Such people tell us that sexuality has nothing to do with children, other than that we must protect children from their own sexual curiosity and from predators (Kincaid 1992).

Yet many teachers behave as if they do consider children sexual beings. They act as if all children were heterosexual until proved otherwise. The teacher who refers to a girl as "your girlfriend" when talking to a boy is making an assumption of heterosexuality and is thereby bringing sexuality into the classroom.

The belief that children are not sexual beings is not substantiated by research. Lively and Lively (1991) maintain that the nature of human sexuality starts at birth or even in utero, forming "the base on which the evolution of children to adolescence is built" (14). Other, external factors, such as the care children receive, also influence their sexuality. From the way children are touched early in their lives, and from the relationships, expressions of feelings, and physical interactions they observe around them, children can experience their bodies as sources of both pleasure and pride (Lively and Lively 1991).

There are no consistent findings in the literature on how a child de-velops a heterosexual, homosexual, or bisexual orientation and identity. Sexual orientation appears to be formed by a complex interplay between biological, social, and psychological situations (Strickland 1995). A compa-rable set of factors converge to construct children's identities: children's ex-periences with their bodies, environmental influences, and their cognitive developmental stage (Derman-Sparks 1987). Although young children may not label their own sexual identities, they can attest to knowing their race, gender, and other characteristics and possess a sense of well-being that includes what we call their eventually emerging sexual selves (Theilheimer and Cahill 1998). Teachers cannot change a child's sexual development that, in adolescence, usually results in heterosexual, bisexual, or homosex-ual orientation. What teachers can affect is a child's sense of identity and how that child feels about him- or herself and others.

Young children are developing images of themselves that influence their understandings and acceptance of their own and others' sexualities. We have coined the term "eventually emerging sexuality" to differentiate between the behavior and "psychic core" (Butler 1996, 60) that identify the sexuality of adults and the unobservable, but evolving, affectional pref-erences and sexual orientation of children. For example, in the film "Both My Moms' Names Are Judy," a girl says her classmates assume she is gay because her mothers are lesbians. She explains that she does not know whether she will grow up to be gay or straight. Her sexuality, though not yet discernible, is developing, will eventually emerge, and may change over time (Sears 1991).

Perhaps with increased media exposure of gays and lesbians and with more out lesbians and gays in many children's lives, children's experience of heteronormativity, the pervasive assumption that all children and ado-lescents are heterosexual, will diminish. Some children know a lot about sexual orientation and take diversity for granted. Eleven-year-old Joshua lives with his straight mother and father in San Francisco. His mother told one of us that he corrected her when she talked about his growing up and getting married. "Mom," Joshua asked, "how do you know I'm not going to be gay?"

Many young children know that men and women live with and love same-sex partners, although they may never have been directly told (King 1997). They may wonder about what it really means, and children coming from heterosexually headed households may make comparisons with the behavior of the adults they know best, trying to understand lesbian and gay relationships. Casper and Schultz (in press) record a conversation between a three-year-old and his aunt, in which he queries her about her relationship with her female partner. His questions such as, "Did you fall in love?" tell us that, within the framework of what he knows about adult love relationships, he is processing what he sees when he visits her.

Children actively construct their own understandings of sexual orientation in the context of their worlds. The messages and information they receive from parents, teachers, and other children contribute to their thinking, as do the models they see in the media and in their lives. Children need time and willing listeners to help them think about and talk through what they know. Teachers must be prepared to use children's perceptions of their world, integrating gay and lesbian issues into the curriculum.

GAY AND LESBIAN ISSUES IN CLASSROOMS FOR YOUNG CHILDREN

Children learn about gayness from what their teachers do and do not do, from both the knowledge and the ignorance a teacher demonstrates. Whereas some teachers affirm children's experiences and help children advocate for themselves and a fair society, others do not.

The materials teachers select and the words they use may actively communicate a norm of heterosexuality. What teachers do not provide and say also gives a powerful message to children. In many classrooms books, videos, and songs portray adults and children in heterosexual pairings. Even without explicit sexual imagery, heteronormativity is evident in many learning materials. For example, a teacher writes: "Then I explained to Rosie how lucky girls were to have a vagina, because after a girl grows up and gets married and has a baby, the vagina is the place a baby can come out when it is born" (Honig 1998, 2). This teacher forthrightly and accurately described the child's body; however, she assumed that Rosie, like all girls, would marry and have a baby. Rosie may hear repeatedly that little girls grow up, marry men, and become mommies. Rosie is probably not informed of other options and, should she exercise them anyway, is likely to feel she diverged from others' expectations of her and lives outside the norm.

Furthermore, the language teachers use when talking about and to families may not include gay and lesbian parents (Clay 1990). Many early-childhood teachers gather information about children and families with forms that ask for the mother's and father's names. Lesbian and gay parents can cross out a title or hide one parent's existence as if they were a single-parent family. Teachers may be unaware of the possibility that some families may be gay, or they may be too uncomfortable with parents' being gay or lesbian to make room for them in their classroom.

This discomfort, and not knowing quite what to do, can also translate into silence when children hurt one another with homophobic slurs. One of the author's nephews, Paul, has told her about "gay games" children play on the playground of his rural school. In these games children chase and tag one another calling the tagged person "gay." Paul's mothers are lesbians, and he says "gay games" make him sad and insult his family. According to Paul, his teachers do nothing. Perhaps they do not know how to intervene or do not see anything wrong with these games, although they are aware that Paul's parents are lesbians.

Classrooms for All Children

We hope classrooms will be places where there is no stigmatization, denial, or denigration of nonheterosexuality, and where children come to internalize repugnance for prejudice and bias (Herek 1990). Because the best way to know about children is to listen to them and observe them carefully, we propose the following guidelines for teachers when children ask direct questions, such as "Can a girl marry another girl?" (Cahill and Theilheimer 1999):

- Respond to children's questions directly, as ignoring a child's question is disrespectful to the child.
- Delve into the meaning of the child's question by asking further questions and repeating or rewording to be certain the child's intent is fully understood.
- Answer as clearly and honestly as possible, in words the child is likely to understand, without giving more information than is necessary.
- As children talk about their views, elaborate and elucidate.
- Have group discussions to use children's different perspectives to enrich discussion and the knowledge children construct through it.
- Continue to listen and observe carefully to learn what children have understood and to allow their interests, concerns, and knowledge to direct the curriculum.

Because discussions of gay and lesbian topics evoke many adult feelings and recall a history of avoidance, teachers have a special responsibility to answer and discuss children's questions about gay and lesbian issues openly and honestly. Teachers cannot expect questions to be resolved immediately; as with other complex topics, the same questions may emerge again to be examined repeatedly by the children.

In addition to capitalizing on the knowledge and questions children bring, teachers have responsibility to make sure the curriculum is inclusive of everyone, whether children raise questions or not. Updating materials to include a multitude of family configurations, including those with gay and lesbian parents, counters what is otherwise a pervasive message of heteronormativity. The children's book *Anna Day and the O-Ring* (Wickens 1994), for example, tells the story of a dog-owning urban family whose son receives a tent for his birthday. The simple story tells about the child's birthday, exuding the warmth of a loving family of two mothers, their child, and the family dog. This book is an example of how inclusive literature offers alternatives to heteronormative messages. It tells a story that could happen in any family. That the family includes lesbian mothers is incidental to the plot, just as heterosexual family constellations are to other stories.

Teachers can tell children about the lesbian and gay people they know or know about. In the video *It's Elementary*, a teacher and children brainstorm ideas about gays and lesbians. They listen to music by musicians such as Elton John and Melissa Ethridge. In a discussion the teacher points out that the musicians are gay. This is one example of how a teacher might formally teach about gays and lesbians. Alternatively, a teacher may be able to share, informally, simple details children might want to know about a well-known gay man or lesbian.

Teachers who put themselves in other people's shoes, then examine the classroom environment, can arrive at insights. Teachers can imagine themselves a child whose parents are gay or lesbian, then look at the classroom and its materials through those eyes. A teacher might look around their room and think about how a gay or lesbian adult might recall his or her experience as that teacher's student. A teacher can view the room, in addition, from the point of view of a gay or lesbian family member. These perspectives may suggest changes. Some simple alterations, such as using "family member" instead of mother or father on the forms teachers send home, can make everyone feel welcomed.

Because early-childhood teachers work with children to establish guidelines that keep everyone safe, it follows that homophobic slurs break the community's rules. If such behavior occurs, teachers should interrupt it and hold individual or community meetings that engage children in solving the problems at the root of the behavior. Children may be repeating homophobic comments with an understanding of their power, but not of their meaning. Good teaching practice unpacks the meaning of children's comments with the children and recognizes the power of which children, too, are aware.

These teachers offer models of active resistance to prejudice as they bring homophobic slurs to the classroom community's attention. Teachers also can provide children with language that enables them to stand up for themselves and other people when they are confronted with homophobia. Together, teachers and children can critique the heteronormative representations around them. Young children have keen understandings of what it means to be treated unfairly, as is evident when a class wrote letters about the "Love Makes a Family" exhibit in their school. One read: "There's some kids that live with two moms. I bet they feel pretty bad about this adult fight and I bet they want the posters up too, cuz it's like their families"(Lyman 1996/1997, 17).

It is tempting to turn to gay and lesbian parents as resources, and some family members may want that role. Not everyone, however, will want to be regarded as gay or lesbian by the families and the children in the classroom community. Others may be glad to be recognized as gay or lesbian, but may not want to be a spokesperson for your school. The teacher has the responsibility of gathering resources and implementing curricula with the help of those family members and others who wish to offer assistance.

Just as teachers tell families about their curriculum in general, through newsletters, meetings, and informal conversations, they can communicate to families about the ways in which gay and lesbian issues are addressed in the classroom. Open communication can help families and educators work together, although some family members may object to raising any antibias issues in school, and particularly to discussions of gay and lesbian issues. The Anti-Bias Curriculum (Derman-Sparks 1987) provides guidelines for talking to parents about one's antibias work with children in ways that try to understand family perspectives while remaining true to one's own antibias position. The Anti-Bias Curriculum suggests, however, that teachers "may have to make choices about what activities they will stand up for and which they will modify or let go" (54) when parents question activities they fear may "lead to homosexuality." We disagree, firmly believing that an antibias position on gay and lesbian issues is no more expendable than on any other form of prejudice.

Working for a fairer society together with children and families is easier when teachers have allies among their colleagues. Other educators concerned with issues of social justice can offer teachers important sources of support. This work can feel like a personal agenda, especially to a gay or lesbian teacher. Finding others who perceive the importance of including gay and lesbian lives in the elementary-school curriculum can serve as a constant reminder that this is not about one minority group, but about a society that includes all of us.

As Besner and Spungin (1995) have said, "Whether children are heterosexual or homosexual is unimportant. What is important is that children grow to feel good about themselves and what they have to offer as contributing members of the family and society" (69). A classroom that includes gay and lesbian issues in the same way it addresses other topics that are important to children and society can do just that.

REFERENCES

Aboud, F. (1988). *Children and prejudice.* New York: Basil Blackwell.

Baker, J. G., and H. D. Fishbein. (1993). The development of homosexual prejudice and race prejudice in children and adolescents. A poster presented to the annual meeting of the American Psychological Association, Toronto, Canada, August 1993.

Besner, H. F., and C. I. Spungin. (1995). *Gay and lesbian students: Understanding their needs.* Washington, D.C.: Taylor and Francis.

Butler, J. (1996). Sexual inversions. In *Feminist interpretations of Michel Foucault,* ed. S. J. Hekman. University Park, Pa.: Pennsylvania State University Press.

Cahill, B., and R. Theilheimer. (1999). Can Tommy and Sam get married? Questions about gender, sexuality, and children. *Young Children* 54(1): 27–31.

Cannella, G. S. (1997). *Deconstructing early childhood education: Social justice and revolution.* New York: Peter Lang.

Casper, V., and S. Schultz. (In press). *Disclosure, gender, and tentative trust: Gay and lesbian parents, their children, and school.* New York: Teachers College Press.

Clay, J. W. (1990). Working with lesbian and gay parents and their children. *Young Children* 45(3): 31–35.

Derman-Sparks, L. (1987). *Anti-bias curriculum: Tools for empowering young children.* Washington, D.C.: National Association for the Education of Young Children.

Herek, J. M. (1990). The context of anti-gay violence: Notes on cultural and psychological heterosexism. *Journal of Interpersonal Violence* 5(3): 316–33.

Honig, A. S. (1998). *Psychosexual development in infants and young children: Implications for caregivers.* Presentation at the annual meeting of the National Association for the Education of Young Children, Toronto, 19 November 1998.

Katz, P. A. (1987). Variations in family constellations: Effects on gender schemata. *New Directions for Child Development* 38: 39–56.

Kincaid, J. (1992). *Child-loving: The erotic child and Victorian culture.* New York: Routledge.

King, J. R. (1997). Keeping it quiet: Gay teachers in the primary grades. In *Making a place for pleasure in early childhood education,* ed. J. J. Tobin. New Haven, Conn.: Yale University Press.

Lively, V., and E. Lively. (1991). *Sexual development of young children*. Albany, N.Y.: Delmar.

Lyman, K. (1996/1997). Teaching the whole story: One school's struggle toward gay and lesbian inclusion. *Rethinking Schools* 11(2): 14–17.

Miller, N. (1995). *Out of the past: Gay and lesbian history from 1869 to the present*. New York: Vintage.

Ramsey, P. J. (1986). Racial and cultural categories. In *Promoting social and moral development in young children: Creative approaches for the classroom*, ed. C. P. Edwards. New York: Teachers College Press.

Sears, J. T. (1991). *Growing up gay in the south: Race, gender, and journeys of the spirit*. New York: Harrington Park Press.

Strickland, B. R. (1995). Research on sexual orientation and human development: A commentary. *Developmental Psychology* 31(1): 137–40.

Theilheimer, R., and B. Cahill. (1998). A messy closet in the early childhood classroom. Unpublished paper, Las Cruces, New Mexico.

Wickens, E. (1994). *Anna Day and the O-Ring*. Boston: Alyson Press.

· 5 ·

FORBIDDEN FRUIT: BLACK MALES' CONSTRUCTIONS
OF TRANSGRESSIVE SEXUALITIES IN MIDDLE SCHOOL

James Earl Davis

INTRODUCTION

Although black males and black females alike experience negative schooling, some research suggests that the problems facing black males are more chronic and extreme, thus deserving special attention (Kunjufu 1983; Mincy 1994; Polite 1993). Others point to cultural messages about black males and how they are negatively constructed in the media and in everyday life (Blount and Cunningham 1996; Guerrero 1994; Harper 1996; Miller 1996). These images portray the young black male as violent, disrespectful, unintelligent, hypersexualized, and generally threatening. Such messages, without a doubt, carry over into schools and affect how black male students are treated, positioned, and distributed opportunities to learn. In almost every category of academic failure in most public schools, black males are disproportionately represented. One study documents that only 2 percent of African American males enrolled in the public school system of a large Midwestern city achieved a cumulative grade-point average of at least a 3 on a 4-point scale. At the same time, three-fourths of black males in that system had averages below two points (Leake and Leake 1992).

Although the plight of young black males in school is a concern for many, little is known about how school context affects their educational and social experiences. Black males are both adored and loathed in American schools. They are on the vanguard of hip-hop culture and set the standards of athleticism. On the other hand, they experience disproportionate levels of punishment and academic marginality. Toney Sewell (1997) describes this compelling contradiction of being "the darlings of popular youth subculture and the sinners in the classroom" (2) as lead-

49

ing to the formation of a set of specialized behaviors in school. These behaviors have particular consequences for black males, namely, how others construct them and how they see themselves. How do young African American males respond to a context in which they are regarded as both sexy and sexually threatening? How do they purchase a space in schools that is reflective of their masculine identity? The masculine spaces that they build are often in response, consciously or subconsciously, to schools that construct them as academically and socially inferior. Indeed, schools are critical sites for young black males as they make meaning of who they are, what they are supposed to do, and how others perceive them.

One reason commonly mentioned for the alienation and poor academic performance of some black males is that they perceive schooling activities as feminine and irrelevant to their masculine sense of self (Holland 1989, 1992). Others contend that the increased presence of committed and successful black male adults in educational environments is essential for enhancing black boys' academic and social development. In the place of successful interventions, or until such interventions are developed, other socializing agents are at play—ones that are operated by and for black males themselves. The construction of sexualities falls squarely within their domain and is informed by a shared understanding of appropriate masculine behavior and style.

Most research on African American males in the U.S. school system typically centers on "at-riskness" and relatively poor academic performance. Little attention is given to how black males construct personal meaning for their lives in and out of school. Particularly, discussions about how black males make sense of their own masculinity and sexuality and others around them has been noticeably absent. In search of meaningful places for their gendered and sexual selves at school, black males harbor personal expectations that are often disconnected from broader schooling expectations (Holland 1989; Sanders and Reed 1995).

This essay frames a critical discussion of how race, gender, and sexuality intersect in a middle-school setting, and is informed by the social forces and experiences of this context. Based on observations, interviews, and small-group discussions over a two-year period with students at a medium-size middle school (grades 6–8) located in a large suburban county, this essay links constructions of masculinities to an interactive process of being black and male. In providing a reading of a specific middle-school environment, I unravel student narratives about parameters of masculine identity, and about black male representation.

SCHOOLING SEXUALITIES AND MASCULINE TRANSGRESSIONS

A distinct black male–centered cultural space is organized at school around a set of competing and complementary forces. Gender, racial, and sexual identities help frame a masculine middle-school orthodoxy that is dominated by the needs and demands of boys themselves. Black boys at the school clearly understand and embrace an accepted code of masculinized conduct. This code is more than a masculine coping strategy, or a racialized identity formation (Majors and Mancini Billson 1992). Rather, it meticulously connects boundaries of race, gender, class, and sexuality, while maintaining its solid normative masculine core. Simple categorization of black males exclusively by race, class, or sexuality fails to address the complex interaction of these identities. The timidity of teachers, school administrators, and educational researchers to highlight these more complicated social spaces reflects a broader intellectual ambivalence to engage in and problematize this intersectionality (Awkward 1995; Hunter and Davis 1994). However, calls for a more nuanced reading of this complex matrix are emerging. For instance, Marriott's (1996) critique of black cultural and masculinity studies indicts traditional attempts to stabilize as well as juxtapose racial identity and sexuality. He cites new scholarly efforts that allow linkages and continuities of race and sexuality, resulting in a "theorizing of blackness, sexuality and gender as representations articulated in discourse which forestall, if not deconstruct, any notion of identification as a simple process" (198). Similarly, in his profiles of African American gay males, Sears (1995) like others (Beam 1986; Hemphill 1991; Mercer 1994) describes a complex identity-formation process that's often made invisible by rigid lines of sexuality, race, class, and gender. Indeed, the treatment of these identity categories as mutually exclusive social experiences is extremely problematic for work with black boys in school. By essentializing them as being only "racial" obscures the diversity of their multiple subject positions, and also limits our understanding of a multifaceted black male adolescent sexuality that is nurtured, performed, and often perfected at school.

Sexuality is often the subtext of much of the adolescent social jockeying and peer relations in middle school. It is significant that sexuality and its representation regarding young people has a history of censorship and intellectual discomfort, particularly black youth sexuality (Giroux 1998; Mac An Ghaill 1994). That youth sexuality in schooling contexts is consistently represented as deviant and exploitative renders it silent and invisible. Adolescent sexuality continues to be problematic in its representational and realized forms. The sexual allure of adolescents is seen as one that's been controlled by the commercial and sexual exportation of adults. How adolescents make sense of and narrate their own sexuality goes virtually unnoticed (Giroux 1998). Although the sexualized identity of black boys is too often ignored, misunderstood, and rendered silent, it offers an even more compelling sexual representation of youth that are culturally marked as menacing and dangerous.

From all indications it appears that most of the boys at this middle school are not sexually active but are extremely active with their constructions of the masculine and sexual "other." The school culture is clearly heterosexual and normative, wherein boys are expected and encouraged to exhibit an interest in girls and resist dispositions and behaviors not associated with boys. Black males carry a heavier burden of sexuality than do their white male peers at the middle school. Along with the constructed image of troublemakers in and out of class, black boys also hold a special sexualized space at the school. This position is a precarious one and holds different value among various peer groups in the school community. For the most part, strong platonic friendships between black boys and girls are nonexistent, unless the friendship is pretense for sexual positioning or at least the talk of sexualized relations. Generally, interracial dating is taboo. However, there are a few black boys, mostly eighth-graders, who have become the objects of affection for some white girls. As Michael, an eighth-grade black male, states: "Right now black guys are very popular. It seems like white guys have lost their status, they are more invisible. I think a lot of white girls buy into the myth about black guys."

Michael is a very thoughtful and articulate student. He is well liked by teachers and consistently appears on the honor roll. Another black boy mentions him in conversation and says that other students "don't like him because he acts geekie and can't dress." Although Michael does not label himself as one of the popular black guys, he does feel some of the social pressure, imposed within and without the black male peer group, to present himself in a more conforming hyper(hetero)sexualized way at school. A recurring pressure is to date or at least talk about the desire to date white girls. One of Michael's best friends, Juan, admits to liking white girls and takes some pride in his newfound sexualized status: "Before coming to school here, I went to school with all black people. I lived in an all black neighborhood and only associated with other blacks. Now I live in the suburbs, mostly white neighborhood. Since being in a school that's mixed, I've gotten to know all different kinds of people. Before, I really didn't have contact with white girls. But being at this school you get to know them, and I like that."

Michael also feels that a few black boys have become "specialized" and very popular at school, primarily because of the "sex thing." He laments his recent fall from grace. "Last year I was in the most popular in-group at the school, but I was kicked out this year, I don't know why."

In general, the school culture is one that is hyper(hetero)sexualized for black males. Although this cultural atmosphere of hypersexuality is by no means completely attributable to black males themselves, some of them often reinforce (intentionally and inadvertently) racial and sexual stereotypes. The potential benefits of this hypersexualized status make it difficult for most boys to reject this social marking. A few boys do not always adhere to the prescribed "straight" masculine orthodoxy, however. The school's masculine code makes clear what's acceptable masculine presentational behavior, including hallway walk, stride or gait, school attire (particularly sneakers and oversize shirts and pants), lunchroom seating patterns, and how boys carry their books and book bags.

The restrictive sexualized culture of black boys at the school also serves as a policing agent for the enforcement of normative sexuality among boys. Black boys reserve the most severe social punishment for transgressors of the behavioral code associated with interactions among same-sex peers. Transgression is not really about sexual acts or intents per se, but about peer constructions of sexuality that are often based on violating an aspect of the code. The mere act of verbalizing alternative views on sexuality, peer relationships, or masculinity, as well as questioning any aspect of the code, could result in the marked violation of community homosocial expectancies. With this transgression comes the perception that a boy is "gay." This acquired status usually requires the ultimate sanctioning—a banishment from the "black boyhood" to the exclusive company of black girls or, even worse, to the social networks of a variety of white student subcultural groups. Here's part of a conversation I had with a seventh-grader about a black male transgressor:

> s: He's like gay—a real fag. He swishes when he walks and he talks like a girl. Once he came up behind me at the water fountain.
> j: What did he do?
> s: Nothing. He was just there acting like a girl. It made me nervous so I got away from him as far as I could.
> j: What do you mean when you say, "he's gay"?
> s: Ah, you know that he's gay. He likes guys.
> j: So does he say he's gay?
> s: No, he'll say that he is not gay. He says he likes girls.
> j: OK, he's not gay. So he's straight?
> s: No. That's not true. It doesn't matter what he says. He's still gay. He doesn't care what people think about him. That's why he gets into a lot of trouble. He has to fight a lot. People at school can't stand him.

Another student reflects on race and gender constraints at the school in reference to the same transgressive black male: "People make fun of this guy because of the way he walks and the way he talks. He swishes sometimes, so people make fun of him . . . and this voice . . . I wouldn't want to be like him. He tries to be hard and tough 'cause of the way he acts, but people still don't like him. He goes around thinking that he is really hard, but he isn't."

Many labels are used to describe boys who transgress normative male expectations. Most are pejorative slurs that are used by boys to belittle, distance, insult, injure, and sanction. The word *sissy* is a classical descriptive that evokes much emotional reaction. I find this word particularly useful because of its traditional use in black communities. In an effort to take the hate and sting out of the word, Hunter (1993) suggests taking ownership and power over it. He offers the following definition for sissy: "a male (regardless of sexual orientation) who is in some way not masculine, who is in some meaningful way more like women than men tend to be, or are 'supposed' to be" (153). Unfortunately, little attention has been paid to the plight of sissies in school. Black boys who are constructed as sissies by their peers are severely stigmatized because of the cultural weight of a racialized sexual mythology about black males. Black sissy boys occupy a complicated social space in school. Because they defy both a racial and a gender code, these boys are constantly juggling and negotiating their legitimacy and place in these two identity groups. Unfortunately, their efforts are usually fruitless.

Through a masculinized code black boys are engaged in producing and reproducing a representation of an authentic black masculine self. The masculine code creates its own means for resistance to a school culture and climate that excludes and labels them as at-risk city boys with very little academic strength. The code in turn can function as a vehicle wherein their hypermasculine style serves as a form of protest and "in-your-face" hip-hop defiance that usually reinforces negative expectations already held by white teachers and peers. Black boys at this middle school are both victimized and liberated by their constructed identities. Some endure and maneuver racial stereotypes that construct them as hypersexualized, using this tactic for social benefits. Other black boys who do not meet the standards of an acceptable gender identity are relegated to the status of masculine misfit.

BLACK MASCULINITIES GO TO SCHOOL

During the late seventies the following narrative started to emerge: Schools are dominated by women and therefore impose on boys a feminine culture. This recurring message has focused on strategies needed to address the perceived feminization of black boys in schooling. The narrative sees teachers (mostly white women) in particular as imposing feminine standards of behavioral expectations on black boys. The image drawn from this narrative is that of public school classrooms with African American males being demasculinized by white women. Because of particular racial and gender experiences of these teachers, there is an accepted understanding that they are ill prepared to teach black boys about being male and becoming men (Holland 1991, 1992). Moreover, the narrative suggests that these teachers prefer teaching white girls, whose behavioral styles and dispositions are more similar to their own. Connected to growing concerns about the successful passage of black boys to manhood, discussions about the possible extinction of black males evoke powerful rhetoric such as "institutional decimation of black males" and "black males as endangered species."

The crisis narrative and actual data about black males in schools have created a groundswell of activity directed toward improving their educational chances. In almost every school where there are significant numbers of black boys, programs are in place to turn the tide. There are more than two hundred Rites of Passage programs, one thousand mentoring and role-model programs, and about one hundred black male classrooms in U.S. public schools. Although these programs emerge out of concern for black boys' relative lack of educational success, too many of them are, unfortunately, framed narrowly by the crisis narrative. Although the problem is compelling enough to galvanize resources in an effort to "save the black male," subsequent interventions based on this narrative have been characterized as antifeminist and misogynistic. Manhood training programs and other school-based interventions such as black male academies and single-sex classrooms are designed to address problems faced by black male youth. These initiatives by and large are aimed to help boys understand what it means to be a man and counter threats to appropriate masculine development. Too often, however, these programs have not only failed to question patriarchy and men's role in its perpetuation, but have been criticized for their chauvinist curriculum focused on black men taking their rightful place as head of the family and assuming the traditional economic provider role (Oliver 1989; Watson and Smitherman 1991).

Moreover, black boys are recast exclusively as victims, often setting their interests against those of black girls. Teachers (primarily women) are blamed, but most intervention efforts overlook these teachers as potential sources for enhancing the school experience of black males. Clearly the message to teachers in elementary and middle school is that race and gender matter in educating black boys.

CONCLUSIONS

As I have tried to illustrate, middle school is a place where black boys make meaning about their gendered and sexual identities. In the process a cultural milieu is created that forces and feeds upon a masculine hegemony. The dynamic nature of negotiating identity categories is difficult for black middle-school boys. As Shawn, a seventh-grader who captures the feeling of most of his peers, concedes, "It's very hard being a black male at this school." To be sure, the difficulties experienced by black boys at school are not distributed equally. A group of boys, due to their nontraditional masculinities, bear a disproportionate level of antagonism and social harassment.

African American males are caught in a politicized battle over whose masculinity will be honored, valued, supported, and represented in schools. It is clear from this reading of a middle-school culture, that only a "straight" masculinity is really available for black boys. I refer to this as a straight masculinity not exclusively because of its heteronormative nature, although that is relevant. Rather, *straight* describes the restrictive and monolithic masculine proscriptions offered black boys. To be clear, this middle-school culture endorses only a heteromasculinity that's framed by sexualized relationships with girls. How boys position themselves relative to girls, in terms of sexual otherness, is important in maintaining the strictness of the normative masculine school code.

A broader definition of acceptable masculinity is being called for in middle schools. The restrictive nature of the code creates a very rigid sexual dichotomy for black boys. Any thought, action, or response contrary to the straight masculinity norms at the school is considered "gay" and out of bounds of the accepted masculinity—the forbidden fruit of gender nonconformity. The labeling of boys as sissies or their actions as gay is not all about sexuality. *Gay* is viewed as a marginalizing and distancing status for boys at the middle school. So to be gay does not necessarily correspond to a boy's sexual orientation, identity, or experience, but rather reflects a boy's marginalized cultural status and value.

The narrowness of the constructed gender and sexual culture at this middle school parallels our intellectual rigidity in crossing race, class, gender, and sexuality boundaries. Work that seeks to connect and intersect these identity categories is also considered transgressive. Likewise, when boys at the school try to articulate, by words or action, a more complex view about gender identity, they are punished socially for this transgression.

This stigmatizing, restrictive gender code presents unique challenges for black boys, regardless if they are gay or straight. The immediate challenge facing us regarding black boys who are constructed as gay is to provide a safe schooling environment where the fear of violence and insult is minimized. Teachers and school administrators bear a disproportionate role in monitoring violent and disrespectful behavior and language in classrooms and in other social spaces at school. Too often school officials are complicit in the victimization of boys. This is particularly true for effeminate boys who are socially sanctioned for transgressing masculine norms by their mere presence and too often are placed in harm's way of physical threat and violence (Rofes 1994). A zero tolerance policy for violence and hate speech directed toward gay-constructed and sissy boys is necessary for all middle schools. Straight boys also fall prey to a strict and restrictive gender code at school. Conformity to expected behavioral roles not only increases their level of anxiety about any potential of being labeled gay, it also circumscribes the range of social, emotional, and academic experiences in school. Also, the condemnation of border crossing to other ideas of gender identity constrains and dictates the kinds of friendships boys have with each other. School culture in turn suffers from a monolithic developmental zone that stifles creativity, limits academic engagement, and promotes the formation of incomplete identities.

Although it's true that school is an important site of critical social and cultural intervention (Browne and Fletcher 1995; Connell 1993), the intervention has to be clearly thought out in light of where boys are positioned in school. Developing critical work in the area of schooling masculinities suggests that the relationship between black boys, their constructions of self, and school culture, are both more problematic and more complex than have been previously thought (Fordham 1996; Kenway et al. 1998). Indeed, the middle-school years are appropriate to include curricula that focus on antihomophobic, antisexist, and antiracist themes. A rethinking of current course content across the core curriculum, plus areas such as music, art, and physical education, must occur where the creation of safe space, both intellectual and physical, is given priority. In these spaces boys should be encouraged to explore and engage in nontraditional gender projects.

The middle-school lives of African American males are complex. They are in some ways empowering because these students set their own social agenda and resistance strategies. At the same time, however, they experience a repressive, largely self-created culture grounded in hegemonic masculinity that enforces strict gender conformity and ultimately victimizes them.

REFERENCES

Awkward, M. (1995). *Negotiating difference: Race, gender, and the politics of positionality*. Chicago: University of Chicago Press.

Beam, J., ed. (1986). *In the life: A black gay anthology*. Boston: Alyson.

Blount, M., and G. P. Cunningham, ed. (1996). *Representing black men*. New York: Routledge.

Browne, R., and R. Fletcher. (1995). *Boys in schools: Addressing the real issues—behavior, values and relationships*. Sydney: Finch.

Connell, R. W. (1993). Disruptions: Improper masculinities and schooling. In *Beyond silenced voices: Class, race and gender in United States schools*, ed. L. Weis and M. Fine. Albany, N.Y.: SUNY Press.

Fordham, S. (1996). *Blacked out: Dilemmas of race, identity and success at Capital High*. Chicago: University of Chicago Press.

Giroux, H. A. (1998). Teenage sexuality, body politics, and the pedagogy of display. In *Youth culture: Identity in a postmodern world*, ed. J. S. Epstein. New York: Blackwell.

Guerrero, E. (1994). The black man on our screens and the empty space in representation. In *The black male: Representations of masculinity in contemporary American art*, ed. T. Golden. New York: Whitney Museum.

Harper, P. B. (1996). *Are we not men? Masculine anxiety and the problem of African-American identity*. New York: Oxford University Press.

Hemphill, E., ed. (1991). *Brother to brother: New writings by black gay men*. Boston: Alyson.

Holland, S. (1989). Fighting the epidemic of failure: A radical strategy for educating inner-city boys. *Teacher Magazine* 1(Sept./Oct.): 88–89.

———. (1991). Positive role models for primary grade black inner-city males. *Equity and Excellence* 25(1): 40–44.

———. (1992). Same-gender classes in Baltimore: How to avoid the problems faced in Detroit/Milwaukee. *Equity and Excellence* 25(2): 93.

Hunter, A. (1993). Same door, different closet: A heterosexual sissy's coming-out party. In *Heterosexuality: A 'Feminism and Psychology' reader*, ed. S. Wilkinson and C. Kitzinger. London: Sage.

Hunter, A. G., and J. E. Davis. (1994). Hidden voices of black men: The meaning, structure, and complexity of manhood. *Journal of Black Studies* 25(1): 20–40.

Kenway, J., S. Willis, J. Blackmore, and L. Rennie. (1998). *Answering back: Girls, boys and feminism in school*. New York: Routledge.

Kunjufu, J. (1983). *Countering the conspiracy to destroy black boys*. Chicago: African-American Images.

Leake, D. O., and B. L. Leake. (1992). Islands of hope: Milwaukee's African-American immersion schools. *Journal of Negro Education* 61(1): 4–29.

Mac An Ghaill, M. (1994). (In)visibility: Sexuality, race and masculinity in the school context. In *Challenging lesbian and gay inequalities in education*, ed. D. Epstein. Philadelphia: Open University Press.

Majors, R., and J. Mancini Billson. (1992). *Cool pose: The dilemmas of black manhood in America*. New York: Lexington.

Marriott, D. (1996). Reading black masculinities. In *Understanding masculinities: Social relations and cultural arenas*, ed. M. Mac An Ghaill. Philadelphia: Open University Press.

Mercer, K. (1994). *Welcome to the jungle: New positions in black cultural studies*. New York: Routledge.

Miller, J. (1996). *Search and destroy: African-American males in the criminal justice system*. Cambridge, Mass.: Cambridge University Press.

Mincy, R. B., ed. (1994). *Nurturing young black males: Challenges to agencies, programs, and social policy*. Washington, D. C.: Urban Institute.

Oliver, W. (1989). Black males and social problems: Prevention through Afrocentric socialization. *Journal of Black Studies* 20(4): 15–39.

Polite, V. (1993). Educating African-American males in suburbia: Quality education . . . Caring environment? *Journal of African American Male Studies* 1(1): 92–105.

Rofes, E. E. (1994). Making our schools safe for sissies. *High School Journal* 77(1/2): 37–40.

Sanders, E. T., and P. L. Reed. (1995). An investigation of the possible effects of an immersion as compared to a traditional program for African-American males. *Urban Education* 30: 93–112.

Sears, J. T. (1995). Black-gay or gay-black: Choosing identities and identifying choices. In *The gay teen: Educational practice and theory for lesbian, gay, and bisexual adolescents*, ed. G. Unks. New York: Routledge.

Sewell, T. (1997). Teacher attitude: Who's afraid of the big black boy? Paper presented at the Annual American Educational Research Association meeting, March 24–28, Chicago.

Watson, C., and G. Smitherman. (1991). Educational equity and Detroit's male academies. *Equity and Excellence* 25(2): 90–105.

· 6 ·

READING QUEER[1] ASIAN AMERICAN MASCULINITIES AND SEXUALITIES IN ELEMENTARY SCHOOL

Kevin K. Kumashiro

While in elementary school, I internalized many stereotypes and messages about who I was supposed to be and, consequently, read (that is, made sense of) my identities and experiences through these normative lenses. For example, I read myself through a racist lens that viewed white Americans as the norm in U.S. society while stereotyping Asian Americans as the smart, hardworking minority. I read myself through a sexist lens that valued a particular form of masculinity while denigrating other expressions of masculinity and all expressions of femininity among boys. And I read myself through a heterosexist lens that defined heterosexuality as "normal" and normative while characterizing queer sexuality as something to fear, hate, and avoid. As a boy who was Asian American, nerdy, and queer (though I had not yet self-identified as queer), I wrestled subconsciously with these harmful readings.

My responses were paradoxical. I tried to conform to the stereotype that Asian Americans are good students, to compensate for feeling inferior to other boys, and to repress and negotiate my queer sexual desires. But I also tried to avoid admitting to myself, and showing to others, that I was being harmed. I ended up throwing myself into arenas such as academics and music, in which I could and did excel. On the surface, then, I was a school success, but my success was, in large part, a mask—a mask that concealed my feelings of difference and fear of isolation while in school.

While growing up, I needed to view myself through less harmful lenses. Similarly, educators today need to read their students through lenses that help rather than harm them, such as lenses that disrupt racism, heterosexism, and other forms of oppression. Researchers have suggested three helpful ways of reading queer Asian American masculinities and sexualities in elementary school. Here I draw on my own experiences as I describe and critique each one. I argue that educators need to make use of all three approaches if they are to work effectively against the multiple forms of oppression facing their students, especially queer Asian American boys.

READING CULTURAL DIFFERENCE

Many researchers have talked about the genders and sexualities of Asian American boys using a cultural lens to describe their differences. They argue that notions of what is normal and queer vary from culture to culture. For example, mainstream U.S. society defines "masculine" or "real" boys as those who constantly demonstrate to other males aggression, competitiveness, and excellence in a number of arenas, including athletics and physique (Kimmel 1994). "Traditional Asian cultures," however, condemn physical displays of aggression and privilege the mind over the body, such as in Chinese communities where boys have traditionally learned to use their wits, not their fists (Sung 1985). The "typical" Asian American boy, then, might seem queer (or effeminate) by U.S. standards since he lacks the dominant, or hegemonic, form of masculinity, but that is because he exhibits a different form of masculinity, one that is valued in his own culture.

The cultural lens has also been used to differentiate Asian American heterosexuality from the normative heterosexuality. For example, mainstream U.S. society encourages sexualized interactions between boys and girls, such as dating, and even condones those interactions that are overtly sexual and sexist, such as boys' sexual harassment of girls and women, defining such interactions as mere expressions of "natural childhood sexuality" (Walkerdine 1990). In contrast, "traditional Asian cultures" expect that sexual attractiveness, expressions, and interactions will be underplayed, subtle, and private, and that boys in particular will control their sexual desire so as not to distract from making learning their top priority (Sung 1985). The "typical" Asian American boy, then, may appear queer (or asexual) by U.S. standards, but by underplaying his sexuality while hyperachieving in academics, he also exemplifies traditional Asian values.

The cultural lens has even been used to differentiate Asian American queers from other queers. Chan (1995), for example, argues that psychological models used to describe the "stages" of queer sexual identity development are based on Western conceptualizations of sexuality and on the experiences of white American queers. "Traditional Asian cultures," however, value different expressions of sexuality, and do not consider public expressions of queer sexuality and participation in queer communities to be the highest stages in, or the "achievement" of, an individual's sexual-identity development. Some queer Asian boys privately express same-sex attraction, but publicly appear heterosexual (such as by dating girls) and refrain from "coming out" and identifying as queer. The "typical" Asian American queer boy, then, may appear abnormal with an "unachieved" queer identity, but he is normal within some Asian queer subcultures.

Educators who use the cultural lens expect that many Asian American boys—straight and queer—will value and exhibit different masculinities and sexualities (compared to white American boys) because they come from different cultures. They also help all their students develop an understanding of cultural differences. More educators need to take this responsibility and ask, "In general, what are ways in which Asian American boys are culturally different from the mainstream?" And, more broadly, "What are ways in which other marginalized groups are culturally different from the mainstream?" Already there exist numerous helpful resources for educators interested in learning and teaching about the cultures and histories of Asian Americans[2] and queer Asian Americans.[3]

The strength of this reading strategy is its ability to acknowledge and affirm, rather than obscure and denigrate, differences among students. In particular, a boy raised to underplay his sexuality, refrain from physical aggression, and avoid athletics will not be pathologized as abnormal and inferior compared to the white American norm, but valued as normal and desirable by "traditional Asian" standards. He will not be admonished to behave the ways boys in the United States are "supposed" to behave, but will be encouraged to be himself, explore his own interests, and take pride in his own cultural traditions and heritage. As I reflect on my own elementary-school experiences, I remember no reading strategy offered to me that disrupted the only ones I knew—ones that defined me as not only different from, but inferior to, other boys because I was not big and strong, nor aggressive and athletic. I needed to see myself in a way that did not make me feel ashamed. I needed a cultural lens that could help others see me, and help me see myself, in affirming ways.

The cultural-difference approach, however, does have several weaknesses. First, it essentializes Asianness, grouping together a vast range of cultures, histories, and identities. Notions of a "traditional Asian culture" may *describe* some Asian Americans, but by failing to recognize that cultural groups are tremendously diverse and that cultures change over time and from place to place, they can also *prescribe* how all Asian Americans ought to be. For example, some researchers argue that Asian American students are "succeeding" in schools because "traditional Asian cultures" value education. Not all Asian Americans, however, do well academically, and not all value academic achievement (Lee 1996). Second, the approach fails to disrupt the status quo. Defining Asianness as "culturally different" allows white American heterosexuality and masculinity to remain the norms that Asianness is different from. Because heterosexual Asian American boys "underplay" their sexuality, theirs is actually a deviant heterosexuality. Similarly, because they lack hegemonic masculinity, such as with nerdy, passive students (or exhibit a hypermasculinity, such as with Asian gangs), theirs is actually a *deviant* masculinity. Third, it can absolve educators from their responsibility to work against the harm experienced by their students. Because Asian cultures traditionally confine all sexual expression to the private realm, educators can argue that challenging sexism and heterosexism by discussing issues of sex and sexuality in the classroom is culturally inappropriate.

The cultural-difference reading strategy, then, is helpful for achieving certain goals, but if used uncritically, it can also be harmful.

READING DIFFERENCES CRITICALLY

Offering a more complex understanding of the dynamics of oppression, some researchers suggest that reading queer Asian American masculinities and sexualities requires looking through not a cultural lens (which gazes outwardly), but a critical lens (which critiques within). They examine U.S. society not only for ways in which Asian American masculinities and sexualities are labeled "deviant" (processes of "Othering"), but for ways in which whiteness and heterosexuality are normalized (processes of privileging), and suggest that the harm experienced by queer Asian American boys results not only from cultural insensitivity and individual prejudice, but from social structures and competing ideologies.

One form of structural/ideological oppression that queer Asian American boys confront is a white-dominated racial hierarchy. Mainstream U.S. society often defines white Americans as the "real" or "authentic" Americans, while stereotyping Asian Americans as perennial foreigners, despite the long history of Asians in the United States. For example, I am often asked, "Where are you from?" to which I answer, "Hawaii" (where I was born and raised), only be to countered with, "No, where are you *really* from?" as if my home can be only in Asia. Defining Asians as outsiders helps keep white Americans at the center of U.S. society. In turn, the perennial-foreigner stereotype helps to reinforce the fear of an Asian invasion and conquest, that is, the "yellow peril" (Okihiro 1994). Mainstream society often views Asian-outsiders as threats to white-insiders, such as recently arrived refugees who "invade" a town and "drain" its financial and educational resources—resources that would otherwise go to the "American" (that is, white) children.

When Asian Americans are recognized as "American," we are insidiously called the "model minority." Reinforcing the racial hierarchy, we are cited as proof that the United States is a meritocratic society, is not racist, and that other minorities (students of color) could also succeed and achieve the "American dream" if they only worked as hard (Lee 1996). Paradoxically, examples abound of racial oppression experienced by Asian American students—both visible injuries, such as discrimination, harassment, and violence, and invisible ones, such as psychological harm. Even high-achieving students face difficulties, as my own experiences illustrate. Yet because of our supposed "success," our problems are often unexpected and overlooked, by others and ourselves.

A second form of structural/ideological oppression that queer Asian American boys confront is a sexual order characterized by the normalization and expectation of straightness (that is, heterosexism) and the fear, hatred, and intolerance of queerness (homophobia). Mainstream U.S. society, through popular culture, the media, even schools and families, often privileges heterosexuality as "normal," "moral," "healthy," and "natural," while Othering queer sexuality as abnormal, sinful, an illness, and a crime. This Othering is not merely ideological—legal statutes and various policies often forbid and prosecute expressions of queer sexuality. As a result, queer students experience a range of injuries, from verbal abuse ("fag," "dyke") and physical violence (gay-bashing), to marginalization in the curriculum (for example, never learning about queers, or learning about them only in the context of AIDS), to institutionalized silencing (such as the absence of antiqueer harassment policies, or the failure of educators to acknowledge queer parents, or the lack of role models and resources for queer youth). And they respond in a variety of ways, some of which reflect the harm, such as dropping out of school, depression, and suicide, and some of which mask it, such as overcompensating or "hyperperforming" in academics, extracurricular activities, and/or heterosexual activity.

Because queer Asian American boys confront (at least) two structural/ideological forms of oppression (namely, racism and heterosexism/homophobia), some researchers conclude that they are *doubly oppressed* or "doubly marginalized" (Hom and Ma 1993). They argue that understanding their experiences requires reading their racial and sexual identities simultaneously, or looking simultaneously at racist forms and heterosexist forms of oppression. I, for example, in the beginning of this chapter, discuss my educational experiences primarily in terms of simultaneity (looking through a racist lens, and a sexist lens, and a heterosexist lens).

Educators who read differences critically and simultaneously recognize that, in society and in schools, racism, heterosexism, and other forms of oppression do play out in ways that privilege certain groups and marginalize others. They also understand that these dual processes of privileging and Othering are often invisible because they are couched in what many call "common sense" (Apple 1995). For example, to many people, it is common sense that men have the "final authority" in households, that men fall in love with (only) women, and that white men constitute (and should constitute) the majority of U.S. history textbooks. Yet these social structures and ideologies are "common sense" only because they have been defined as natural and left unchallenged (that is, naturalized) over time. More educators need to learn about and critique (and help their students learn about and critique) the history and harmfulness of commonsense ways of privileging and Othering different groups in society. They need to ask, "How has society come to this way of thinking and operating? And what effects do these assumptions have?"

Furthermore, more educators and students need to engage in resisting and challenging such oppressive structures and ideologies, beginning with changes in their own school's culture and environment. Queer Asian American boys (and all marginalized groups) need schools to provide safe spaces (free from harassment and discrimination), supportive spaces (with people who affirm and advocate for them), and empowering spaces (with various resources). Because the status quo is harmful, schools that focus on only academic goals risk being complicit with various forms of oppression. Schools must provide social and psychological support, and engage in social and political transformation.

The main strength of the critical reading strategy is its ability to offer a more complex understanding of oppression. It looks at not only the Othering of Asianness and queer sexuality, but also the privileging of whiteness and heterosexuality, and ways in which these dual processes are often couched in the language of common sense. Furthermore, it looks simultaneously at students' multiple identities and experiences with multiple forms of oppression. In particular, it recognizes that a queer Asian American boy may have a radically different experience in school compared to a straight Asian American boy, solely because they have different sexualities, and likewise compared to a queer white American boy because of different racial identities. The critical lens gets educators to expect that some of their students might be queer and Asian American (or some other combination of marginalized identities), and to ensure that their antiracist pedagogies are not heterosexist, their antiheterosexist pedagogies not white centered, and so on. In other words, it helps educators address multiple forms of oppression simultaneously.

The critical reading strategy, however, does have a major weakness: It relies on an additive model of oppression. The experiences of queer Asian American boys cannot be captured by, and are more complex than, the sum of Asian American and queer experiences. Queer Asian American boys confront additional forms of oppression.

READING FOR DIFFERENT CITATIONS

Queer Asian American boys experience oppression not only in mainstream U.S. society, but in communities traditionally marginalized in society, such as racism in queer communities, and heterosexism in Asian American communities (Wat 1996). However, the racism and heterosexism playing out in these communities do not replicate the racism and heterosexism in mainstream society. Although they have generally the same meanings as those in mainstream society, and though they carry the powers to produce similar results (that is, they often harm people in similar ways), they are slightly different; they add something new.[4] In other words, the racism and heterosexism in traditionally marginalized communities refer to, reflect, and draw on (cite) the racism and heterosexism in mainstream society, but they also supplement them, in that they add a new dimension and carry excess (Butler 1997).

For example, the heterosexism in Asian American communities is similar to that of mainstream society, but it has something extra, namely, a racialized dimension. As with mainstream society, Asian America normalizes heterosexuality and denigrates queer sexualities and queer individuals. This is how the heterosexism of Asian America cites that of mainstream society. However, unlike mainstream society, Asian America often assigns racial markers to different sexual orientations. In particular, the "traditional Asian values" of getting married, having children, and passing down the family name, imply that being a virtuous or real Asian American requires, at least for adults, the performance of heterosexuality (by marrying a different gender, bearing children, and so on). In other words, heterosexuality in Asian America is racialized *as Asian*; it is an Asian value. Similarly, queer sexuality is often attributed to white Americans, such as with the notion that queers are supposed to be white: If an Asian American is queer, that individual is not a real Asian, is more white than Asian, has the "white disease" (Wat 1996). In other words, queer sexualities in Asian America are racialized *as white*; they are characteristic of white Americans. Queer Asian American boys, then, do confront heterosexism in Asian American communities, but it is a racialized form of heterosexism.

As I reflect on my own childhood, I realize that my sexual repression and confusion resulted from my internalizing both the heterosexism of mainstream society and the racialized heterosexism of Asian America. I had feelings for boys, but told myself I was merely "curious" about them, not attracted to them. Instead, I paid heed only to my attraction for girls. In part, I did not want to be queer, but also in part, I did not even consider being queer a possibility, perhaps because I saw no queers who were Asian American. Not until going to college did I meet other queer Asian Americans, learn about queers in Asian history, and start to critique both the heterosexist "traditional Asian values" and the racist-heterosexist notion that only white Americans are queer. Not until unlearning the racialized heterosexism of Asian America did I start coming out to myself.

Queer communities, too, can be oppressive spaces, where a form of racism plays out that cites the racism in mainstream society but carries some excess, namely, a queered dimension. Like mainstream society, queer communities privilege whiteness while Othering Asianness. Also like mainstream society, queer communities often assign a gendered marker to different racial identities, stereotyping white American men as masculine and Asian American men as feminine (and passive and weak). However, unlike mainstream society, queer communities often give this gendered form of racism a hypersexualized dimension. In particular, whereas being both Asian and male is often read in mainstream society as unmasculine (wimpy, nerdy) and, therefore, sexually undesirable, it is often read by other queers as "exotic" and, therefore, hyperdesirable. In fact, some queer (often older, white American) men actually fetishize queers who fit the stereotype of the feminine, Asian American, youthful boy (Kumashiro, in press). Thus, within queer communities queer Asian American males do confront racism, but it is a queered form of racism.

Educators who look at ways in which certain forms of oppression cite and supplement other forms gain a more nuanced understanding of how queer Asian American boys experience oppression differently in different cultural spaces. Why is this significant? Recognizing that unique forms of oppression play out in marginalized communities forces educators to re-think what it means to challenge oppression. Traditionally, educators expect that Asian American boys can turn to their Asian American families and communities to find relief from racial oppression, and similarly, that queer boys can turn to their queer "families" and communities to find relief from heterosexism and homophobia. But boys who are both queer and Asian American face the paradoxical situation of belonging to both communities while finding solace in neither. With racialized heterosexism in Asian American communities, and queered racism in queer communities, they often feel excluded from, and unsafe and unsupported in, both communities. Even their identities can leave them with a sense of exclusion and paradox: They cannot be both queer and Asian American if queers are "supposed" to be white and Asians are "supposed" to be straight.

REWORKING HARMFUL READING PRACTICES

Educators can help challenge oppression by helping to change traditional reading practices, by helping to disrupt the associations between Asianness and straightness, queerness and whiteness, queerness and abnormality, and so forth, and create associations that are less prescriptive and derogatory. In other words, educators need to help change the harmful ways queer Asian Americans (and straight white Americans, and other groups) are read and treated in Asian America, in queer communities, in mainstream society, and so on. But how do we do this? How do we change the harmful ways in which we read one another and ourselves?

To change reading practices, educators and students must find ways to enter into the processes of citing and supplementing. Earlier, I argued that a community associates certain identities with certain attributes because, over time, those associations are naturalized within that community, such that it is "common sense" to think that way (for example, heterosexuality is normal, queer sexuality is abnormal). However, when many members of a community begin to supplement the meanings of identities or structures in the same way, the associations do change (people no longer see queer sexuality as abnormal, and queers as criminal). For example, many queers have appropriated the term *queer* such that it still cites a deviation from the norm but, when used with other queers, rather than carrying a hateful, derogatory sentiment (which is what it used to and still does cite for many people), it often carries a feeling of self-empowerment. In effect, they have entered into the citational processes of the term *queer*, supplemented it, and changed the meaning of queerness and the social and political power of queers. Although different situations will call for different strategies, this is the type of effort in which educators and students need to engage.

Thus, besides reading through culturally appropriate lenses, and besides reading through lenses that are critical of multiple forms of oppression, educators need to teach themselves and their students to read through lenses that change citational practices. Such strategies, I argue, will benefit not just queer Asian American boys, but all students harmed by oppressive reading practices.

NOTES

1. I use the term *queer* to signify a deviation from what is commonly considered "normal" (that is, how people generally are) and normative (how people ought to be) in terms of both sexual orientation and gender. Asian American boys, then, can be queer in at least two ways: They can have a queer sexuality, meaning they do not self-identify and/or are not identified by others as heterosexual; and they can exhibit a queer gender, meaning they do not express the form of masculinity that society expects of boys.

2. For example, the Asian American Curriculum Project (www.best.com/~aacp/) lists numerous resources for both students and teachers.

3. For example, see Eng and Hom (1998), and the "Queer Asian Pacific Resources" website (www.geocities.com/WestHollywood/Heights/5010/resources .html).

4. I develop these arguments more thoroughly elsewhere (Kumashiro, in press).

REFERENCES

Apple, M. (1995). *Education and power.* 2nd ed. New York: Routledge.

Butler, J. (1997). *Excitable speech.* New York: Routledge.

Chan, C. (1995). Issues of sexual identity in an ethnic minority: The case of Chinese American lesbians, gay men, and bisexual people. In *Lesbian, gay, and bisexual identities over the lifespan,* ed. A. D'Augelli and C. Patterson. New York: Oxford University.

Eng, D., and A. Hom. (1998). *Q&A: Queer in Asian America.* Philadelphia: Temple University.

Hom, A., and M. Ma. (1993). Premature gestures: A speculative dialogue on Asian Pacific Islander lesbian and gay writing. *Journal of Homosexuality* 26(2/3): 21–51.

Kimmel, M. (1994). Masculinity as homophobia. In *Theorizing masculinities,* ed. H. Brod and M. Kaufman. Thousand Oaks, Calif.: Sage.

Kumashiro, K. (In press). Supplementing normalcy and otherness: Queer Asian American men reflect on stereotypes, identity, and oppression. *Qualitative Studies in Education.*

Lee, S. (1996). *Unraveling the "model minority" stereotype: Listening to Asian American youth.* New York: Teachers College.

Okihiro, G. (1994). *Margins and mainstreams: Asians in American history and culture.* Seattle: University of Washington.

Sung, B. (1985). Bicultural conflicts in Chinese immigrant children. *Journal of Comparative Family Studies* 16(2): 255–69.

Walkerdine, V. (1990). *Schoolgirl fictions.* London: Verso.

Wat, E. C. (1996). Preserving the paradox. In *Asian American sexualities,* ed. R. Leong. New York: Routledge.

· 7 ·

"MY MOVING DAYS":
A CHILD'S NEGOTIATION OF MULTIPLE LIFEWORLDS
IN RELATION TO GENDER, ETHNICITY, AND SEXUALITY

Maria Pallotta-Chiarolli

For Steph, for your questions, your insights, your love

"*Hi my name is Stephanie Chiarolli and I would like to tell you about my family's moving days.*" So begins my daughter's story, written when she was eight years old. A story that documents, through her eyes, a world of mobility and ambiguity when one is "queerly raised." My male partner and I are her biological parents. We identify as heterosexual, and our child is "queerly raised." She travels within and between multicultural and multisexual worlds as well as undertaking geographical journeys: to and from Adelaide, where she was born, raised principally by Italian migrant grandparents while we worked full time, and continues to maintain close family and friendship networks; to and from Sydney, where her father lived for two years while she was three and four and where she attends queer events with her parents' friends; and to and from Melbourne, where her father is now primary care-giver supported by a network of multicultural and multisexual friends as my work takes her away at regular intervals.

To be "queerly raised" is to be in motion. Not only and not necessarily geographical motion, but shifting and sliding, negotiating and maneuvering, between and within "lifeworlds" (Cope and Kalantzis 1995). These sociocultural constructs and sites are based on categories such as gender, ethnicity, and sexuality. To be "queerly raised" is to interrogate the taken-for-grantedness of such fixed categories and the way society divides people into "normal" and "abnormal," "natural" and "unnatural," according to their locations within those categories. To be "queerly raised" is possibly to have heterosexual parents, such as ourselves, constructing a nonheteronormative space, and subverting the wider society's heteronormative

71

framework. To be "queerly raised" is to thrive in the destabilization and disruption of normalizing discourses of family, gender, and compulsory heterosexuality. It is an upbringing that encourages stability in mobility, security in change, clarity in ambiguity.

Yet, what happens when a child is raised "queerly"—where multiculturalism and multisexuality are normative constructions in the child's familial and community worlds—and then attends a schooling institution where sexual diversity is still constructed as "deviant"? How do these children interrogate and negotiate their lifeworlds?

Using the writings, experiences, and life circumstances of the first ten years of a third-generation Italian Australian girl called Steph, this chapter explores the kinds of understandings, negotiations, and dilemmas "queerly raised" children experience as they "move" between many sites, and their both conflicting and complementary discourses. For example, what happens when one has grown up attending and participating in the Sydney Gay and Lesbian Mardi Gras only to find that doing a show-and-tell on the event evokes increasing harassment from peers and silencing strategies from teachers with each year of elementary school? How does a child respond to sex education at school that perpetuates a heteronormative reproductive discourse, when the child is part of a community wherein peers are being raised by same-sex couples or being conceived without heterosexual physical coupling? How does a child respond to AIDS phobia at school when HIV-positive persons, and grieving over AIDS-related deaths, have been a part of one's life since birth? What effect does this multipositioning and moving between worlds have on the child's understandings of her own gender and sexual development?

Here is an excerpt from Steph's story entitled "My Moving Days":

> *I go to Sydney sometimes especially at Mardi Gras time and have fun with Mum and her friends. We go to interesting shops and restaurants. I was in the Mardi Gras one year pretending to be Alan and Malcolm's daughter. I wore my purple fairy costume and waved a wand and the gay flag. Lots of people took pictures and I was on the news. At first I was shy because there were so many people and I forgot to wave. Then I started waving. Before it was our turn to move, I saw my Mum waving to me from where her dancing group was getting ready to join in the Parade.*
>
> *I love my life. It's exciting.*

"Queerly raised" children have insights into the lives lived in the gaps, on the borders, and on the hyphens of interwoven categories and social ascriptions. Steph is an insider/outsider/no-sider situated by others and situating herself beyond, within, and between monolithic categorizations and polarizing definitions. She sees what is often silenced, denied, invisibilized in the wider heteronormative worlds of her school, media, and the wider society. She explores the gaps and inconsistencies, pastiche and ambiguities, within which she and other "queerly raised" children exist. She interrogates definitions of Truth, Reality, Purity, and Identity constructed by dominant social discourses, thereby revealing the Truths, Realities, Impurities, and Identities that these discourses say do not exist at all or exist only in forms they can control and distort as being "wrong" or "strange."

Getting ready for school one morning, seven-year-old Steph asks, "What's artificial insemination?"

I ask, "Were you interested in what Uncle Matteo was saying last night?" I had been chatting to a gay Italian friend, Matteo, about his daughter, a baby he'd had with a lesbian and his plans to have another. Steph had been sitting with us silently listening.

Steph nods. "If they don't have sex, how can they have babies, that's all I wanted to know, really. At school we learned that it takes a man and woman who are married to each other to have a baby, but Uncle Matteo is gay and he isn't married. But I know he's had a baby."

I explain how many gays and lesbians are now becoming parents without having sex with each other. And this leads to a chat about women's decisions about having sex and babies, and that leads on to how women should never let anyone exploit their sexuality. And this leads to a conversation about what else was missing from the "sex education" lessons at school—the clitoris! We talk about the book Steph has at home showing where the clitoris is. The question comes: "But why didn't they show it in the book at school? I looked for it but the teacher acted like nothing was there. I know it's there." Steph has been taught that it is the clitoris that gives her pleasure when she masturbates.

Steph picks up her schoolbag. She's ready for another day at school, and as we head out the door, she says with a scornful snort, "They don't say all the truth at school but I know it anyway."

Three interwoven social processes of "coming out/going home" are undertaken by "queerly raised" children:

- the critiquing and interweaving of socially ascribed categories, truths, and labels imposed on one by the sites of power such as educational and religious institutions;
- the crossing, bridging and bordering of communities, or "worlds," such as ethnic, queer, and feminist communities, and the regulations and codes of those communities;
- the employment of personal agency, including strategies of adaptation, negotiation, resistance and subversion.

Because Steph was born into a multicultural family, multisexuality or sexual diversity has been part of her life as far back as she can remember through her parents' friendship circles. Indeed, her birth, baby years, and childhood have become public knowledge in Australia. My book *Someone You Know* details my pregnancy while a dear friend was living with AIDS (Pallotta-Chiarolli 1991). Jon died when Steph was just under a year old, and she makes frequent appearances in the text. For example, when she was four months old, Jon held her in his arms, trying to shake off the irrational fear that he was passing on some illness to her, wanting so much to be her "Uncle Jon" throughout her life but knowing he would possibly never see her again.

Seven-year-old Steph is getting frustrated with kids at school who play games where they spread "AIDS germs" to each other. She tells her teacher her Mum is a writer who has written a book about AIDS and gets me invited to her school to speak to children about my work as a writer and writing about AIDS. She then asks to read my book about "my Uncle Jon who isn't really an Uncle but is really my Uncle." Over a few days, she reads the whole book, engrossed, her lips often moving silently as she tries to pronounce or understand some of the words, her face flushing happily when she comes across herself in it. When Steph has finished, she looks perturbed. I begin to wonder whether reading about a gay family friend dying of AIDS was all too much for a seven-year-old. I ask, "Was there stuff in the book that you'd like to talk about, that worried you?"

Steph shrugs and looks miserable. "You said I looked yucky when I was born. I wasn't yucky when I was born."

I explain what babies look like when they're born and my obviously feeble attempt at humor in my book. Steph smiles and accepts my explanation and apology. I add, "Is there anything else, about AIDS or death? About Uncle Jon being sick?"

Steph shakes her head. "Uncle Jon looked yucky too, didn't he?"

"Yes, he did. But it didn't matter. He was my friend. I loved him."

"I didn't know I looked yucky too. A good yucky. But you still loved both of us."

That same year another close friend dies of AIDS. We go to visit Uncle Duane in hospital a couple of weeks before he dies. Duane says hastily, "Please don't let Steph in. I don't want her to get frightened when she sees me. I couldn't bear her reaction." He raises a feeble hand as if to hide his emaciated face.

I step outside to where Rob is sitting with Steph. She leaps up, "Can I go in now?"

"Uncle Duane would prefer if you stayed here."

"Huh? Why?" She looks shocked and sad.

"Because he's very sick—"

"I know. That's why we've come to visit. I'm s'posed to help him play Nintendo."

"You know about Uncle Jon and AIDS and what AIDS does to the way people look."

"They look yucky."

"Well, Uncle Duane thinks you may be scared of him."

Steph's eyes fill with tears. She shakes her head sadly, mystified. "No I won't. Why would I be scared? It's a good yucky."

But I insist as it's Duane's wish, and I hear Steph's loud whimpers to her Dad as I go back in to Duane.

Duane can hear her and asks, "Is Steph all right?"

"Not really, Duane. She really wants to see you. She says she knows what you'll look like and she won't be scared."

Duane sighs. "OK. I'd really like to see her too."

Steph rushes to him, kisses him on the cheek, and gives him a big hug. Rob and I watch the relief and joy on Duane's face. Steph sits on Duane's bed and helps his fingers press the Nintendo remote control.

"Queerly raised" children are agents. People are, and always have been, active agents in the constitution of their unfolding social worlds (Davies 1991). Rather than seeing socialization as a "printed circuit" in which children are programmed to behave in the "right way," "the daydreaming and the questioning, the funneling and the digging, the adopting of now this stance and now that stance, the recurrent problems and the turning-points" need to be documented and acknowledged as modes of agency (Plummer 1975, 14). Their personal world is "an emergent, situated, negotiated one where considerable variation becomes possible"(50).

When Steph is three, I am tucking her into bed one evening and am about to read her a children's version of the Swiss Family Robinson. "No, I'll read it to you," Steph says, which means she'll tell the story through the pictures.

There is one picture where the parents stand in the middle of their sons, one son next to his father, and two, with arms around each other's shoulders, next to their mother. Steph describes the family, pointing to the people as she goes: "This is the mother. This is the father. This is the first son," pointing to the boy on his own. "This is the second son"—and then to the third son next to his brother—"and this is the second son's boyfriend."

She dares to mix; she dares to cross the borders to introduce into language . . . everything monologism has repressed. . . . The necessity of re-naming so as to un-name.(Trinh 1991, 14)

Circumstances that tend to influence the level and nature of a child's agency include:

- access to knowledge, mentors, and a culture that construct and articulate the child's "queer" social locations;
- critical awareness of the ignorance of the taken-for-granted belief-claims constructed as "knowledge" in the broader heteronormative world;
- mechanisms and strategies available to help the child become a disseminator of knowledge, thereby challenging that taken-for-grantedness and heteronormativity;
- the feeling that one is supported and part of a larger collective agency.

By the time she's eight, Steph has been to three Mardi Gras and been in one of them. Her teachers have gotten used to Steph writing about these occasions in her journal or shouting happily on a Friday afternoon, "I'm going to Sydney to the Mardi Gras." In grade 3 Steph even does a show-and-tell on Mardi Gras. The security guy at the parade had allowed her to stand outside the barricades so as the parade went by, Steph was handed all sorts of things like flowers, streamers, balloons, and posters by passing drag queens and all sorts of other queer people. So she has ample demonstration material.

The teacher admits to me later that she'd been worried about it and had voiced this concern in the staff room, to which Steph's first teacher at this parish suburban Catholic school had said, "Oh, don't worry. She knows how to handle it. And the kids are used to her. She's teaching them a thing or two."

When I ask her how her show-and-tell went, Steph's happy about it but adds scornfully, "But a couple of boys made stupid noises when I talked about the drag queens and tranys, and you know what, some asked me what a 'Mulligrub' was. They don't know about the Mardi Gras! Can you believe it?"

"So what did you say it was?"

"I said it was like a Christmas pageant, only bigger and better. And I said how come they didn't know what it was because it was on TV. Everyone watches the Mardi Gras, don't they, Mum?"

Her teachers begin to call her "a political activist" around the school and comment on her awareness of so many social issues. For it's Steph who tells the girls that it's a dumb game to dare each other to run up to the school fence and yell out "I'm a lesbian!" She can't understand the dare. She quite happily stands at the fence and yells out, much to the shock of passersby, "I'm a lesbian!"

Often she hears words like gay and lesbian being used in other "weird" ways, and she tells the kids what they mean. Like the time she's walking down the street with me and one of her school friends. Steph's feeling happy and runs up to a streetlight and hugs and kisses it. Her friend yells, "You're a lesbian!"

Steph looks at her incredulously. "Lesbians don't kiss poles. Lesbians are women who love women."

These sorts of comments usually silence friends, who are shocked, stunned, and curious all at once. Indeed, she's so used to it all that there's no shock or novelty value in it for her. Like the time I sit down with lesbian friends to watch a video on young gay and lesbian people. Steph sits and watches for a while, then wanders off to her bedroom and returns with Enid Blyton's The Magic Faraway Tree.

Michelle, one of our friends, tries to stifle a giggle. "Is that more interesting than the video, Steph?"

Steph nods matter-of-factly.

Steph's taken-for-grantedness is tested just before we set off to her fourth Mardi Gras, when she's ten. She's been telling everyone for weeks about her trip to Sydney but is now finding that she's being called a lesbian and is being told that "your parents hang out with freaks" by some boys. These same kids are also beginning to harass her, pulling her off play equipment and making sexually explicit comments to her. The girls are beginning to stay away from her because they don't want to be harassed as well, they tell her, or to be seen as lesbians if they hold Steph's hand or touch her in any way.

The harassment is particularly severe on the Friday before we leave for Sydney. Steph walks dismally out of the classroom looking weary and dejected, and before we leave, we make an appointment with the principal to discuss the situation when we get back on Monday.

> What has happened, is a sort of overrun *[debordement]* that spoils all those boundaries and divisions and forces us to extend the accredited concept, . . . [but] it still will have come as a shock, producing endless efforts to dam up, resist, rebuild the old partitions, to blame what could no longer be thought without confusion, to blame difference *as* wrongful confusion! (Derrida, in Kamuf 1991, 256–57)

Over the weekend Steph forgets about the harassment and enjoys herself immensely. As we watch the parade, she suddenly asks, "Mum, did everyone in this parade get teased when they were at school?"

"Yes, I think most of them would have. They often faced horrible situations. You've heard Matteo, Luc, Michelle, and Madelaine talk about what they went through at school and how they handled it."

"And they're happy now?"

"They still face prejudices, but they are strong and confident, celebrating together and fighting prejudice together."

Steph nods reflectively. I give her a hug. "So don't forget that, Steph. You're not the only one that's been hassled, and it actually isn't your fault, and you really know the truth about the things they're hassling you about and know nothing about. You know this world here."

She nods again, this time with a proud smile. But she doesn't do a show-and-tell that year, even though the principal and teachers deal effectively with the harassment after Steph explains to the principal that being labeled a lesbian isn't the problem—it's that the boys mean something very negative by it and are hurting Steph.

But a couple of weeks later when a gay couple comes to stay who are very close friends and visibly present themselves as camp, Steph asks them to go to her school on Open Day and visit her in her classes. Indeed, she makes sure they get up early that school morning by taking them breakfast in bed! They do attend, and despite the wary looks and stifled giggles from some of her ex-harassers, Steph proudly escorts them around and happily plays along with their camp comments. The teachers are supportive, telling Steph how lucky she is to have such loving and caring family friends.

At the end of the year, for a variety of reasons, Steph decides to change schools to a single-sex school to begin her year five. She loves the facilities and the fact that "There are no boys." She still keeps her old friends, plays netball for her old team, and goes to a lot of her old school's events, all the while making new friends. So she now inhabits two school worlds quite comfortably.

Mardi Gras comes around only four weeks after she's begun at her new school. She's going to march as the daughter of two lesbian friends, one of whom she particularly likes, as they share the same adoration of Sporty Spice! She'll be holding her "Two Mums + Baby = A Family" poster. When I ask her if she'll be able to handle any reporters who may ask her questions about her Mums, Steph says, "Of course! I'll just answer like there were two of you!"

Rob and I decide we won't ask her about what she'll say at her new school. Maybe she'll decide to silence her "Mardi Gras world" and "queer life" in this new school. But for about a week before, Steph's been letting her new teachers and her new friends know, doing some of the explaining she's been used to, and getting interested and positive feedback. Even her class teacher exclaims, "Wow! I wish I was going with you! Have a great time, and tell us all about it on Monday!"

> Freedom grows in the cracks. People create options, choices, alternatives for themselves. (McGregor 1980, 313)

Lugones (1990) uses the image of "playfulness" to describe ambiguity, openness, and irreverence to norms and divisions. A "queerly raised" child can "travel" between these "worlds" and inhabit more than one of these "worlds" at the very same time.

One evening, as we wait for Steph's computing class to begin, three girls around twelve years old come cheerily in to collect some material for their next class. They look confident and speak assertively, arms and hair swinging. I notice Steph has taken my hand and is squeezing it.

I look across and notice a faint shy blush on her face. "What's up, Steph?"
Steph is still staring at the girls. She whispers, "Which one do you like?"
"All of them. They look like really nice, smart young women."
Steph persist. "No! I mean, which one do you like?"
"Which one do you like, sweetie?"
Steph nods her head toward the long-haired girl in jeans and T-shirt who's doing most of the questioning in articulate computer-speak. "Do you like her too?"
"Yes, I do," I reply.
Steph smiles slightly, pleased, still not taking her eyes off the girl.
"What're you feeling, Steph?"
Steph smiles shyly. She shrugs and looks at me with embarrassment. I squeeze her hand. "It's okay, Steph. She's gorgeous, and if you think that, that's fine. Enjoy those feelings, there's nothing wrong with them."
In the meantime, Steph also has crushes on two boys. Getting out of the car one afternoon with a friend who's come to play, she looks at the houses across the street and declares, "I wish Peter lived there and Anthony lived there. Then I could see both of them."
Her friend looks scornfully at her. "You can only love one person."
"Who says?"
"That's the way it is. Unless you're a lesbian."
"If I was a lesbian, I'd want Peter and Anthony to be girls. Anyway, maybe I'll love no one. Maybe I'll love girls or boys, or both. Maybe lots of both!" And she laughs cheekily as her friend remonstrates.

Children are living in societies that are increasingly acknowledging the realities of the world's multiracial, multicultural, multisexual composition. They are developing skills of critical perception, critical thinking, the negotiation of differences, and the passion for social justice that engage with diversity rather than reconstruct it as homogeneity. They are simultaneously "coming out" and "going home"—that is, assertively striding out while constructing a secure base. They are interweaving "lifeworlds," positioning themselves and others as home sites of confluence and intermixture, rather than as having to assimilate to one "world" at the expense of another. Nor are they "intersecting" within themselves two or more neat and homogenous "worlds" with distinct chasms between them. They are acknowledging the differences *within* as well as *between* categories.

Schools and teachers can act as cultural mediators between children and family/community, children and mainstream society, and children and social services/organizations/community groups that cater to their ethnic, gender, and sexual identities (Pallotta-Chiarolli 1995, 1996, 1998a). More spaces need to be provided in schools for "queerly raised" children to cross borderlines and expand boundaries, to explore the contradictions and complementarities inherent in the construction of their multiple social positionings as end products of larger sociopolitical and cultural forces; beginnings of new inscriptions into society, politics, and culture; and resistances to discriminatory institutions such as education and church. All children need to be encouraged to gain broader and more understanding visions of themselves and others who coexist with them in their schools, their immediate worlds, and the worlds beyond their perception.

Steph's writing and experiences of agency exemplify children's great potential to demonstrate and transcend categorical limitations, oppressions, and the splitting of concurrent realities inherent in the heteronormative, Anglocentric, and phallocentric need to homogenize, categorize, and simplify. Their recognition of themselves and others as multiplaced persons, constantly undertaking "coming out/going home" journeys, can do much to challenge ethnocentric, sexist, and homophobic perspectives.

As I write this chapter, Steph's "Moving Days" continue to take new directions. One of her friends, a girl in her early teens, has now confided to Steph and to us that she thinks she's a lesbian. She can't tell her own parents, she says. She can't tell anyone else at school. Steph has now become her confidante, and we can hear them chat into the night during sleepovers. Steph's friends now begin to embark upon their own journeys, and Steph has to decide how she'll travel with them. It looks as if Steph knows the course to navigate: one of love and support. As fourteen-year-old Khizran Khalid (1998, 265) writes,

I'm the voice of tomorrow.
I'm the one who will make a difference.
I'm the one who will see tomorrow.
But can you take the time to listen?

REFERENCES

Cope, B., and M. Kalantzis. (1995). Why literacy pedagogy has to change. *Education Australia* 30: 8–11.
Davies, B. (1991). The concept of agency: A feminist poststructuralist analysis. *Social Analysis* 30: 42–53.
Kamuf, P., ed. (1991). *A Derrida reader: Between the blinds.* New York: Harvester Wheatsheaf.
Khalid, K. (1998). The voice of tomorrow. In *Girls talk: Young women speak their hearts and minds,* ed. M. Pallotta-Chiarolli. Lane Cove, Sydney: Finch Publishing.

Lugones, M. (1990). Playfulness, "world" travelling, and loving perception. In *Making face, making soul/haciendo caras,* ed. G. Anzaldua. San Francisco: Aunt Lute Books.

McGregor, C. (1980). *The Australian people.* Sydney: Hodder and Houghton.

Pallotta-Chiarolli, M. (1991). *Someone you know: A friend's farewell.* Adelaide: Wakefield Press.

———. (1995). "Can I use the word gay?" In *Boys in schools: Addressing the issues,* ed. R. Browne and R. Fletcher. Lane Cove, Sydney: Finch Publishing.

———. (1996). "A rainbow in my heart": Interweaving ethnicity and sexuality studies. In *Schooling and sexualities: Teaching for a positive sexuality,* ed. L. Laskey and C. Beavis. Melbourne: Centre for Education and Change, Deakin University.

———. (1998a). "Coming Out/Going Home": Australian girls interrogating heterosexism and homophobia. In *Everybody's special: A handbook on sexuality education,* ed. L. Beckett. Brisbane: Association of Women Educators.

Plummer, K. (1975). *Sexual stigma: An interactionist account.* London: Routledge and Kegan Paul.

Trinh T. Minh-Ha. (1991). *When the moon waxes red.* New York: Routledge.

· 8 ·

WHAT HAPPENS WHEN THE KIDS GROW UP? THE LONG-TERM IMPACT OF AN OPENLY GAY TEACHER ON EIGHT STUDENTS' LIVES

Eric Rofes

INTRODUCTION

Exactly twenty years ago I was a sixth-grade teacher facing a frightening situation. My successful career teaching at an elite private school in the Boston suburbs had come into direct conflict with my budding avocation as a gay activist. The two years since I'd graduated from college had been spent living a double life: mild-mannered prep-school teacher during the day and spirited community organizer at night. I ricocheted between writing plays about Beowulf or sketching floor plans for medieval sugar-cube castles, and writing radical political analysis for Boston's *Gay Community News* or launching social programs for queer youth. The stress was incredible, but I was twenty-three years old and caught up in the excitement of gay liberation in the 1970s. Who could resist? (Rofes 1985).

The conflict exploded later that spring when I came out to the head of the school in a note enclosed with my contract for a third year teaching at the school. A lengthy series of soul-searching meetings took place with various committees of the school's board, but finally I was informed that I could remain at the school only if I promised to continue to do my gay organizing under a pseudonym (Eric Rogers is the one I had been using) and avoided photographers and television cameras when the issue at hand was homosexuality. As my departure from the school became public, word leaked out to the parents and students in my class that I was leaving because I was gay. Resistance mounted, debates ensued, but I left nevertheless. Anyway, that summer I had more important tasks to do than prepare lesson plans: I took a position as a key national organizer for the first gay march on Washington, to be held in October 1978.

A few months later, just before the new school year was starting, I received a phone call from the Fayerweather Street School in Cambridge. They'd heard I'd been successful at another local school and they knew I'd left the previous position, although they hadn't heard why. Would I apply for a position heading up their sixth-to-eighth-grade program?

At the end of a lengthy, upbeat interview with the head of Fayerweather, I took a deep breath and asked her if the school would hire an openly gay teacher. She replied that she'd just hired a lesbian teacher the week before and didn't think it was a big deal, but that I'd have to run it by the hiring committee, as they were the body with decision-making authority on this matter. I met with this large committee later that week. They queried why I'd left my previous position; I spilled the beans. This seventeen-member committee—including several ten- and eleven-year-old students—then engaged in a long, thoughtful discussion about whether my being gay mattered. They finally decided that they were interested in hiring the best person possible for the position (recent teachers at the 6-7-8 level hadn't lasted more than a year), and that sexual orientation wasn't a big deal.

Hence I embarked on a wild five-year odyssey as an openly gay teacher at a progressive independent school in Cambridge. I taught many of my students for three years in a row, and I got to know their families well. Each year I'd find some excuse to come out to the students and their parents sometime during the fall and answer their questions. Because I had been a founding member of the Boston Area Gay and Lesbian Schoolworkers, and was the only openly gay K–12 teacher in New England at the time, I frequently found myself on television, interviewed on issues ranging from Anita Bryant's antigay campaign, to the antigay Briggs Initiative (banning gay-positive teachers) in California. At this innovative, open-classroom school, my students were interviewed on local and national television about their gay teacher. One group of students even authored a best-selling book called *The Kids' Book of Divorce* (Rofes 1981), which included a chapter titled "Loving Your Gay Parent."

I recall appearing on a television talk show as a gay teacher during that time and being confronted by an agitated, red-faced man from the audience who insisted my openness with my students would "turn them all gay." Although I was able to respond quickly and insist that teachers' sexual orientation had no influence on the future sexuality of their students, I recall that I froze inside when I heard this man's accusation. Though my response was the popularized retort at the time, and still dominates progay rhetoric about gay teachers today, inwardly I felt dishonest making such a claim.

Did we have any real evidence that the environment created by openly lesbian and gay teachers did not spawn greater numbers of queer kids? Should we be upset or delighted if it did? I wondered how my students at age eleven, twelve, or thirteen truly experienced having an openly gay teacher, and how it would affect them in the long haul. I have since wondered if they reflected on this experience over the years, and, if so, how they thought my openness about being gay influenced them. Did any of them turn out to be gay? As they grew older, did they even remember my heartfelt coming-out talks? Has my influence been felt in any way: as a committed teacher, a gay man, a caring friend? Or am I just another schoolteacher with an overblown sense of his effects on his students?

HETEROSEXUAL ADULTS WHO'D HAD AN OPENLY GAY TEACHER TWO DECADES AGO

Once I realized that my former students—now in their late twenties and early thirties—would make an excellent pool of subjects for a study of the impact of gay teachers on their students' future lives, I made a great effort to identify, locate, and communicate with them. This was not an easy task, especially since the school at which I'd taught did not have a long-term system in place for maintaining contact with graduates. So I checked phone books, internet directories, and sent many letters to the addresses of my students from two decades earlier, only to have most of them sent back marked "Return to Sender."

Yet my curiosity propelled me forward, and I found myself driven to seek answers to a range of questions. What do my kids-turned-adults remember about being a sixth-, seventh-, and eighth-grader and having a gay teacher? Do they think having a gay teacher affected them in any way? Do they believe having a gay teacher influenced their current sexual identity, relationship status, or whether they currently have children? I was able to locate and receive survey responses from eight former students, three women and five men, all white and between the ages of twenty-nine and thirty-two. Hence while this is an interesting cohort to sample, I couldn't pretend it was in any way a representative or definitive pool of subjects.

I had mixed feelings on discovering that all of my former students who'd responded identified as heterosexual. At first I felt disappointed. Had my openness and the occasional accompanying controversies turned my students away from homosexuality? Then I felt relief: That red-faced man in the audience at the talk show was wrong! Mostly I was left confused and wondering whether students who might have grown up to be gay, lesbian, or bisexual had been especially difficult to locate because they'd moved away from their families, as I did when I was in my twenties.

Two of the women who responded to the survey are married, as are two of the men. The third woman and one additional man are together in an unmarried, live-in relationship. This struck me as especially ironic, as they had both been my students but in different years. Looking back, I realized they seemed suitable for each other, as both had an especially bizarre and cynical sense of humor. Five of these former students live in the greater Boston area, and two others live in New York City and Montana. I was surprised to find one former student living in the same small town in Maine that I live in. Always an outdoorsman, Nick, before the age of thirty, had acquired a small piece of land and built his own house a short walk from the Maine coast. A delightful salmon dinner at Nick's home enlivened the research for this chapter.

My former students hold a range of jobs, including park ranger, outdoor educator, songwriter/producer, freelance illustrator, software engineer, university development officer, securities partnership tax practitioner, and furniture artist. I was surprised to learn that Max was a park ranger, but I shouldn't have been: The affable manner and generosity of spirit I remember him having as a sixth-grader surely assist him in his work. I had a difficult time fitting the idea of thirty-two-year-old Hannah crafting furniture alongside the shy, cerebral thirteen-year-old I'd taught two decades earlier.

GAY TEACHERS CAN INFLUENCE STUDENTS

Contrary to arguments I had made when these adults were children, and contrary to the statements of many gay-rights advocates denying that gay teachers will "influence" children (Jennings 1994; Homosexual teachers 1978), all my former students surveyed felt altered by the experience. When I asked "Do you think having an openly gay teacher affected you in any ways?" the respondents answered that this early experience served to "normalize" for them gay men and lesbians, as well as their open gay relationships, and to reduce their own homophobia.

Two young men exemplify this "normalization" perspective. Max Lockwood, the National Park Service ranger, succinctly responded to this question by writing, "Having a gay teacher made me believe that there is nothing wrong with being gay." Nick Rathbone, my newly discovered neighbor in Maine who works as an outdoor educator, shared a similar perspective: "Introduced to a *real live* gay person at this age, I think it has always just seemed normal to me that some people you meet will be gay and some won't."

Hannah Gittleman, the furniture artist and teacher living near Boston, explained how having an openly gay teacher served her during her high school years:

> It made me open to other gay people I met later (other gay teachers in high school, for example). When other people in high school were whispering and all wound up about teachers who they thought were gay, I hadn't really thought too much about it. It wasn't a big deal for me because I had already had a teacher who was gay. I felt like these other students were so immature.

Two other women discussed how this reduction of homophobia affected their personal and professional relationships with significant gay people in their lives. Laura Forbes, whom I remember as a sociable girl who was often the center of adolescent drama in her social group, argued that having an openly gay teacher made her more able to forge meaningful friendships with gays and lesbians as she grew older:

> It made me not homophobic, or even not the type of homophobia where Cambridge-liberals-who-see-having-a-gay-friend-as-a-status-symbol-type-of-homophobic. It more has affected family members, friends, and co-workers (close and acquaintances) who are gay because they have one less person being weird about their sexuality around them—me. That's important.
>
> It's like that butterfly effect theory. Through just me, Eric slightly helped a handful of strangers two decades later. I can just be friends with gay people (if they're nice). I don't need to go through a "training period." They don't need to explain themselves. That's a relief. I am a minivacation in the heterosexual world.

Laura insisted having an openly gay teacher had helped her form stronger relationships with friends and family members who are gay:

> It has helped me *tremendously*. I wonder if I'd be able to have real and close relationships with some people who I cherish if not for this experience. It was harder to be gay twenty years ago. It's a lot easier for kids now, but there's a chance I could have been uncomfortable around gay men or women, and I'm glad I was always spared that.

I wasn't surprised to learn that Heather Peck, now thirty-three years old, was a securities partnership tax practitioner and a mother of two sons. She'd seemed both ambitious and family oriented as a child. Yet she was surprised to receive the survey because she hadn't thought about her year in my class for quite some time. Heather also was surprised to realize that her first child's care arrangements may have been influenced by the early experience of having a gay teacher:

> I never really thought about how having a gay teacher in the eighth grade affected me until I received this survey. In looking back on the years since Eric was my teacher, I have probably been much more accepting of people who were gay, albeit not consciously. I put my newborn son in the care of a gay man for the first 1½ years of his life. Some people questioned that decision, but he received better care from that man than any day-care center could have ever provided.
>
> I never once worried about any misconduct or about my son being gay because of the care provider he had. I don't know if that was partly due to the experience I had with Eric, or if it is totally unrelated, but it didn't hurt my ability to accept difference in people's lifestyle choices.

All eight respondents agreed that having an openly gay teacher at a young age had made them more open not only to gay people, but also to the full range of human diversity. Several students believed their openness as adults to a broad range of people was enhanced by this childhood experience. Hannah Gittleman summed up this perspective nicely: "I also think that I'm probably more open to other kinds of people in general as a result of having a middle-school teacher who was gay."

Likewise, Nick Rathbone felt his ability to get along with others was enhanced by this experience. This is particularly important for his work with Outward Bound, where a cooperative spirit is critical to the collaborative wilderness experience:

> I think it did help. I feel I have an easy time dealing with pretty much anyone. Their sexual identity doesn't make me uncomfortable. And I'm glad it doesn't—that's a lot of people to be uncomfortable around!
>
> Schools should teach our children what exists in the world around them. This world has gay people in it. It has black people too. And Chinese. And pianists. Honestly, we aren't in a position right now to be turning down any good teacher who is willing to do the job.

Two of the young men not only felt more open to diversity but believed their views about political activism and discrimination may have been affected by having a gay teacher who was known to be involved in social-change work. John McClain, a twenty-nine-year-old software engineer, described how his current political views may have been affected by his elementary and middle-school experience:

> Yes, I think it has had a profound effect on how I view human relationships. If any two consenting adults love each other, I can't imagine

discriminating against them because of it. Now, Fayerweather was a very liberal school, as are my parents (especially on social issues), so I am pretty sure I would have felt this at some level; however, I don't think I would have felt it as strongly if I did not have a person to tie it back to.

Brian Claflin believes he was most influenced by seeing a politicized gay man who was his teacher:

> I'd had other gay teachers, but I suppose in Eric's case he offered an example of a gay man who seemed very responsible and active in politics, and I think it was this side of the experience that was remarkable. He did not seem to fit any stereotype any kid had about homosexuality. It was not the fact of Eric's being openly gay that was remarkable. He was a strong personality and an effective authority. That made him notable as a person, but that and his sexuality had no real bearing on one another.

In addition to believing they were less xenophobic because they'd had this early experience with a gay teacher, several students felt that their understanding and experience of their sexuality had been affected, but not in the way the red-faced man feared. In response to my question, "Did you ever wonder if you were gay because you had a gay teacher?" all eight former students answered no. Caleb Brown, a graphic artist in Montana, was among those offering additional comments. He argued that because of the ways he understood the formation of sexual orientation, he did not believe a gay teacher's identity exerted any influence over his own:

> I didn't think that "gayness" could be transmitted. I was not interested in exploring my sexuality (in so far as wondering about orientation) in 6–8th grade. In high school I wondered if I would ever have a girlfriend, and sometimes wondered if I was gay when I didn't, but I never linked that questioning to my gay teachers.

Yet several former students thought that this early experience influenced their understanding of sexuality in general. Laura Forbes suggested that one effect of having an openly gay teacher was "I was more comfortable with my entire sexuality probably." Forbes stated,

> It helped that my teacher was so lovable and warm (despite trying and failing to make me a good speller). Twelve-year olds are squeamish and easily embarrassed (at least I was). I also respected him. This is all-important because it all, coupled with his seeming security in his sexuality and self-respect, was a definite influence in my shaping opinion of the entire spectrum of sexuality.

John McClain recalled a critical incident during which his participation in a discussion about gay teachers for one of the many media pieces that focused on our class forced him to consider his own sexual identity when he was in his early teens:

> There was one odd event when Eric was on another local TV talk show and my mother and I were in the audience, specifically because I was a former student of Eric's. At one point the host asked me my sexual preference, which left me in a bit of a bind because I wanted to help dispel the whole notion that gay teachers lead to gay students, but at that point did not feel comfortable announcing my sexual preference on TV. I ended up announcing my sexual preference and have seemed to survive anyway.

Nick Rathbone did not share Laura's and John's belief that their understanding of their own sexuality was, in part, influenced by having a gay teacher. He experienced his teacher's sexual orientation fully divorced from his own: "I guess I didn't really connect that *gay* had to do with sexuality. If Eric was it, it certainly couldn't have anything to do with my sexual feelings (Since day #1: strong and for women)."

Hence, the kids–turned–adults present perspectives that differ significantly from the arguments of both antigay polemicists who claim gay teachers will produce students who grow up to be gay, and gay-rights advocates who insist a teacher's open homosexuality or lesbianism will have no influence on their students.

DIVERSITY AND COMPLEXITY OF HUMAN BEINGS

This limited sample of former students suggests that openly gay teachers *can* make a difference in their students' lives. These students clearly believed their years with me influenced the development of their moral views on homosexuality and their acceptance of human diversity. Some students believed that their understanding of and experience of their own sexuality had been affected by having a gay teacher and engaging in early discussions of sexual orientation. Others felt that witnessing a teacher who was politically active as a gay liberationist affected their views about political activism and discrimination against gay people.

There may be several important implications of these findings. First, they suggest that the public may hold powerful misconceptions about the impact of an openly gay teacher on students' lives. Although some studies show that American citizens support laws protecting lesbians and gay men from job discrimination (Schmalz 1992), others indicate that a large portion of those polled begin to hedge around the question of job protections for gay teachers (Yang 1998), frequently due to the question of "influence." The kids-turned-adults who responded to this survey provide evidence that a gay teacher is not likely to "turn children gay." Likewise, they provide evidence that refutes long-standing misconceptions that gay teachers are no different from heterosexual teachers.

Second, although the central debate on gay teachers frequently focuses on the development of children's sexual orientation, it may be more appropriate to debate the influence of gay teachers on children's moral and political development. Gay teachers might not turn children gay, lesbian, or bisexual who otherwise would embrace heterosexual identities, but we might make children less homophobic and less xenophobic. Although researchers have long probed kids' identity development (Kohlberg 1981; Schulman 1985; Langford 1995), the past two decades of research into children's moral development have failed to engage gay and lesbian issues or suggest ways in which students' broader values and sense of morality might be affected by having an openly gay teacher.

Finally, the greatest influence of openly lesbian, gay, and bisexual teachers may be on students' relationship to political activism and social movements. By witnessing up close the importance of political advocacy on a teacher's job security and social position, children's understanding of the importance of activism and its relevance to their lives might be enhanced. What better pedagogy for empowerment could there be than for children to participate in public education and media advocacy about cutting-edge issues that directly relate to their social worlds and their schooling?

Too often educators promoting critical pedagogy, who take seriously the powerful sources of oppression that are active forces in children's contemporary lives, discuss social change and activism distanced from children's social worlds in elementary and middle schools (McLaren 1989; Shor 1992). The findings from this study might encourage advocates of a pedagogy of empowerment to focus on sociopolitical issues related to schools (the rights of gay teachers, but also broader issues of freedom of speech, job security, and curricular freedom) as central to their teaching.

How do we find ourselves in a place where spokespeople for the lesbian and gay movement, or gay teachers themselves, repeatedly insist "gay teachers are no different from straight teachers" or that their gayness is "incidental" to their teaching? (See Griffin 1992, 181.) Is this part of the same assimiliationist trend that took hold when gay liberation was transformed into the more politically palatable gay-rights movement and we began to put forward arguments that lesbian mothers were no different from their heterosexual counterparts (Hotvedt and Mandel 1982; Patterson 1992), that gender nonconformity had no relationship to lesbian, gay, or bisexual

sexual orientation (Besner and Spungin 1995, 13–14), and that the position of sex in gay men's lives and cultures was no different from that of heterosexual men? (Besner and Spungin 1995, 17–18; Nava and Dawidoff 1994, 32–39, 53–56.) When this same assimilationist trope is applied to lesbian and gay teachers, it might very well serve to exorcise the very qualities that make gay people critical as educators.

Likewise, though some advocates ground their arguments in the support that gay teachers and gay-oriented curricula might offer lesbian, gay, and bisexual students (Harbeck 1997, 8; Lipkin 1995, 31–52), the actual utility of gay teachers might be much broader. Max Lockwood, the park ranger, clearly believes the potential benefits are distributed more widely than only to those students who may grow up to be gay. "Having an openly gay teacher taught me to be receptive to diversity and about the complexity of human beings," he wrote in his final comment on the survey. "I think it would benefit all children and society if they had openly gay teachers."

References

Besner, H., and C. Spungin. (1995). *Gay and lesbian students.* Washington, D.C.: Taylor and Francis.

Griffin, P. (1992). From hiding out to coming out: Empowering lesbian and gay educators. In *Coming out of the classroom closet,* ed. K. Harbeck. New York: Haworth.

Harbeck, K. (1997). *Gay and lesbian educators: Personal freedoms, public constraints.* Malden, Mass.: Amethyst Press.

Homosexual teachers the issue in Proposition Six. (1978). *San Jose Mercury News,* 15 October.

Hotvedt, M., and J. Mandel. (1982). Children of lesbian mothers. In *Homosexuality: Social, psychological, and biological issues,* ed. W. Paul, J. Weinrich, J. Gonsiorek, and M. Hotvedt. Beverly Hills: Sage.

Jennings, K. (1994). *One teacher in ten.* Boston: Alyson.

Kohlberg, L. (1981). *The philosophy of moral development.* San Francisco: Harper and Row.

Langford, P. (1995). *Approaches to the development of moral reasoning.* Mahwah, N.J.: L. Erlbaum.

Lipkin, A. (1995). The case for a gay and lesbian curriculum. In *The gay teen,* ed. G. Unks. New York: Routledge.

McLaren, P. (1989). *Life in schools: An introduction to critical pedagogy in the foundations of education.* New York: Longman.

Nava, M., and R. Dawidoff. (1994). *Created equal: Why gay rights matter to America.* New York: St. Martin's Press.

Patterson, C. (1992). Children of lesbian and gay parents. *Child Development* 63: 1025–42.

Rofes, E. (1981). *The kids' book of divorce: By, for, and about kids.* Lexington, Mass.: Lewis.

———. (1985). *Socrates, Plato, and guys like me: Confessions of a gay schoolteacher.* Boston: Alyson.

Schmalz, J. (1992). Gay politics goes mainstream. *New York Times Magazine,* 11 October, 41.

Schulman, M. (1985). *Bringing up a moral child.* Reading, Mass.: Addison-Wesley.

Shor, I. (1992). *Empowering education: Critical theory for social change.* Chicago: University of Chicago Press.

Yang, A. (1998). *From wrongs to rights: Public opinion on gay and lesbian Americans moves toward equality.* Washington, D.C.: National Gay and Lesbian Task Force.

• Part 3 •

CURRICULUM

In this section the chapters examine notions of elementary curricula within a range of disciplines and from a variety of perspectives. Eschewing a "tacos and tepees" approach to multicultural education, wherein stereotypic representations of a culture are introduced into the curriculum in an attempt to say "We've done multiculturalism," these chapters take a far more rigorous approach to how issues of sexual diversity might play out in classroom curricula and pedagogies. Collectively, these chapters ask such questions as, In what ways is the elementary school curriculum heteronormative? What are subject-specific examples of the ways in which this content is being incorporated into the curriculum? How can educators draw from popular culture to inform pedagogical practices that embrace difference and interrogate (con)texts? How does "normal" get defined through the curriculum, and how can we change what it means? These chapters are based on the assumption that the salient question is no longer, Should we include this material? but rather, What are a variety of ways to include this material?

In chapter 9 Will Letts starts by defining heteronormativity and then proceeds to examine the ways in which the pedagogies and curricula of elementary school science embody this normalizing discourse. Using the construct of "heterogender," the chapter examines "the ways in which heteronormativity becomes part of the hidden curriculum in science class, and thus for the most part exists in silence." Why does recognizing heteronormativity matter? Because when "issues of language, of resources for the construciton of broader, varied identities, of a more socially situated view of school science, and of social justice" are all brought to the forefront of discussions about classrooms, then teachers, administrators, parents, and students can recognize and attend to this aspect of the daily practice of schools.

Mara Sapon-Shevin describes a variety of types of children's music that can be used "to teach against homophobia" in chapter 10. She examines music "that does not inscribe compulsory heterosexuality" with the hope that we can move "from homosexuality and same-sex relations as 'remarkable'" to a view where they are viewed as "'unremarkable,' or normal." To achieve this goal, Mara examines songs that deconstruct gender and gender roles, that help adults explain homosexuality to children, and that explicitly address homosexuality and sexual preference.

In the next chapter Jim King and Jenifer Jasinski Schneider are "interested in finding a place for gay and lesbian perspectives in the daily reading and writing of elementary classrooms." By examining classroom talk, reading, and writing practices, this chapter locates a perspective for including, and making integral, lesbian and gay themes in teaching. Further, they assert that using this perspective "can be a productive way to open composing and response behaviors [the core of elementary literacy efforts] so that they more closely match the lives of our students."

Adding to this discussion of elementary literacy practices, Wayne Martino explores "the possibilities for using texts to interrupt straight thinking in the elementary English classroom." He notes that such a "potentially disruptive reading practice can hardly be achieved by simply providing texts that are inclusive of gay and lesbian characters." By examining teachers' strategies and responses and students' reactions to a particular novel, Wayne draws attention to the "very significant ways in which this novel could be used to assist teachers in their attempts to interrupt straight thinking." Such a strategy could enable students "to move beyond positions of mere acceptance and tolerance of the *other* to encourage students to think about what we take for granted as *normal* and *natural*."

In the final chapter in this section, Kevin Colleary explores "teacher understandings about gays and lesbians in the elementary social studies curriculum." To this end he investigates the ways that the teachers envision these issues as explicit versus implicit in the curriculum, how they engage in "waiting rather than creating" opportunities for inclusion, and how the teachers' own lack of knowledge around gay and lesbian issues in the curriculum impedes even the most motivated among them from including this material. He uses teachers' views to illustrate the important issues that must be addressed "if we are going to begin to break the insidious cycle of silence that has existed throughout the history of elementary education."

Focusing on issues of silence, absence, heteronormative discourses, and homophobia, as well as affirmation, visibility, possibilites, and inclusion, the five chapters in this section envision different configurations of elementary school curricula, in hopes that they generate discussion and challenge more traditional views about what can (and cannot) be talked about with young children.

How to Make "Boys" and "Girls" in the Classroom: The Heteronormative Nature of Elementary-School Science

William J. Letts IV

Although the ever-growing body of critique of the natural sciences—from feminist, antiracist, postcolonial, poststructuralist, and even queer perspectives[1]—has had some effect on what science content is taught, many people in classrooms still hold more traditional views of science. They see science, even school science, as directly reflecting the truths in nature, as being objective and value neutral, and therefore as above reproach.

But what these many critiques have painted is a very different picture. Science is socially constructed, value laden, and context bound. This, however, is not always easy for educators to accept. As David Hess notes, "Too frequently we have been taught to see culture as a corrupting force in the production of science and technology, and to see anthropological, sociological, and historical approaches as airing the 'dirty laundry' of how social forces have impinged on a field of human endeavor that should somehow be asocial" (1995, 259).

But acknowledging that science is rooted in and emanates from culture doesn't diminish the power and utility of what we call modern Western science—it is a set of our best explanations for natural phenomena. The modern Western sciences have brought us many useful concepts—scientific rationality, objectivity, and method—and these critiques of science attempt to "rehabilitate some of [these] traditional central philosophic underpinnings" (Harding 1998, 191). However, they also challenge the notion that science is the same everywhere (that it is "universal") and that it is a direct reflection of the "truths" in the natural world (that is, an unmediated mirror of nature).

In this chapter I examine and critique one aspect of elementary-school science: its heteronormative nature. I want to start to examine the ways in which heteronormativity becomes part of the hidden curriculum in science class, and thus for the most part exists in silence (Fine 1993; Silin 1995). This chapter is intended to "break the silence" on at least one way (via school science) that discourses of sexuality get normalized, incorporated into the hidden curriculum, and policed in schools (Friend 1993).

Chrys Ingraham develops a notion of heteronormativity as "the view that institutionalized heterosexuality constitutes the standard for legitimate and prescriptive sociosexual arrangements" (1994, 204). That is, heterosexuality is the norm—unmarked, unspoken, presumed (Epstein and Johnson 1994), and compulsory (Rich 1993)—against which all else is judged as different, other, abnormal. Heteronormativity is ultimately an issue of power in the classroom in that it references and reinforces a certain "culture of power"—heterosexuality (Delpit 1988). But it also often brings with it a "silencing" that renders invisible what is considered normal and "diverts critique away from economic, social, and educational institutions which organize class, race, and gender hierarchies" (Fine 1987, 158).

I also draw on Ingraham's notion of heterogender, as opposed to simply gender, which is "the asymmetrical stratification of the sexes in relation to the historically varying institutions of patriarchal heterosexuality. . . . Heterogender confronts the equation of heterosexuality with *the natural* and of gender with the cultural, and suggests that both are socially constructed, open to other configurations (not only opposites and binary), and open to change" (1994, 204). So what my analysis gains by relying on the conception of heterogender is a reflection of the intertwined and interdependent nature of gender and sexuality, an acknowledgment that both are socially constructed, and that both are pliable and open to change.

A critique of elementary-school science as heteronormative is not an antiheterosexuality stance. I am not advocating that we deny it as an option for children, nor am I trying to deliver a message, either overtly or covertly, that heterosexuality is a bad thing. Instead what I am doing is taking a stand against hegemonic heterosexuality, that is, the version of heterosexuality that essentializes, naturalizes, and obscures its own presence—causing it to be taken for granted (Epstein and Johnson 1994, 1998). Like homosexuality and bisexuality, heterosexuality is socially constructed (Steinberg, Epstein, and Johnson 1997; Wilkinson and Kitzinger 1993).

It is also important to point out that the critique being leveled is not about bad teachers or negligent curriculum producers. Rather, the focus here is on the institutional production and maintenance of structures that perpetuate heteronormativity, mostly unbeknownst to those involved in its perpetuation (Epstein and Johnson 1998). This does not absolve each of us—whether administrator, teacher, staff member, parent, or student—

from working to identify and eliminate this bias, but it does shift the focus from trying to locate and change the "bad" or heterosexist people to a stance that presumes that each of us might unknowingly be perpetuating the heteronormativity.

In what follows I will examine heteronormativity in elementary-school science through both its pedagogies and curricula to illustrate my argument.

PEDAGOGICAL INSTANCES

The following two pedagogical instances are taken from videotaped classroom observations conducted as part of a large school science reform project. Although they are not intended to be representative of all elementary science classrooms, I think they are typical of what goes on in science class.

The first example is taken from a transcript of a sixth-grade lesson in a unit on insects. In this lesson the students were investigating body characteristics and various behaviors of a large species of cockroach. Students worked in groups of four, and each group had a single cockroach that was about five centimeters long. This snippet is taken from the interaction in one cooperative group.

> ASHLEY: Here, do you want it? [to Sam]
> SAM: No!
> ASHLEY: Take it—everyone has to.
> CARMEN: Come on, just take it. *She's* holding it.
> [Ashley hands the roach to a visibly nervous Sam. After several seconds the roach starts to run up Sam's arm, and in response he starts flailing his arms, sending the roach flying across the room.]
> ASHLEY: Oh my god, what a baby!
> LARA: Sam!
> MR. WILTON: [from across the room] Sam, grow up. It can't be that bad.

Sam is clearly not playing by "the rules," as they are implicitly, if not explicitly, defined in this classroom. As is made clear to him, if a girl can touch the roach and he refuses to, then he is a "baby" who needs to "grow up." As Gail Boldt (1996) notes, "to be a boy associated with girls interests and desires is constructed as a step away from power and possibility" (119). And in this instance even the girls held the roach, while Sam (initially) refused to, retreating even further from power and possibility. Sam's reluctance to hold the roach and eventual (over)reaction as it crawls up his arm evoke the idea that "feelings are, for the most part, forbidden to boys in schools and to (appear to) be a macho stud is, for the most part, required" (Epstein and Johnson 1998, 181). Taunting boys who refuse to engage in activities that *even girls* can do is a common misogynist put-down strategy used against boys. But beyond this, it is also implicated in discourses of homophobia (Epstein 1997; Epstein and Johnson 1998), because in Sam's case he is worse than a girl, he is a baby. This infantilization of Sam seems to work to humiliate him, to police his own enactment of his heterogender, and to coerce him into behaving in ways that boys are expected to behave in science class.

A second classroom example is taken from a transcript of a fourth-grade unit on the human body (Full Option Science System, 1993). Students are forming groups of four in order to engage in an activity called "Counting Bones," in which students will feel certain body parts, like the leg or the hand, and try to determine from this experience how many bones are in that part of the body. This snippet of dialogue picks up as the teacher is giving directions for the activity.

> MS. MARKER: Okay, when I tell you, get into groups of four, according to your gender. I want to see either a group of four boys, or a group of four girls. Each group member will then be the subject of examination of a certain body part. Listen to the four parts. Listen. The leg and foot, that's all number one. Two, the arm and hand. Three, the head, and four the neck, shoulders, and hips. Neck, shoulders, and hips are all number four. Did you get that? Any questions? [Silence from the class.] All right, then, start forming groups. [After a couple of minutes Nissa approaches Ms. Marker.]
>
> NISSA: Ms. M., there are no more girls left. Can I get in a group with Drew and Jeremy?
>
> MS. MARKER: No, sweetheart, you need to be with girls. . . .
>
> NISSA: Why?
>
> MS. MARKER: . . . . so why don't you get in that group, Dana's group?
>
> DREW: But there are only two of us, we need more people.
>
> MS. MARKER: That's all right, dear. You and Jeremy just trade off feeling body parts.
>
> DREW: But we want Nissa!
>
> MS. MARKER: I'll bet you do! Now, let's go, you two, get going.

When the researcher filming this lesson asked why she divided the groups according to sex (because this is not even mentioned in the teacher's manual for the module), Ms. Marker stated that because they would be feeling each other's body parts, she thought it would be "safer"[2] to form the groups that way. But safer for whom? Although she freely admits this to an adult observer in her classroom, when Nissa asks about it, her question is ignored. The teacher's manual suggests that each group investigate only a single body part, and that each student within the group feel their own body to count the bones. It is interesting that Ms. Marker made two alterations to the directions as presented in the teacher's guide, the most interesting having the students feel other students' bodies. In a way, Ms. Marker created a problem that she then set out to solve. But even if we ignore her decisions to deviate from the directions in the teacher's guide, the incident still warrants analysis.

This classroom incident shows how teachers' pedagogical decision making can be heteronormative. The teacher called for the formation of same-sex groups (though she referred to it as "gender"), feeling that it was somehow "safer" to have children of the same sex feeling one another's bodies than to allow mixed-sex groups to engage in this activity. This is a case where the notion of heterogender is particularly useful. From knowing their sexes, Ms. Marker then infers their gender and sexuality—and these inferences dictate how she organizes the activity. This organization seems to be consistent with the assumption or expectation that "there are certain ways that boys *by nature* feel and behave and certain things that they like, and that these are often different than the behaviors, feelings, and likes that girls *by nature* have" (Boldt 1996, 117). Her fear seems grounded in the assumptions that few children—too few to be concerned with— are gay or lesbian (or even have feelings of attraction to members of the same sex) and that any touching of bodies done by members of the opposite sex is necessarily an instance of sexual, or sexualized, touching. Both assumptions normalize heterosexuality, and as a result, the framework from which she makes pedagogical decisions seems rooted in the notion that heterosexuality is universal *and* is a salient feature of these fourth-graders' lived experiences. This is not to argue that fourth-graders are not sexual, or sexualized, beings, only that a decision predicated on the assumption that anything they do is foregrounded by heterosexual desires and motivations is a faulty one.

CURRICULAR INSTANCES

Gina Ingoglia's (1989) *Look Inside Your Body*, a trade book about inside and outside appearances aimed at early-elementary children, begins with a picture of a traditional nuclear family. Later in the text, marked by a tab that depicts the silhouette of a high-heeled shoe and a man's dress shoe, is the section "How are boys . . . and girls different?" The pictures show a girl dressed up in high heels and a boy dressed up in a shirt, necktie, and men's

shoes. Below that are pictures of a girl sitting on the toilet and a boy standing at the toilet. The text reads,

> Everybody belongs to the female sex or the male sex. Girls and women
> are females. Boys and men are males. Women can become mothers. Men
> can become fathers.
>   Girls and boys are born with some body parts that are the same and
> others that are different. The way boys and girls urinate is different. (11)

On the facing page there are two almost identical drawings of naked bodies except one figure has the vulva pictured and labeled and the other has
the penis pictured and labeled. Both bodies are the same size, have the same
hair cuts, have breasts (as evidenced by nipples) drawn and labeled, and
have navels drawn and labeled. The text to accompany these pictures reads,

> When girls urinate, the liquid leaves through an opening, a tiny hole, in-
> side the vulva. Boys don't have a vulva. Boys urinate through a little tube
> inside the penis. Girls don't have a penis.
>   When girls and boys grow older, some body parts change. Everyone
> has breasts. But as girls become women, their breasts grow larger. As
> boys become men, hair grows on their chests, and beards grow on their
> faces. Boys and girls change inside, too. After all the changes take place,
> they are grown-ups. (12)

This perhaps seemingly innocent text is fraught with examples of the
ways in which heteronormativity manifests itself. Starting with the first illustration and description of the family, this work is predicated on a certain version of normalcy—that of a heterosexual nuclear family with op-
posite-sex parents, grandparents, and "2.5" children. Delivering a message
by what is *not* written or depicted, this trade book uncritically normalizes
a certain version of a family.

Further, it normalizes the dichotomy of two sexes—male versus female—which has been increasingly challenged (Connell 1999; Fausto-
Sterling 1992, 1993; Lorber 1994; Van den Wijngaard 1997) as simplistic
and overly biologically deterministic. The text does this by reducing the
differences between males and females to the visually apparent anatomy, in
a move that seems to deny the social construction of the sexes and rely
solely on anatomical markers of difference—markers that aren't even jus-
tified on the basis of which gonads, ovaries or testes, are present, but rather
on whether there's a penis or vulva present and visible. The text describes
both sexes initially having breasts, but whereas the females' grow more
pronounced "as girls become women," the males' seem inexplicably to be
replaced by chests, upon which hair grows "as boys become men." So the

text dwells on what it deems significant visible physical markers to describe how men and women are different. As Robert Connell (1999) notes, "The body may not match the dichotomous imagination.... It seems, then, that we need to look harder at the conception of dichotomy, and the place to start is the conception of distinct types of bodies" (450).

In addition to negating the lives and experiences of intersex[3] peoples, this dualistic classification system focuses on differences between these two categories, holding them as somehow more salient than other schemes for describing people. It seems to make more important distinctions between males and females (for instance, "How are boys . . . and girls different?") rather than, say, focusing on the range of differences that exist *within* the category of female. Granted, male and female genitals are different, providing a basis for us to sort people into one of two sexes. But this sorting makes the categories of "male" and "female" seem as if they are "natural" categories, as opposed to socially constructed distinctions that were devised to distinguish people, just as we might distinguish them by eye color. This point is illustrated by the way that the text naturalizes the manner in which boys and girls urinate, as if there is something distinct, unique, and important about these socially constructed routines. Boys don't have to stand to urinate (nor do girls have to sit—they could squat); that's just how they get conditioned.

But beyond this contested "biological" terrain of sex, the issue I want to raise here for consideration is the automatic slippage that superimposes dichotomous notions of gender—femininity and masculinity—onto "biological" sex in such a way that makes gender also seem dichotomous, discrete, polarized, and "natural"—in effect, making it heterogender. There are more ways to think critically about gender than the broad categories "male" and "female" provide us, such as the importance that gender plays in an individual's life. To ignore this complexity and multilayeredness of gender makes it seem as if gender is naturally, or biologically, occurring (essentializes it), and as if a person is some comprehensible embodiment of either "masculine" *or* "feminine" (oversimplifies and reduces it).

A second example of curriculum is taken from Helene J. Jordan's *How a Seed Grows* (1992), a book aimed at preschool- and kindergarten-aged children. The book describes the life cycles of plants, from seed to mature plant. At one point in the book, in a section describing the different rates at which different seeds grow, the text reads, "Some seeds grow slowly. These are the seeds of an oak tree. An oak tree grows very, very slowly. Suppose you planted an oak tree seed. You would be a father or a mother, or even a grandfather or a grandmother, and the oak tree would still be growing" (6).

This text illustrates another example of invoking heteronormativity by presupposing that all children will become parents. Although this is not a bad goal (nor is it necessarily limited to heterosexuals), and many children will ultimately likely subscribe to it, it becomes problematic in the classroom when it is presented as the only option—as what is assumed will happen to everyone. In this book this contextualization occurs when the text is read with its accompanying illustration, which pretty obviously represents a set of (married) parents and a set of (married) grandparents. It becomes the standard by which other life trajectories are judged as "not normal." Instead, this could easily have been presented as one of several viable options—marrying and having children, being a single parent, adopting a child, having a child with your same-sex partner—removing its assumed naturalness and normalcy.

In addition to examining science trade books, I also want to look at the National Science Education Standards document (National Research Council 1996). I will cite two sections from the NSES to support my argument that school science is heteronormative. The first selection comes from the "Principles and Definitions" section of the document, under the heading "Science Is for All Students." The text reads, "This principle is one of equity and excellence. Science in our schools must be for all students: All students, regardless of age, sex, cultural or ethnic background, disabilities, aspirations, or interest and motivation in science, should have the opportunity to attain high levels of scientific literacy" (20).

Of the myriad factors that are deemed salient identity categories affecting access to, interaction with, and achievement in school science, any mention of sexuality is missing. This is odd, if for no other reason than it seems that sexuality (or more precisely, "deviant" sexualities) would have a profound impact on all of these aspects of science. Following Joseph Tobin (1997), I characterize such a statement of the "equity and excellence" principle as "missing"—missing as in uncharted, unexplored, undiscovered, lost, disappeared, repressed, unspeakable/unthinkable, overlooked, and, finally, depleted. The heteronormativity in this case is manifested in the silence around issues of the sexuality of science learners. The absence of any mention that sexuality as a salient category to the discussion of the ways in which students learn (or fail to learn) science keeps in place the presumed norm, heterosexuality. The end result is that issues of sexuality remain invisible.

Later in this same section is the guiding principle "School science reflects the intellectual and cultural traditions that characterize the practice of contemporary science." This section then affirms the commitment of the standards to having all students attain high levels of scientific literacy—not only by learning science subject matter, but also by learning about "the nature of science, the scientific enterprise, and the role of science in society and personal life" (National Research Council 1996, 21).

But, interestingly, the document is devoid of *any* of the critiques of the enterprise of science cited in the first endnote, let alone mentioning the heteronormative nature of science or the impact that the study of sexuality has had on the structure and practice of science. This constitutes, following Alberto Rodriguez (1997), a "discourse of invisibility" regarding the ways that certain dominant identity categories—white, male, middle-class, straight— have shaped and continue to shape science, but remain unremarked and unnoticed as having such effects. I take as problematic the notion that school science should reflect the intellectual and cultural traditions that characterize the practice of science. Freed from the aforementioned critiques, this seems a biased, partial, and uncritical view of the nature of modern science. Without an acknowledgment of the (hetero)sexualized, racialized, classed, and colonial roots of modern Western science, this guiding principle may advocate for something that is a far cry from what the authors of this document intended—a false vision/version of science that is completely disconnected from the social contexts that created it, and that work still to sustain it.

WHY DOES RECOGNIZING HETERONORMATIVITY IN SCIENCE MATTER?

The recognition that elementary-school science can be heteronormative in both its pedagogies and its curricula points to several things that teachers (and parents, administrators, and students themselves) can do. First, the preceding examples point to the importance of language in all that we do. Language is a powerful tool that can convey both explicit and implicit meanings. We deliver messages by what is said, but also by what is left unsaid (Fine 1993; hooks 1994). With this in mind, a careful examination of the types of language being used and the ways in which it is used seems essential to exposing and disentangling the heteronormative nature of school science. For instance, in the previous example with the roaches, instead of contributing to the denigration of Sam, the teacher could have explicitly focused attention on the comments that were made about his behavior, with an eye toward exposing the hidden ways in which such comments work to enforce normative gender roles. A brief, but frank, discussion could have moved the effects of such language into plain sight, allowing for critical analysis and the presentation of alternative ways of interacting. Teachers and students (and others) need to be much more self-conscious about what the words they utter (and don't utter) are saying to students in the classroom.

Another issue raised by this work is the opportunities that arise for teachers to guide children to thinking critically about the sexual dualities that permeate our culture, and science in particular—male versus female, heterosexual versus homosexual, natural versus cultural. Again, I acknowledge that classifying people by their sex, for instance, is a prominent practice that is useful in some contexts. But I am suggesting that teachers can help students destabilize these dualities and think about them critically, so that even when they rely on them, they are consciously aware of what they are doing, rather than blindly and uncritically falling back on them. Teachers (and administrators, parents, and, of course, students themselves) can resist the alluring dichotomy of "sex" with examples of, discussions about, and teachings about the myriad multiple and shifting gender identities that are available to "both" sexes. And not all of these genders need to be unquestionably, silently constructed as heterogenders. This needn't only be an intellectual exercise, for expanding acceptable definitions of categories like "boy" and "girl" that are so polarized may create more viable spaces for children to exist and more acceptance of those children who currently construct themselves outside of the narrow ranges of what is currently acceptable (Boldt 1996; Rofes 1994).

Because schooling provides the contexts through which students' identities are constructed, refined, resisted, and altered, attention must be paid to the ways in which certain subjects, in this case science, provide resources for, or erect barriers to, students' constructions of subjectivities, or identities. As Peter Redman writes, "if the formal and hidden curricula are recognized as important sites in which young people learn about sexuality, then schools have an obligation to ensure that this learning is positive and useful" (1994, 142). And Deborah Britzman writes, "to better understand the contradictory meanings of these [identity] categories in terms of sexualities requires that we address the availed and disavowed gendered and sexual representations that formally and informally circulate in schools" (1997, 185). The issue here is not, for instance, whether certain students are gay or straight, but what identities are validated and made available to students and how these children take them up in their identity formation (Davies 1993; Epstein and Johnson 1998; Lemke 1995). Thus, the issue moves from being one unique to science class, to one that can impact identity formation more broadly.

To this end, one way that teachers (and others) can provide more resources for the varied constructions of identity is to thwart the dominant presentation of science as a "master narrative," one that was created by, and is sustained by, only certain types of people, one that goes unchallenged and unquestioned. Instead of seeing science in a dogmatic way, students can be helped to develop a critical stance toward it (Brickhouse 1994), one in which they are concerned with evidence, methodology, and context, rather than blindly accepting any claims made in the name of science, or obsessing about "correct answers." This is teaching that "enables transgressions—a movement against and beyond boundaries" (hooks 1994, 12), and it is the kind of teaching, I believe, that is long overdue in our science classrooms.

Finally, I conclude that a recognition of the heteronormative nature of elementary-school science, as well as an acknowledgment of the ways science is gendered, classed, colonialized, and racialized, can lead to a knowledge framework that more accurately reflects concerns for social justice (Sleeter 1996). A greater awareness of our subject and the ways in which we teach it offers us more insights into and resources for constructing a liberatory pedagogy for science (Osborne and Barton 1998). This, in turn, can lead to a discipline that will "attract more diverse students into science and. . . . prepare both scientists and citizens for active participation in shaping the sciences of the future" (Brickhouse 1994, 407). A concern for social justice may finally bring in those students for whom school science is "another world" (Costa 1995).

But if these issues of language, of resources for the construction of broader, varied identities, of a more socially situated view of school science, and of social justice are unconvincing, let us recall and reflect on the words of Suzanne de Castell and Mary Bryson as we decide whether to take action, or to remain silent/silenced—"because silence *does* equal death, and because in not speaking we are ourselves complicit in very real acts of violence, very real assaults against very real people" (1998, 245).

Notes

I would like to thank Nancy Brickhouse, Taj Carson, and Steve Fifield for their careful readings, insightful comments, and useful critique of earlier drafts of this chapter.

1. Examples of these critiques include Gould 1981; Haraway 1989; Harding 1991, 1993, 1998; Keller 1985, 1992; McKnight 1997; Rosario 1997; Schiebinger 1989, 1993; Terry and Urla 1995; and Tuana 1989.

2. It is important to add that even if Ms. Marker's concerns for a "safer" grouping scheme were rooted in fears of possible parental complaints or a concern over the occurrence of sexual harassment, either of which might occur as a result of mixed-sex groups, these fears are still rooted in a system that assumes boys and girls are attracted to one another, and that frames sexual harassment as occurring between people of opposite sexes. Heterosexuality is still taken as the norm.

3. Anne Fausto-Sterling (1993) has written about five sexes, rather than just two, highlighting that there are "intersex" people born with ambiguous "sex," having

physical characteristics of both sexes (referred to as pseudohermaphrodites). As Marianne van den Wijngaard (1997) explains, "In most cases of pseudohermaphroditism, a deviation of the genital organs can be observed at birth. The baby's clitoris may be shaped like a penis, or the penis may be so small that it resembles a clitoris. Sometimes the labia or testes of these children are not properly developed either" (87).

REFERENCES

Boldt, G. M. (1996). Sexist and heterosexist responses to gender bending in an elementary classroom. *Curriculum Inquiry* 26(2): 113–31.

Brickhouse, N. (1994). Bringing in the outsiders: Reshaping the sciences of the future. *Journal of Curriculum Studies* 26(4): 401–16.

Britzman, D. P. (1997). What is this thing called love? New discourses for understanding gay and lesbian youth. In *Radical in<ter>ventions: Identity, politics, and difference/s in educational praxis*, ed. S. de Castell and M. Bryson. Albany: State University of New York Press.

Connell, R. W. (1999). Making gendered people: Bodies, identities, and sexualities. In *Revisioning gender*, ed. M. M. Ferree, J. Lorber, and B. B. Hess. Thousand Oaks, Calif.: Sage.

Costa, V. B. (1995). When science is "another world": Relationships between worlds of family, friends, school, and science. *Science Education* 79(3): 313–33.

Davies, B. (1993). *Shards of glass: Children reading and writing beyond gendered identities*. Sydney: Allen and Unwin.

De Castell, S., and M. Bryson. (1998). Don't ask, don't tell: "Sniffing out queers" in education. In *Curriculum: Toward new identities*, ed. W. F. Pinar. New York: Garland.

Delpit, L. D. (1988). The silenced dialogue: Power and pedagogy in educating other people's children. *Harvard Educational Review* 58(3): 280–98.

Epstein, D., ed. (1994). *Challenging lesbian and gay inequalities in education*. Philadelphia: Open University Press.

———. (1997). Boyz' own stories: Masculinities and sexualities in schools. *Gender and Education* 9(1): 105–15.

Epstein, D., and R. Johnson. (1994). On the straight and narrow: The heterosexual presumption, homophobias, and schools. In *Challenging lesbian and gay inequalities in education,* ed. D. Epstein. Philadelphia: Open University Press.

———. (1998). *Schooling sexualities.* Philadelphia: Open University Press.

Fausto-Sterling, A. (1992). *Myths of gender: Biological theories about women and men.* New York: Basic Books.

———. (1993). The five sexes: Why male and female are not enough. *The Sciences,* March/April, 20–24.

Fine, M. (1987). Silencing in public schools. *Language Arts* 64(2): 157–74.

———. (1993). Sexuality, schooling, and adolescent females: The missing discourse of desire. In *Beyond silenced voices: Class, race, and gender in United States schools*, ed. L. Weis and M. Fine. Albany: State University of New York Press.

Full Option Science System. (1993). *Human Body*. Chicago: Encyclopaedia Britannica Educational Corporation.

Friend, R. A. (1993). Choices, not closets: Heterosexism and homophobia in schools. In *Beyond silenced voices: Class, race, and gender in United States schools*, ed. L. Weis and M. Fine. Albany: State University of New York Press.

Gould, S. J. (1981). *The mismeasure of man*. New York: W. W. Norton.

Haraway, D. (1989). *Primate visions: Gender, race, and nature in the world of modern science*. New York: Routledge.

Harding, S. (1991). *Whose science? Whose knowledge? Thinking from women's lives*. Ithaca: Cornell University Press.

———, ed. (1993). *The "racial" economy of science: Toward a democratic future*. Bloomington: Indiana University Press.

———. (1998). *Is science multicultural? Postcolonialisms, feminisms, and epistemologies*. Bloomington: Indiana University Press.

Hess, D. J. (1995*). Science and technology in a multicultural world*. New York: Columbia University Press.

hooks, b. (1994). *Teaching to transgress: Education as the practice of freedom*. New York: Routledge.

Ingoglia, G. (1989). *Look inside your body: A poke and look learning book*. New York: Grosset and Dunlap.

Ingraham, C. (1994). The heterosexual imaginary: Feminist sociology and theories of gender. *Sociological Theory* 12(2): 203–19.

Jordan, H. J. (1992). *How a seed grows*. New York: HarperCollins.

Keller, E. F. (1985). *Reflections on gender and science*. New Haven: Yale University.

———. (1992). *Secrets of life, secrets of death: Essays on language, gender, and science*. New York: Routledge.

Lemke, J. L. (1995). *Textual politics: Discourse and social dynamics*. London: Taylor and Francis.

Lorber, J. (1994). *Paradoxes of gender*. New Haven: Yale University Press.

McKnight, J. (1997). *Straight science? Homosexuality, evolution, and adaptation*. New York: Routledge.

National Research Council. (1996). *National Science Education Standards*. Washington, D.C.: National Academy Press.

Osborne, M. D., and A. M. C. Barton. (1998). Constructing a liberatory pedagogy in science: Dilemmas and contradictions. *Journal of Curriculum Studies* 30(3): 251–60.

Redman, P. (1994). Shifting ground: Rethinking sexuality education. In *Challenging lesbian and gay inequalities in education*, ed. D. Epstein. Philadelphia: Open University Press.

Rich, A. (1993). Compulsory heterosexuality and lesbian existence. In *The lesbian and gay studies reader*, ed. H. Abelove, M. A. Barale, and D. M. Halperin. New York: Routledge.

Rodriguez, A. J. (1997). The dangerous discourse of invisibility: A critique of the National Research Council's National Science Education Standards. *Journal of Research in Science Teaching* 34(1): 19–37.

Rofes, E. E. (1994). Making our schools safe for sissies. *High School Journal* 77(1/2): 37–40.

Rosario, V. A., ed. (1997). *Science and homosexualities*. New York: Routledge.

Schiebinger, L. (1989). *The mind has no sex? Women in the origins of modern science.* Cambridge, Mass.: Harvard University Press.

———. (1993). *Nature's body: Gender in the making of modern science.* Boston: Beacon Press.

Silin, J. G. (1995). *Sex, death, and the education of children: Our passion for ignorance in the age of AIDS.* New York: Teachers College Press.

Sleeter, C. E. (1996). *Multicultural education as social activism.* Albany: State University of New York Press.

Steinberg, D. L., D. Epstein, and R. Johnson. (1997). *Border patrols: Policing the boundaries of heterosexuality.* London: Cassell.

Terry, J., and J. Urla, ed. (1995). *Deviant bodies: Critical perspectives on difference in science and popular culture.* Bloomington: Indiana University Press.

Tobin, J., ed. (1997). *Making a place for pleasure in early childhood education.* New Haven: Yale University Press.

Tuana, N., ed. (1989). *Feminism and science.* Bloomington: Indiana University Press.

Van den Wijngaard, M. (1997). *Reinventing the sexes: The biomedical construction of femininity and masculinity.* Bloomington: Indiana University Press.

Wilkinson, S., and C. Kitzinger, ed. (1993). *Heterosexuality: A "feminism and psychology" reader.* London: Sage.

· 10 ·

USING MUSIC TO TEACH AGAINST HOMOPHOBIA

Mara Sapon-Shevin

"'A' my name is Alice and my husband's name is Albert. We live in Alaska and we sell apples."

"The farmer in the dell, the farmer in the dell, hi-ho the derry-o, the farmer in the dell. The farmer takes a wife, the farmer takes a wife, hi-ho the derry-o, the farmer takes a wife."

"Suzi and Matthew sitting in a tree, k-i-s-s-i-n-g. First comes love, then comes marriage, then comes Suzi with a baby carriage."

Through jump-rope songs, playground chants, records and tapes and school music classes, children are exposed to music as part of both the formal curriculum of school and the "informal" or hidden curriculum.

But unlike other school curricula, the messages and underlying assumptions of children's music are rarely subjected to the same level of analysis and critique. Whether because music is the province of the "music teacher" and outside the "real curriculum," or because the activities of singing and listening to music are considered less serious than the more academic content students are expected to master, it is not common enough for teachers to look seriously at what students are learning from the words they are singing.

One of the few aspects of music education that has received critical examination relates to issues of multicultural education, particularly issues of diversity reflected in holiday music. Although in most schools there is still a "holiday concert" (in some cases still called a "Christmas concert"), there is increasing recognition of the fact that not all children celebrate Christmas and that music representing other cultures and religions should be represented in schoolwide celebrations. In many schools such "inclusion" still does not go beyond the inclusion of the compulsory "I Have a Little Dreidel" for Chanukah, although there are a growing number of sources of multicultural music (Page 1995).

111

If there has been progress in recognizing that not all children are Christian and that music should reflect that diversity, what about the assumption that all children are heterosexual or come from Mommy-Daddy families? How are gender roles and sexuality inscribed through children's music? What messages do children get about who boys are, what girls should be like, what kinds of love and relationships are possible? Acceptable? Laudable?

In this chapter I examine children's music that does not inscribe compulsory heterosexuality in terms of the students themselves, or heterosexual marriage and nuclear, traditional families as the only sources of parenting or family relationships.

Although there are an increasing number of children's songs that celebrate diversity in general (Ruth Pelham's "Under One Sky," Patricia Shih's "The Color Song," Tom Hunter's "Family of Woman and Man"), I was able to discover relatively few children's songs that specifically address homosexuality or same-sex relationships or partnerships.

I do not mention the lack of songs in this area merely to frame the limitations of this examination. Rather, the absence of a significant number of examples is the essence of the problem; examining the limited songs available can illuminate the dilemma that frames this chapter: How does one move this issue from "invisibility" to "visibility" in ways that both call attention to and yet normalize same-sex relationships and homosexuality?

Daphne Patai (1991) discusses the concept of "surplus or excessive visibility." Patai argues that for members of underrepresented or oppressed groups, there is no "middle ground," no "normal" representation. Historically silenced or underrepresented groups must choose between invisibility (there are no lesbian parents, no gay teenagers, no bisexual teachers) and surplus visibility (Why do you always have to flaunt your identity? Why must you bring up your issue again and again?). The choice is "between silence and the accusation that we are making excessive noise."

When heterosexuality is assumed and silence is the norm, then disrupting sexual-orientation hegemony may seem forced or artificial. We rarely hear a teacher say, "You know, Billy has both a mother and a father and they all live together in an apartment." And yet if a teacher comments "You know, Billy has two mothers and they all live together on Euclid Avenue," then one wonders about the speaker's intent.

This is the double bind that is represented by some of the songs shared here. If we just say "family," or "parents," then the predominant assumption is that *family* means nuclear family and *parents* means a mom and a dad. But to *name* the other somehow seems aggressively strident. Why are we talking about sexual-preference issues in the context of a song about having a dog, or going on vacation?

If our goal is to move from "remarkable" to "unremarkable" (or normal) in our depiction of homosexuality and same-sex relations, then how do we do this without *remarking* about it? If having two mothers is "normal," then why bring it to children's special attention in a song or a book?

An examination of the early children's literature in the area of disabilities illustrates the same dilemma and, perhaps, some of the same "developmental" process. Many early books about children with disabilities were of the "remarkable" variety. The books were "about disability" more than they were about children with full lives who happened to have disabilities.

The "second generation" of children's books on disability came much closer to making disability simply a part of the landscape—visible, but not the defining feature, present but not strikingly highlighted. The children's books were about something else, but there were children in them who used wheelchairs, had hearing aids, and experienced other challenges.

Much of the early children's literature on homosexuality fits into this same pattern. *Heather Has Two Mommies* (Newman 1989), *Gloria Goes to Gay Pride* (Newman 1991), *Daddy's Roommate* (Willhoite 1990) are all books specifically about having same-sex parents and/or coping with the attendant discrimination. The next generation of books is shifting, I believe, to include people or characters who are gay or lesbian as part of the overall story, but not as the story itself. Striking the balance between visibility and distorted hypervisibility is a challenge that will remain with us as long as there is societal oppression based on sexual preference; there is little surprise that it is difficult to both "name" the other and imply that the "other" is not an "other"!

I will discuss here songs in four categories: (1) songs that address issues of gender roles and that overtly challenge expectations of how girls and boys should behave; (2) songs that are written primarily for adults and that deconstruct issues of sexuality, sexual preference, and relationships that could be useful for the adults who parent, teach, or work with younger students; (3) songs primarily intended as consciousness raising or discussion pieces that could be used with upper-elementary and older students; (4) children's songs, meant to be sung by children, that might be used in music classes, children's choruses, or other such instances.

For each of these categories I will share some relevant portions of the lyrics and then discuss the content of the song as well as possible teaching applications.

SONGS THAT DECONSTRUCT GENDER AND GENDER ROLES

The ways in which both boys and girls are confined to specific roles and activities (and punished for deviating) are directly related to homophobia. The boy who doesn't play football but prefers to draw or has a stamp collection; the girl who wears overalls and climbs trees and eschews jewelry and makeup—both are suspect, and, within school, often isolated or harassed. Although not every boy who plays with dolls is or will assume an identity as "gay," "bisexual," or "transgendered," the fears surrounding nonnormative sex-role behavior are directly related to homophobia. Addressing issues of rigid sex-role stereotyping and exploring the ways in which societal expectations and norms are imposed by schools, media, parents, and other institutional structures can be a useful first step in challenging compulsive heterosexuality.

One of the earliest songs in this category was recorded following the publication of a children's book by the same title, "William's Doll" (Rodgers and Hanick). The song tells the story of a young boy who wants a doll, a request that is met with discomfort, scorn, and derision by those around him, including taunts of "sissy" from one of his friends. The boy's father attempts to channel the boy's interests into more "appropriate" toys (a basketball, marbles, and a baseball glove), but William is not dissuaded. Finally, William's grandmother arrives to visit and explains to William's distressed father that William needs a doll so that he can learn to be a "good father" someday.

The song explores not only the "norms" of male behavior but also hints at the ways in which homophobia begins early—through torment by and isolation from other males.

Peter Alsop has written several wonderful songs about issues of gender and gender identity, including "It's Only a Wee-Wee." The chorus says:

> *Oh, it's only a wee-wee, so what's the big deal?*
> *It's only a wee-wee, so what's all the fuss?*
> *It's only a wee-wee and everyone's got one,*
> *There's better things to discuss*

The verses explore the ways in which children's roles are shaped by their gender and the illogical reactions adults have to children who violate these rigid expectations. The song concludes:

> *Grown-ups watch closely each move that we make*
> *Boys must not cry, and girls must make cake*
> *It's all very formal and I think it smells!*
> *Let's all be abnormal and act like ourselves!*

The song could be a useful tool for unpacking traditional, rigid assumptions about gender identity and the limits imposed by cultural norms and stereotypes. "If you get confused, they'll say 'Look in your pants,'" humorously illuminates the way in which sexual identity becomes coercively linked to both gender identity and inflexible, oppressive behavioral expectations.

SONGS FOR ADULTS STRUGGLING WITH EXPLAINING HOMOSEXUALITY

Before adults (teachers or parents) can work with students on developing broader understandings of love, sexuality, and relationships, they will need to explore their own upbringings, biases, and (mis)understandings about homosexuality and other forms of sexual expression. One of the major challenges adults face in working with children lies in "explaining" both homosexuality and homophobia to children. This is a delicate task. If children are unaware of prejudice and discrimination against people whose sexual orientation is "nonstandard," then "introducing the topic,"—"You know, some people don't feel this kind of loving is okay"—risks reifying the discrimination as somehow inevitable or justifiable. If children are already aware of homophobia and heterosexism, then the conversation can be helpful in discussing how to recognize this form of discrimination and how to be an ally to those who are being oppressed.

Following an experience in which my own daughter asked me, "Who's my other mom?"—reflecting on the two loving mothers that one of her friends had—I wrote the song "Mama, What's a Dyke?" The song attempts to address the difficulties of "explaining" prejudice to children, and is sung as a dialogue between a mother and a daughter. It includes the following two verses:

Mama, what's a dyke?
I heard it at school.
The kids said Karen's mom was one,
They sounded pretty cruel

Well, you know our friends
Diane and Sue
The ones we gave your jacket to
For little Mary Lou

But Mom, I still don't get it,
They're just a family.
And sometimes I wish
That I had two mommies

Mama, what's a faggot?
They hit Darren really hard.
They said that he was one of them,
And chased him round the yard.

Well you know Mike and Bill,
We went camping last fall
You had a lot of fun with them
When you were playing ball.

But Darren is my friend,
And Mike and Bill are great.
Next winter they said
They'd teach me how to skate.

Finally, the child in the song concludes:

Mom, I think I just don't get it,
You keep talking 'bout my friends.
You don't explain the nasty words
Or why it never ends.
My friends are really different,
But in most ways we're the same.
I think they should call all of us
By our own names.

The song attempts to capture the parent or teacher's dilemma. The mother explains the discriminatory terms with reference to people her child already knows and loves, and yet is unsuccessful in "explaining" how such negative name-calling "makes sense." Because, of course, it doesn't "make sense," more than any other discriminatory, prejudicial behavior, the child is left with her own (previous) acceptance of diversity but not able to make the connection to the nasty, abusive behavior she has witnessed.

Pat Humphries's song, "People Love," addresses the particularly insidious form of bigotry when people say, "I don't have any problem with this, but what would we tell the children?" This inability to take responsibility for their own feelings and judgments (by blaming their discriminatory decision on their children) both substantially underestimates children's abilities to be thoughtful and supportive and allows the adults to collude with existing patterns of oppression without owning that decision. The song asks:

What will we tell our children if they see you talk?
People who love each other talk.
A gentle whisper when we walk
People who love each other talk

Would you rather teach them fear
To hate and to betray
Or will you show them love can grow in many different ways
People love, people love, people love

Lastly, "Home Is Where the Heart Is" (Fingerett) tells the story of a mother explaining to her daughter about the gay couple down the street, one of whom is dying of AIDS. When the daughter expresses concern for how the remaining partner will survive, the mother reassures her that "home is where the heart is, no matter how the heart lives" and that they will help support Martin.

SONGS FOR USE WITH OLDER STUDENTS (AND ADULTS)

Songs in this category tell stories and can be used to initiate productive discussions with listeners. These songs are generally appropriate for upper-elementary students and older.

Bob Blue's "Chromosomophobia" makes the direct connections between rigid conceptions of gender identity and biological determinism and then links that connection to discrimination against same-sex couples. The song explains that whereas men have a Y chromosome, women have two X's, but that it seems strange that we attribute a whole set of characteristics and expectations to the presence or absence of a single chromosome. With regard to relationships, the song asks:

And when people love each other,
And decide to be together,
How absurd it is for someone to imply
That the love is not legitimate unless one of the lovers
Has two X's and the other has a Y!

Fred Small's "Scott and Jamie" tells the true story of two gay men who adopt two young boys and form a close and loving family. Then, devastatingly, the children are removed from their home by social services when the parents are deemed "unacceptable" based solely on their sexual identities.

Laura Berkson's song, "Marie," tells the (also) true story of two girls from Salinas, California, who fought their school's policy and won the court-ordered right to attend their school's senior prom together, as a couple.

Waltz her around the floor, Marie.
You're dancing for all that you believe.

Although your intentions have raised a few questions,
The answers can set us all free.
So waltz her around the floor, Marie.

Two songs by Romanovsky and Phillips can also be used to good effect with older students. "One of the Enemy" is about the pain of a gay teacher who feels that he cannot "come out" to his students, even when he sees his gay and lesbian students suffering and desperate for support and role models. And "Love Is All It Takes to Make a Family" explores the pain of a father who is threatened with disconnection from his children because of his sexual orientation.

CHILDREN'S SONGS ABOUT HOMOSEXUALITY AND SEXUAL PREFERENCE

Fred Small's "Everything Possible" was among the first (and remains one of the best-known) songs that explicitly addresses same-sex relationships. Although many performers have recorded the song, teachers who have attempted to sing the song with children have made visible the still powerful resistance to such open exploration of possibilities. The song is a lullaby and explores the many possibilities open to all young people. It includes the following verse:

There are girls who grow up strong and bold.
There are boys quiet and kind.
Some race on ahead, some follow behind,
Some go in their own way and time.
Some women love women, some men love men,
Some raise children, some never do.
You can dream all the day, never reaching the end
Of everything possible for you.

And it concludes with a chorus:

You can be anybody you want to be,
You can love whomever you will.
You can travel any country where your heart leads
And know I will love you still.
You can live by yourself, you can gather friends around,
You can choose one special one;
And the only measure of your words and your deeds
Will be the love you leave behind when you're done.

There are several children's songs that address different kinds of families, and the songs vary in the extent to which they name lesbian or gay families explicitly, and the extent to which they also name the oppression along with the difference. The tension between "naming" and "normalization" becomes clear in an analysis of these possibilities.

In Uncle Ruthie Buell's "The Family Song," which is also about diverse families, one of the verses is:

> *Susie and her brother*
> *Live with their mother*
> *And someone who their mother loves a lot*
> *And they've got a cat named Rover*
> *And a dog who won't roll over*
> *And I'll tell you something else that they have got*
> *A family, a real family*
> *There may be dirt upon the floor*
> *The roof might leak above*
> *But they're a family, a real family*
> *That's living in a house that's made of love.*

In Bill Harley's song, "Family," the chorus sings:

> *Family is just people living together*
> *Family, learning to get along*

One verse reads:

> *Jamie's got two sisters*
> *Sometimes that's no good*
> *Tommy doesn't have any at all*
> *Sometimes he wishes he could*
> *Sarah lives with her father*
> *Her mom is far away*
> *And Terry's house has got an extra room*
> *And her mom's friend is coming to stay*

Are these references "prominent" enough, or are they too subtle? It is difficult to know. When the Syracuse Community Choir's Children's Chorus performed Uncle Ruthie's song, they changed the words to "Susie and her brother live with their mother and a woman who their mother loves a lot" (deciding that "someone who their mother loves a lot" wasn't explicit enough to imply a same-sex relationship). Bill Harley reports that he has received letters from both gay couples (supportive) and people on the religious right (uncomfortable), so perhaps even somewhat opaque references are noticeable to those who either seek affirmation of their situation or who are troubled by that same affirmation.

The children's song "Love Makes a Family" (David and Jenny Heitler-Klevans) describes different kinds of families in the neighborhood, all of which are filled with love, including an adoptive family, a family with three generations in the same house, a child who divides her time between two families, and a childless couple. The verse about same-sex parents says:

> *The kids up the street have two moms and no dad.*
> *Some people tease them, they say that it's bad.*
> *The way people treat them, it makes me real mad.*
> *'Cause their house, it is filled with love.*

This is one of the few "singable" children's songs that addresses this topic more explicitly, and it is commendable on that count. David Heitler-Klevans shared with me that there has been a wide range of reactions to their song, from wild enthusiasm to censorship. Some of the other children's performers who have performed the song have left out the lesbian verse when sharing it with children, and there have been a number of schools, both public and private, that have requested that Two of a Kind (Jenny and David's group) either not include "Love Makes a Family" in its program, or leave out the "two moms" verse. When schools make this request, they generally say that most of the parents in their school communities would be fine with the subject, but that the few parents who would be upset would make life so miserable for the school that it just wouldn't be worth it.

The song exemplifies the dilemma identified earlier: how/when/ whether to introduce same-sex relationships linked to the information that such relationships are sometimes perceived negatively. Although the song's clear intent is to show that same-sex families can fill their houses with love, one wonders about the necessity and results of naming the discrimination this explicitly: What are the benefits and drawbacks of mentioning that this family is teased or that people say that "it's bad"? Can a sensitive teacher use the verse to discuss homophobia and oppression based on sexual identity? What about children in the class or audience who do live with two moms or two dads? Will such a song affirm their reality (yes, they tease me too), or will it introduce discrimination into the discussion when it isn't (yet) part of that child's (or his/her classmates') understanding of that difference? While David reports that one lesbian friend thought that the verse's focus on homophobia was good because it was "true," and that the song was a good way to deal with the experiences faced by kids with various kinds of families, other lesbians with whom I spoke are uncomfortable with linking "two moms" to negative reactions, in contrast to the other "different" kinds of families, who aren't associated with negative portrayals. The issue is tricky: How can we represent same-sex partnerships as normative or unremarkable in a world in which they must be remarked upon in order to become part of the conversation? And how explicitly should we name homophobia at the same time that we talk about homosexual relationships?

It would appear that the challenge is to "name" the issue but to do so in a way that implies acceptance. Perhaps the song that comes closest to "naming" the difference but contextualizing that difference within many kinds of differences is Sarah Pirtle's "Sing about Us." In this song there are many verses possible (and ideas are given for writing new ones). Each verse talks about a different "kind" of difference (food preferences, nationalities) and concludes with a chorus:

> *Sing about us. Tell me again.*
> *You don't have to be just like me*
> *to be my friend, be my friend.*
> *You don't have to be just like me*
> *to be my friend.*

When Sarah sings this song with children, she writes new verses to reflect the diversity of the class. When working with a kindergarten class, she was asked by one of the mothers of a student to make sure that her son's family was not omitted, and that the song somehow express the idea "We Have Two Moms." Her request resulted in this verse:

> *In some families we live with our grandparents.*
> *In some families we live with our Mom and Dad.*
> *In some families we have two homes.*
> *You know, love makes a family.*
> *In some families we live with our Mom.*
> *In some families we have two Moms.*
> *In some families we have a foster Mom.*
> *Every family is a good family.*

Sarah reports that the children smiled in recognition when their particular family configuration was mentioned, and that a child spoke up (a child other than the boy with lesbian parents), saying, "I have two Moms. And I have two homes. There's my Mom and my step-Mom."

Similarly, Ruth Pelham's song, "Under One Sky," whose chorus is "We're all a family under one sky, we're a family under one sky," and which is a "zipper" song designed for call and response, can easily incorporate verses relating to family differences:

> *We have one mom*
> *We have two moms*
> *We live with our dads*
> *And our moms and dads too.*

CONCLUSION

The challenge before us as educators, parents, songwriters, and performers is clear. We must write, perform, and play children's music that affirms multiple possibilities for young people. We must make sure that children grow up hearing about families and people with whom they can identify, knowing they are not alone, and that they will find support and community for their identities and their decisions related to sexual orientation. The role of popular culture in embedding messages and conveying acceptance cannot be overestimated. Children receive daily messages that shape their thinking and their understandings of themselves and others.

The four alternative "messages" we might hope to convey are these: (1) Not everyone is heterosexual, and this is true about children and young adults as well as adults. You are not alone if you are questioning your identity.

(2) Not everyone lives in a family with a mother and a father. There is lots of variation, including gay and lesbian parents, and these families can be loving, good families too. You are not alone if you live in a "nonstandard" family.

(3) Sexual orientation isn't dichotomous or fixed. There is not simply a heterosexual/homosexual dichotomy; it's more complex than that—there are people who are bisexual, transgendered, and so on. And people's sexual and gender identities may change over time.

(4) Homophobia is real and present in our society. It is linked to other oppressions (sexism, racism, classism), and it is important to understand those linkages. Working against homophobia is important work, and you need not do it alone. "Straight" people can be allies, and differences in sexual orientation need not keep us apart and isolated.

What a wonderful day it will be when we hear children chanting on the playground, " '*A' my name is Alice and my partner's name is Annette. We live in Amarillo and we make armchairs.*" Until that moment arrives, we must be vigilant in examining the music that our students and children are exposed to, and in consciously promoting a wider range of musical and life choices for our children and ourselves.

REFERENCES

Fink, Cathy. (1993). Everything's possible: Making choices. *Pass It On: The Journal of the Children's Music Network* (15) Fall.
Newman, Leslea. (1989). *Heather has two mommies.* Boston: Alyson Wonderland.
————. (1991). *Gloria goes to gay pride.* Boston: Alyson Wonderland.
Page, Nick. (1995). *Sing and shine on! The teacher's guide to multicultural song leading.* Portsmouth, N.H.: Heinemann.
Patai, Daphne. (1991). Minority status and the stigma of "surplus visibility." *The Chronicle of Higher Education,* 30 October.
Willhoite, Michael. (1990). *Daddy's roommate.* Boston: Alyson Wonderland.

MUSIC REFERENCES

The author gratefully acknowledges permission to quote the lyrics included in this chapter.

Alsop, Peter. It's only a wee wee. On *Uniforms.* Flying Fish Records, 298/1983. © 1981, Moose School Music (BMI), 800-696-5480.
Berkson, Laura. Marie. On *Laura Berkson.* Brave Ann Music, 41 Potter Lane, Kingston, RI, 02881, 401-782-8625, <braveann@ids.net>. Words and music © 1986 by Laura Berkson/Brave Ann Music.
Blue, Bob. Chromosomophobia. In *The Mister Blue Songbook,* available from J. Gordon, 810 Kater St., Philadelphia, Pa., 19147, 215-625-8892.
Buell, Uncle Ruthie. The family song. On *Take a Little Step.* 1731 S. Sherbourne Dr., Los Angeles, Calif., 90035, 310-838-8133.
Fink, Cathy, and Marcy Marxe. Everything possible. On *Nobody Else Like Me.* Rounder Records, One Camp Street, Cambridge, Mass., 02140, <www.rounder.com>.
Fingerett, Sally. Home is where the heart is. Four Bitchin' Babes. On *Buy Me, Bring Me, Take Me: Don't Mess My Hair,* Vol. 1.

Harley, Bill. Family. On *You're in Trouble*. Round River Records, 301 Jacob St., Seekonk, Mass., 02771, <www.billharley.com>.

Heitler-Klevans, David and Jenny. Love makes a family. On *Love Makes a Family*. 130 N. Nippon St., Philadelphia, Pa., 19119-2427, <www.twoofakind.com>.

Humphries, Pat. People love. (Not yet recorded.) Contact Pat at <movingfwd @mindspring.com>.

Hunter, Tom. Family of woman and man. On *Connections*. The Beech Center on Family and Disabilities.

Pelham, Ruth. Under one sky. On *Under One Sky*. Gentle Winds 1012. Music Mobile, P.O. Box 6024, Albany, N.Y., 12206, 518-462-8714.

Pirtle, Sarah. Sing about us. In *Linking up: Using music, movement, and language arts to promote caring, cooperation and communication*. Cambridge, Mass.: Educators for Social Responsibility, Discovery Center Music. Words and music © 1998 by Sarah Pirtle, Discovery Center Music.

Rodgers, Mary, and Sheldon Hanick. William's doll. (based on a book by Charlotte Zolotow). On *Free to Be You and Me*. Marlo Thomas and Friends. Arista Music.

Romanovsky and Phillips. One of the enemy. On *Be Political, Not Polite*. Fresh Fruit Records.

———. Love is all it takes. On *Be Political, Not Polite*. Fresh Fruit Records.

Sapon-Shevin, Mara. Mama, what's a dyke? (Not yet recorded.) Contact Mara at <msaponsh@mailbox.syr.edu>.

Shih, Patricia. The color song. On *Big Ideas*. Glass Records.

Small, Fred. Everything possible. On *Everything Possible*. Flying Fish Records. ©1983 Pine Barrens Music (BMI).

———. Scott and Jamie. On *I Will Stand Fast*. Flying Fish Records.

· 11 ·

LOCATING A PLACE FOR GAY AND LESBIAN THEMES IN ELEMENTARY READING, WRITING, AND TALKING

James R. King and Jenifer Jasinski Schneider

As the title for this chapter suggests, I am interested in finding a place for gay and lesbian perspectives in the daily reading and writing of elementary classrooms. It is different work from that related to the question "Should we include (permit) gay and lesbian themes in classroom language arts?" More subtly, I am interested in exploring *how* we use gay and lesbian content, which is an important, co-occurring message that comes with our choices to include these lives in classrooms. In this chapter I discuss the significance of teachers' stances toward the use of gay and lesbian themes and content in elementary classroom discussions, in writing, and in reading.

UNDERSTANDING LITERACY AND ITS TEACHERS

The language arts include reading, writing, listening, speaking, and visual expression (National Council of Teachers of English 1996). However, it is common practice to define literacy as reading and writing. For some, these are not separate disciplines, but related and mutually supportive processes. Indeed, writing with an awareness of future audience causes young writers to read their own work from another's presumed perspective. At this point, few teachers of young students have not heard of this interrelationship between reading and writing.

If a broad definition is accepted for literacy, then there is much to consider in the ways that we teach it. Newer, broader conceptions of literate competence suggest that students' intertextual use (Spivey 1997) of multiple texts (written, oral, and performative), as well as multiple interpretations of those texts, are desirable outcomes for language-arts instruction. How we understand children, their language competence, our role in facilitating their linguistic performance, and our role as culture broker when we do intend to facilitate students' literacy growth, are the real issues in what counts as literacy in classrooms. We are responsible for what we choose as instruction and for what we don't choose for our children.

How teachers see themselves in relation to curriculum, to children, and to the larger culture strongly influences what counts in reading and writing: what is "permissible" in children's talk, what is "productive" in children's reading, what is "prohibited" in children's writing. For each of the following sections on oral language, reading, and writing, I include both direct and less direct approaches to the infusion of gay and lesbian content. Both approaches can be productive, but for different teacher purposes.

Locating Gay and Lesbian Themes in Classroom Talk

One common dilemma that all elementary teachers share is students' use of abusive verbal labels, in this case ones that are predicated upon sexual orientation. Responding to students' use of derogatory language such as *fag, faggot, dyke,* or *lezzie* can actually open up discussion on why such talk is harmful and unacceptable. I understand this necessary work with elementary-aged children within a larger commitment I have made toward teaching about diversity and respect for all, and toward developing a classroom community based on inclusion and equality. Such acrimonious talk deserves our attention as an act of hostility and verbal abuse.

The instance of abusive talk based on presumed sexual orientation in schools is astoundingly common. The follow-up and correction by teachers who hear such talk is troublingly rare. As occasions for teachable moments in oral language, our intervention must do more than punish or shame. In fact, I would submit that we not intentionally punish this behavior at all. If teachers are working for the transformation of their students within language-arts activity, punishment will not change their beliefs. We must mediate new understanding about language and the rights of people to choose the ways that they are represented. To me this requires that we lead students to question abusive talk and help them renegotiate and redefine their standards for acceptable talk. But, more important, it also requires that we go beneath the surface to examine why we (all) use bigoted, stereotypic thinking and talk, and how we might learn other practices from each other.

In a second-grade classroom this year, I overheard one child accuse another of being "gay." I wondered to what extent the labeler was aware of the meaning of his label. I also considered that, regardless of the degree of knowledge, the intent was to demean the other student with a label I understood to pivot on sexual orientation. So the first task was to bring to the surface the illocutionary intent (to demean). This, to me, is productively handled as a community issue ("In what ways have we agreed to talk to each other in this family? . . . How is what you said different? . . . What can you do about it now?"). The second issue is in pulling apart the values that use homosexuality as a lever, as a cultural "bogeyman," that is used to control others. It is important to learn from the student what he or she meant with the term. If the child does not understand the underlying sexual dimorphism behind "gay is bad, straight is good," then it makes little sense to deconstruct the reasoning that allows for this partisan "knowing" and the destructive use of that knowing to hurt or control others. So it may be for the use of *fag* with young children. It is a "bad" word that conjures for them instant linguistic authority. But it does so at others' expense. So punishing may be the very payoff (negative power) for the use of *gay*. My friend Jenifer, who is also a professor of literacy, describes the following childhood incident: "I vividly recall when I was in second grade, a boy told me to say a word that he had spelled out: b-i-t-c-h. I pronounced the word for him, and knew immediately from his reaction, and those of his friends, that I had said something bad. I didn't know what it meant, but I knew that it was bad. He tried to tell the teacher on me. Fortunately, she believed me."

Jenifer is now an adult and still remembers the incident. Part of her vivid memory is the fear she felt in anticipation of her teacher's reaction. Her peer drew her into a linguistic power play. If young Jenifer was also to learn from these communication events so common in our classrooms, punishment is exactly not the thing for the teacher to do. A more productive approach seems to be addressing the intent to demean, and the compliance of an unsuspecting victim, and not the potentially misunderstood content that was embedded in the term chosen to demean.

In contrast to a naive use of *fag*, when there is some sense of what it means to be "a fag" or "a lez" embedded in the accusation, an interrogation of those notions may be productive. Overt examination of "Is it (necessarily) bad to be gay or lesbian?" with a class of second-graders is a concrete discussion. It can be based on gay and/or lesbian people known to the students, members of the immediate class's extended families, and narratives from children's background experiences. Perhaps with fifth-graders we would interrogate how *faggot* as a label for homosexuality necessitates that the underlying idea—homosexuality—must be kept negative. Students might begin to examine the mechanisms behind sexist, patriarchal notions of masculinity. After all, if homosexuality is simply okay, then the accusation "What are you, queer?" loses its bite and becomes a flaccid piece of language.

One aspect of language that we know well is that we learn it through use. If we are interested in speaking and listening as components of the language arts, then speaking and listening about issues and topics that are important to students is productive use of teaching time. Convening talk about language use is reflexive work on language, and that is language arts. The productive move is teachers' reframing of the significance of what is happening as we talk about using labels and the content behind a given label. If the talk is seen as a broader process-level goal of "learning to interrogate labels," or "questioning the propaganda techniques of categorizing people," this is the work of critical thinking. As such, it is firmly within even the most traditional classroom curricula. What we often fail to do is push the discussion to a critical level, where we can examine with our students how labeling works on an essentialized, bigoted reduction of a person to a label, and that that picture is inaccurate and incomplete.

I think that this discussion is potentially more productive in achieving the desired behavioral change than simply punishing. Another concern that I have about authoritarian treatments, such as punishment, is that the talk gets silenced, and therefore continues as a powerful language. Of course, I also recognize that in some classrooms, where teachers themselves have referred to targeted students as "fags," we cannot expect any of this interrogation. This advocacy is crucial. But it alone won't cause a transformation in the ways our students think about gay and lesbian people. We must also look for occasions to convene conversations on homosexual lives as a social fact. Yet these occasions are not a part of most planned elementary curricula. Another way to infuse the language arts curriculum with gay and lesbian lives is through a less direct method.

If we simply demonstrate an interest, a discussion ensues. Our students are interested in others' lives, lives that may be different, or lives that may be the same. For me the teaching role here is to legitimize, or make public, the conversation on gay and lesbian lives by inviting these potentially risky discourses into our classes. It is a consistent theme or belief in child-centered language arts that the lives of children are the center of the language learning. Furthermore, these young lives are part of, and embedded in, a culture that appears to have limitless curiosity about gay and lesbian lives. So be it. But the talk must also be reconvened and simultaneously legitimated in classroom discussions. This would be a satisfying bit of linguistic and curricular justice.

GAY AND LESBIAN LIVES IN LITERATURE: READING (THE) QUEER

Literacy learning that matters the most uses students' reading and writing to help them make sense of their places; it helps them see the possibilities in their daily worlds. Teaching "reading" is about reading this world (Freire and Macedo 1987) in teaching approaches that are centered on individual students and their outside-of-school lives. Often called critical literacy (King and Brozo 1992; Lensmire 1994), these approaches to teaching reading and writing can be seen as displacing literacy as the goal in favor of using it as a lever for social transformation, with teacher-mediated practice on the lever as the literacy learning agenda. Consequently, texts that readers use to make meaning must matter, must be provocative, and must connect with students' outside-of-classroom lives. Choosing literature for children with explicitly gay and lesbian themes, characters, and situations is a direct approach to including part of many children's home lives. For other young readers, teachers' choices to include gay-and-lesbian-themed literature would provide a point of contrast or difference. Characters may be lesbian or gay, or the storyline may focus on issues that result from gay identities. The approach, then, is a direct involvement with literature that has gay and/or lesbian content.

A less direct approach to locating gay and lesbian presence in reading can be found in our responses to literature, any literature. For many teachers the important part of reading is teaching students by using their responses to what they have read. Reader response, as this method is called, is a widely accepted practice in secondary and postsecondary literacy (Rosenblatt 1991), which has been working its way into elementary classrooms. Both response groups and literature circles are small groups that have read the same story and convene to discuss it (Goier 1996). A major premise of this teaching approach is that readers understand their reading more deeply when they have connected the content of the literature with some aspect of their personal lives. Connection here can be identification, contrast, catharsis, or any of a variety of positionings that relate the reader as a person to the text as a representation of the reader's world. Students' personal relationships to narratives were positively related to the students' continued, independent reading (Purves and Beach 1974; Sabo 1980). Readers of all ages work from a desire to rebuild themselves within the characters of the text (Bruner 1986). Sensitive teachers, who successfully scaffold readers' bridges between textual and nontextual worlds, occupy a powerful place when they facilitate young readers.

What does it mean if a teacher who convenes reader response does so with a goal of gay and lesbian representation? From a reader-response perspective, interpretation that uses gay or lesbian perspectives can add to the complexity and possible personal connections for readers. These are the interstices that Bruner claims enrich narrative ways of knowing texts, and knowing ourselves within those texts.

To ask students in a literature circle the follow-up question "What would it mean if . . . ?" and then to include same-sex relationships, or to bring a focus to a quasi-erotic friendship between same-sex friends in a story seems dangerous, irresponsible, or even unethical. In a graduate seminar on critical literacy, which I taught a few years ago, my students, all elementary teachers, labeled their sense of fear in such teaching "the ax." Teaching in this way, they told me, could cut them loose from their jobs. Yet none of them, even after they conducted follow-up interviews at their respective school sites, had knowledge of any teacher who had been cut for "risky teaching" (King et al. 1997). These same teachers, as well as the rest of us, would have little hesitation in discussions of ethnic identities, class differences, or even reparative strategies for the gender chasm. What is so scary about the homosexual possibilities in literature? The responses I have heard from undergraduates are, at their most positive, "It's different."

In their written and spoken responses to direct depiction of gay and lesbian themes in children's picture books, my students teach me about their fears and their limits regarding the teaching of homosexuality with their future students. For many of these undergraduates, homosexuality, even in children's literature, is about only sex. And because it is "inappropriate" to teach sex in elementary classrooms, homosexuality is relegated to the taboo list, the books come off the library shelves, and the talk is silenced.

The first problem in this argument is the mistaken reduction of all talk about homosexuality as talk about sex. Why is it that others, including teachers, insist on making us only what they imagine to be our sexual lives? Because of our "sexual difference," we are made into places where others can project and transfer their shame, because homo-*sex*-uality is about sex. It seems to me that the location of sexuality in homosexuality is exactly not in the character of the homosexual, but in the minds of those who would banish this theme from literacy discussion. From my perspective, dislocating homosexuality from within a discourse of sex is where productive talking in elementary classrooms must begin.

Starting a counterdiscourse is appropriate, and interpreting literature from gay and lesbian sensitivities and awareness is one way to start. Further, we cannot avoid discussing the cultural aspects of gender, sexual orientations, and sexual diversity that are redolent in children's and young adults' literature and lives. In literature that engages children, the sexual orientations of characters are concrete facts in most stories. And that "fact" is universal heterosexuality. Clearly, this is an unbalanced portrayal. And, finally, the explicit use of gay and lesbian lives is common (some would say ubiquitous) on television, in advertising, and on talk shows. Elsewhere I have argued that these "texts" are daily events that shape the background knowledge, or schema, that our students bring to our classrooms (King 1997). Elementary children do consider sexualities—theirs and others'—talk about it, and some practice with it. When we refuse to talk about it, the value of sexual talk of all kinds increases on the black market of linguistic transactions. Ultimately, we are responsible as teachers for what we choose *not* to teach children.

Teaching homosexuality is precisely about difference, learning from difference, and broadening the ways we understand others. The combined fears of sexual taboo and job insecurity (either real or imagined) have proved sufficient to keep homosexuality in the classroom closet. We can no longer afford this heterosexist elitism. Our students already know better (and worse).

GAY AND LESBIAN THEMES IN WRITING

In child-centered writing we invite our students' lives into the classroom. Process writing (Calkins 1994) maintains that students' investment in writing, both process and product, is learned from ownership, or personal connection with the content of the writing, along with its intended audience. The degree to which young and emerging writers engage with their topic is an indicator, if not a determinant, of their participation as an author. Children's outside-of-school lives are converted into texts for the purposes of their learning. Lives become pedagogical texts (Gilbert 1989).

What are the permissible texts? Can students write about anything? On the children's own behalf we make decisions about what are and are not appropriate "stories" for their compositions. When I was teaching in fifth grade, I had a group of students who wrote about torture, death, and dismemberment. Their graphic depictions included blood, consumption of human organs, and limitless explicit accounts of victims pursued by demons. The professional books I was reading at the time suggested that the fascination my students had with the horror genre would dissipate. It didn't. I finally stopped them with a "no more blood and guts rule" for writing.

When I reconsider their fascination now, I think through Bettelheim's (1975) analysis of folktales, and children's psychotherapeutic use of the "safe fear" in a text. Fear that is contained, controlled in texts, is fear that is different from the chaotic threats in the real world. I'm not sure how such understanding would have affected my "no more blood and guts" edict. What I *do* know is that their continued choice irritated me, and I stopped it.

Of course, my rules as a teacher do not stop anything my students can imagine. I simply closed one of the ways that they were able to express the real-life issues that might have compelled them to be authors. Here is the secret of the child-centered approach to writing. It is an intractable problem for all teachers. Our choices as teachers of writing say much about what we value, what we fear, and how we expect those values to be adopted by our students. One of the lessons here is that children's lives are only partially admissible for our appropriation. Kids learn what is okay to broach with given teachers and within given writing assignments. It is the hidden curriculum in elementary writing.

One way that gay and lesbian texts come into writing classrooms is through teachers' direction. A process-drama approach to writing (Jasinski 1996) encourages children to write for different audiences, imagining themselves as multiply positioned writers. Student writers in a process-drama classroom may be sent on imaginary journeys, through enacted trials, across inhabiting bodies, and into lives different from their own. Students write in role from other people's perspectives. The intent is to help them understand and work with difference, viewing the world from multiple perspectives. Process drama may also use literature as "pre-text" (O'Neill 1995), or as background knowledge, to set the scene for spontaneous dramatic encounters, during which composing may result.

A process-drama approach engages children in their real responses to lives they imagine. Like response to literature, emotional experiences that children have lived become the context from which they write about experiences they may not have had. Consider the following scenario for a fifth-grade writing project that I have borrowed from *Twilight of the Golds*, a recent movie:

> You and your spouse (husband or wife) have recently learned that you will have a baby together. Several members of your family (an uncle, a sister) are homosexual. When you ask your pediatrician about the likelihood that your baby will be gay or lesbian, he suggests that there is a conclusive genetic test that will determine the eventual sexual orientation of your child. What will you do?

My colleague, Jenifer, thought that my example was too heavy-handed and offered the following:

> How about reading the novel *Number the Stars* by Lois Lowry. Either before, during, and/or after reading, students can investigate the Holocaust

to find out what groups were targeted. Then they can participate in scenes where they take on various roles. For example, you (the teacher) could take on the role of the Nazi party youth leader, who recruits and then conducts an orientation. In this role, you could dish out propaganda—gently at first—convincing them of the evil of Jews, gays, Gypsies, and so on. Then you can lay it on thick. The drama would go from there. In drama, the teacher frames the scenario and then it evolves. Children could also write in the role of the characters of the story. The students could imagine that they were schoolchildren in 1943. They would write in role as a child in 1943 from their own perspectives.

What Jenifer is telling me is that I can simulate the gay experience using imaginary contexts and characters. She is teaching me about being more subtle with children. Playing in character roles creates language that can be transformed into text, and teachers can anticipate a diversity of responses to such a dilemma. It is the contestation of the differences that opens up learning opportunities about sexual orientations, the values we hold about them, and how other beliefs exist around our own.

There are certainly more direct ways to include gay and lesbian content in classrooms. A few models are available from recent work in adult literacy and the learning projects of older students. In a recent seminar in anthropology on my campus, the students completed a group oral-history project on a local AIDS care network. The project paired students, who were learning fieldwork methods, with informants who were stakeholders in the agency. The students completed a written account of the agency's history for a course project. A recent ethnographic study of a gay softball team explored the relationships that developed between the researcher and her husband (a member of the team), and the other players on the team (Tillman-Healy 1998). When I read this study, I was spellbound. I am not prone to weep during these academic reads but did so, repeatedly, gratefully.

If such research is possible for adults, can it be converted for younger researcher-writers' inquiries? I think so. In the past, language-arts instruction has connected students to the lives of elders through classroom-based projects. Wigginton's (1986) Foxfire approach with high school students is renowned, Puckett's (1989) criticisms notwithstanding. It is productive to use oral history and ethnography to move language arts into the social worlds of "the other." For me the challenge is to find ways to engage young students in documenting gay and lesbian lives as opportunities for students' learning. And as with any alternative learning, teachers must arrange for interactions with individuals who are appropriate for young students. This is so with any field-based learning for kids.

Project approaches, with real-world outcomes, can also bring gay and lesbian lives and understandings into children's writing (Willinsky 1990). When we turn our kids' writing into a project, we follow the project for its passion and its interest, and trust that learning writing happens when the writers practice with feedback and guidance. What these previous examples have in common is their potential for locating gay and lesbian stories, and the use of projects as an anchor for learning. There is intention to teach "gay and lesbian" by virtue of the project focus.

CONCLUDING THOUGHTS

In writing this essay I had help. Jenifer read and responded to my writing several times. The chapter emerged through this dialogue. Readers will have noticed our different stories in the final vignette. Mine is direct, while Jenifer's is less so. In other parts of the chapter, I have argued for less direct approaches to including gay and lesbian perspectives in teaching language arts. But in both direct and indirect approaches, the teacher chooses.

In *Playing in the Dark: Whiteness and the Literacy Imagination*, novelist Toni Morrison (1992) argues that "white" American literature is possible only through the presence of an unacknowledged black consciousness in our nation's history, culture, and, particularly, literature. She makes a compelling case that dominant culture is defined by what it is not. If we use Morrison's approach, literature that is premised on normative heterosexuality tacitly uses homosexuality to define itself. More concretely, Gifford (1995) presents a reasoned model for the figure of the homosexual as character/role/perspective in American literature. Homosexuality has always been part of the culture. It is written into the margins of literature (King 1997). Using this perspective in teaching elementary children can be a productive way to open composing and response behaviors so that they more closely match the lives of our students.

REFERENCES

Bettelheim, B. (1975). *The uses of enchantment: The meaning and importance of fairy tales*. New York: Vintage.

Bruner, J. (1986). *Actual minds, possible worlds*. Cambridge, Mass.: Harvard University Press.

Calkins, L. (1994). *The art of teaching writing.* Portsmouth, N.H.: Heinemann.

Freire, P., and D. Macedo. (1987). *Literacy: Reading the word and world.* South Hadley, Mass.: Bergin and Garvey.

Gifford, J. (1995). *Dayneford's library: American homosexual writing, 1900–1913.* Amherst, Mass.: University of Massachusetts Press.

Gilbert, P. (1989). Student texts as pedagogical texts. In *Language, authority, and criticism: Readings on the school textbook,* ed. S. deCastell, A. Luke, and C. Luke. London: Falmer.

Goier, R. (1996). *Reader response groups in elementary classrooms.* Ph.D. diss., Northern Illinois University, DeKalb.

Jasinski, J. (1996). *Context, genres, and imagination: An examination of the interplay between a teacher's writing instruction and her students' writing behaviors and beliefs in an urban elementary classroom.* Ph.D. diss., Ohio State University, Columbus.

King, J. (1997). Rereading the straight and narrow: Interpretive, pedagogical, and ethical issues in suing a queer perspective in literacy learning. Paper presented at the annual conference of The Center for the Expansion of Language and Thinking, July, Portland, Oregon.

King, J., and W. Brozo. (1992). Critical literacy and pedagogies of empowerment. In *Using inquiry in reading education,* ed. A. Frager and J. Miller. Pittsburgh, Kans.: College Reading Association.

King, J., S. Danforth, S. Perez, and N. Stahl. (1997). Is resistance empowerment? In *Reading: Putting the pieces together. Yearbook of the American Reading Forum,* ed. B. Hayes and K. Camperell. Logan, Utah: American Reading Forum.

Lensmire, T. (1994). *When children write: Critical revisions of writing workshop.* New York: Teachers College Press.

Morrison, T. (1992). *Playing in the dark: Whiteness and the literary imagination.* Cambridge, Mass.: Harvard University Press.

National Council of Teachers of English. (1996). *Standards for the English language arts.* Urbana, Ill.: National Council of Teachers of English.

O'Neill, C. (1995). *Drama worlds.* Portsmouth, N.H.: Heinemann.

Puckett, J. (1989). *Foxfire reconsidered: A twenty-year experiment in progressive education.* Urbana: University of Illinois Press.

Purves, A., and R. Beach. (1974). *Literature and the reader: Research in response to literature, reading interests, and the teaching of literature.* Urbana, Ill.: National Council of Teachers of English.

Rosenblatt, L. (1991). Literary theory. In *Handbook of research on teaching the English language arts,* ed. J. Flood, J. Jensen, D. Lapp, and J. Squire. New York: Macmillan.

Sabo, F. (1980). Students' self-selected reading choices after being exposed to oral reading and discussion in one of Purves's four categories of response to literature. Ph.D. diss., University of Pittsburgh.

Spivey, N. (1997). *The constructivism metaphor: Reading, writing, and the making of meaning*. New York: Academic Press.

Tillman-Healy, L. (1998). Between gay and straight: Ethnographic dilemmas and possibilities for friendship. Ph.D. diss., University of South Florida, Tampa.

Wigginton, E. (1986). *Sometimes a shining moment: The Foxfire experience*. New York: Doubleday.

Willinsky, J. (1990). *The new literacy: Redefining reading and writing in the schools*. New York: Routledge.

· 12 ·

"IT'S OKAY TO BE GAY": INTERRUPTING STRAIGHT THINKING IN THE ENGLISH CLASSROOM

Wayne Martino

INTRODUCTION

In this chapter I explore possibilities for using texts to interrupt straight thinking in the elementary English classroom (Britzman 1995; Sumara and Davis 1999). What kind of approach to teaching English will assist students to interrogate the effects of "compulsory heterosexuality" (Epstein and Johnson 1998) without necessarily falling into the trap of merely reinforcing the homo/hetero divide? How can teachers help students interrogate familiar patterns of thinking that often resort to defining sexual identity in oppositional terms and as a stable category?

It is important to emphasize that such a potentially disruptive reading practice can hardly be achieved by simply providing texts that are inclusive of gay and lesbian characters, as Britzman (1995) points out. However, in this chapter I explore the role that such texts might play in the classroom for creating a threshold for "imagining difference" beyond the hetero/homo oppositional way of thinking about sexuality. On the basis of the way students responded to one particular novel, I argue that such inclusive texts may prove to be quite useful for teaching young people to challenge particular stereotypes about gay people and for questioning the limits of normality.

TWO WEEKS WITH THE QUEEN

Two Weeks with the Queen is a novel by Morris Gleitzman (1996) about a young boy named Colin who is sent to London to live with relatives because his younger brother, Luke, is dying of a very rare type of cancer for which there is no cure. While in London he writes a letter to the Queen asking "to borrow her top doctor." Eventually he gets the address of the top cancer hospital in London and visits the cancer ward. In an attempt to speak with the best doctor, he is thrown out of the hospital. As he is sitting on the curb outside, he notices a man sitting on the opposite side of the street crying. He strikes up a friendship with this man, Ted, who is gay and whose partner, Griff, is dying of AIDS. Later he visits Ted at his apartment to find that he has been bashed because he is gay. As he approaches the block of flats, he notices some graffiti on the wall outside—the word *QUEENS* is spray-painted in red. Hence the significance of the title: Colin ends up by spending two weeks with Ted, a different kind of queen, and they become close friends who care for one another.

I interviewed six teachers at one particular school who had taught this novel to students aged twelve to thirteen years. Students were also surveyed to identify the kinds of positions they assumed in response to the issues raised about gay people and their relationships in the novel. I wanted to explore the possibilities of using such a text to interrupt and make available alternative ways of thinking about gay people (see Pallotta-Chiarolli 1995). I was aware of the problems associated with inclusive pedagogies in that they attempt to reverse familiar oppositions—the *other* to heterosexual, which has been excluded, becomes incorporated into the curriculum when adopting such approaches. And, as Britzman argues, this does not enable us to escape or to move beyond the limits of straight thinking. This is because the logic of straight thinking is one that resorts to working with oppositional categories, rather than attempting to blur the boundaries between different kinds of people and their identities (Angelides 1994). Within these limits the existence of the *other* can be understood only in opposition to what it is not! The focus moves away from an examination of how it is that heterosexuality has come to be seen as so normal and natural. Thus merely presenting students with representations of gay and lesbian characters may have the effect of presenting them as just like everyone else while being different at the same time.

While wanting to explore possibilities for using texts to teach queerly, I was also aware of many teachers' fears about raising these kinds of issues in their classrooms for fear of being outed or even losing their jobs (see Pallotta-Chiarolli 1998; Martino 1998c; Curran, Crowhurst, and Halliday 1998). Given this context and this form of surveillance, I was interested when I learned of one particular Catholic school that required all Year 8 students to study *Two Weeks with the Queen* as part of their English course. So I set out to explore exactly what teachers at this school did with this text and how students responded.[1]

The teachers I interviewed were very positive about teaching *Two Weeks with the Queen* and what they were able to achieve. They used the text to open up spaces for active discussions about marginalization and issues related to being gay. They tended, though, to work with liberal humanist notions of identity to personalize the gay characters. In this way, they provided students with an opportunity to challenge particular stereotypes about gay men and to present them in a positive light. For example, Jane makes the following comment about her approach to teaching the novel:

> JANE: It's a really good thing to be able to present the idea of Ted and Griffith as homosexual men as okay especially in a school like this, which is pretty homophobic. It's really a good thing to be able to present that, and for homosexual men to be portrayed in a positive light because it's something that never happens around here. It just never happens, and we have the opportunity to talk about that, and I saw them pass through these one-dimensional stereotypes that the kids have around here, and this is really good.
>
> WAYNE: Can you tell me how you saw the students moving beyond that one-dimensional homophobic stereotype?
>
> JANE: I think the novel positions them to accept that perhaps their "normal" wasn't correct, that their normal perceptions were not correct. The way I did it over a few lessons is we created character charts about Ted and all his character traits and things like that. . . . They described him and things like that, and every time someone wrote down *poofter*,[2] I'd say, well, that's really not appropriate, why do you think it's not appropriate, and sort of dealt with it that way . . . and when they said *poofter*, I'd say, what does that say about his character, how does that change his character? . . . So we're talking about his character, so that doesn't fit in, does it? . . . So that's how we dealt with it. . . . They could see that there was no connection. . . . And also I used my own experiences and things like that. I talked about my own friends and things like that, so that they can see that even I had gay friends and lived with them. . . . We talked about how everyone has different likes and dislikes about all sorts of things. So we just dealt with likes and dislikes. Are we allowed to like and dislike other people, and does it make them different? No! And then I brought up this idea of, where's the difference? Do you think that you can't be friends with someone who likes something different to you? But the boys were embarrassed. That was something I really noticed. The boys were embarrassed. It was something that they found very difficult to talk about.

Jane works with the liberal humanist notion that individual differences are okay and inserts into this framework the whole idea of being gay. She does this by using the character as a means by which to broach the issue of homosexuality—that is, being gay is just like having different likes and dislikes, and there's nothing wrong with that! She also uses her own experiences and mentions the gay friends she has to personalize them for her students in an attempt to move them beyond the one-dimensional stereotypes of gay people as supposedly deviant or abnormal. Her reference to the boys being embarrassed and having difficulty with the gay issue was also reiterated by other teachers and was reflected in the students' responses as well, with at least thirty-five of the seventy boys producing homophobic responses.

This point is highlighted by Anne, who was teaching a single-sex girls' class at this school. She begins by talking about how well the girls responded to the novel:[3]

> Most of the time I devoted to actually looking at Colin's progress of his coming to terms with the idea of death. . . . At the same time we looked at the way that he related the whole idea of homosexuality. How did he realize that this man was gay, and how did they feel about that? They were quite open about it and very tolerant, the girls. Because I said, "What does the book seem to be saying about homosexuality?" They say, "Well, it seems to say okay." I say, "Well, what's okay about it?" Somebody said, "Oh, well, it's just two guys who love each other," which the book presented in that way, I think. They thought that was great. They sort of see no problems at all with that. I did say to them, "Why did he get bashed?" "Why do people bash gays?" And they say it seems to be a problem with the boys. And they could see that. Yes, boys react to this differently. They could see that boys seem to be more obsessed with the idea than the girls. . . . But what they saw was just a kind of love between the two men.

Here Anne comments on the girls' reactions and their apparent acceptance of the gay issues raised in the text. She actually used the novel to create a space for discussing issues about gay characters and noted that students were willing to interrupt dominant ways of thinking about gay relationships. The discourse here is one that revolves around liberal humanist notions of acceptance but appears to move beyond just the idea of tolerating gays. This is made apparent in Anne's account of the students' readings of Ted and Griff as gay men in a loving relationship—"it's just two guys who love each other"—which, she claims, is the view that the book appears to be promoting anyway. In other words, the students actively accepted a gay-affirmative reading.

Anne, however, talks about the high levels of homophobia among the boys and how much harder she had to work to "get them to see the other side of it. . . . They just wanted to laugh and be silly and make sort of gay jokes and things like that." This also emerged in the students' responses to the survey, which I discuss later.

Later on in the interview Anne talks in detail about the bind in which she finds herself. She is aware of the limits imposed by the Catholic school in terms of the kind of critical thinking she can pursue with her students:

> But it's homosexuality that is a problem because it is forbidden. . . . I think they'd prefer we didn't discuss it at all. The problem is that the realities of life, you can't actually avoid it. Kids will ask questions. You have to be able to answer them. And I think actually *Two Weeks with the Queen*, as a text for teaching somebody about homosexuality, was absolutely brilliant because it presents it in a totally acceptable way as just being a love . . . but as for the more sexual side of it, which I feel is private anyway, I don't teach that. I'm not Catholic myself, so I don't know what we're allowed to do, but I think we are pretty limited.

Here Anne discusses what she understands to be the limits of her teaching of *Two Weeks with the Queen* with regard to addressing the issue of homosexuality—she believes she cannot go beyond directing her students to accept the love that exists between Ted and Griff. However, within the limits that she believes are imposed on her by the Catholic context in which she teaches, she is able to use the novel to engage students in some kind of critical thinking, and to challenge some of their stereotypes about gay people and relationships. She does this by using the characters in the text to deflect any attention explicitly from her own personal life or moral, ethical position. However, like Jane's approach, hers is informed by a liberal humanist ideology:

> I think it's difficult for some people [to deal with homosexuality]. I don't think I find it particularly difficult because I'm not that close to the Catholic church. But I know other people have difficulty with some of those things. . . . I think the thing is you just have to deflect away from discussing it as a moral issue and discuss it in terms of the character as motivation. I think that's a different sort of question. . . . I deflect to the focus of the text and say, "Why does that person do it?" And sometimes I would say, "How do you feel about that?" Usually they would say, "Well, I'm excited." But I don't start talking about whether it was morally right or wrong. We're not really there to judge. Sometimes kids ask me what I think. I tend to deflect that too. There's no right or wrong. It's up to you. Cut your own life. I just think that it's really not my job to stand there and give judgment.

On this basis it would appear that at times just including texts that focus on gay characters could have some benefit in assisting students to think beyond certain stereotypes of gay people as sexually depraved or deviant. While acknowledging the limits of such critical practices, I want to argue that this approach may well serve as a threshold for undertaking further critical work for getting students to interrogate the naturalization and normalization of compulsory heterosexuality (Epstein and Johnson 1998, Martino 1998b). In an attempt to move beyond liberal humanist positions in teaching about character, efforts must be made to direct students' attention to how characters are constructed in such a way as to challenge the dominant view of what is considered to be "normal."

Jason, another teacher, who taught the novel to a class of boys, reinforces many of the claims made by Anne. He talks about the boys' resistance, initially, "to the homosexuality in the book" and in a similar way appears to use the text as a means by which to challenge the students' thinking; but once again his approach is underscored by a dominant liberal ideology:

> There was a lot of resistance from the boys initially, and I do emphasize initially, with the homosexuality in the book, with Ted and Griff. And it wasn't so much a resistance—well, I think maybe *resistance* is the wrong word—I think more of a misunderstanding about it, I suppose, or a nonunderstanding of it and therefore a . . . quite embarrassed—almost childish, naive—sort of view of it. And I mean, that's to be expected, I suppose. I mean at a Catholic school it's very hard to talk about homosexuality, because technically we're supposed to teach that it's a disease, and it says that in the Vatican II document. I don't agree with that, so we broached the subject very briefly and we had a discussion on who knew anyone that was homosexual, and no one actually knew anyone that was homosexual in class. We talked about what it meant to be homosexual, and what sort of things they had to put up with and what was different than perhaps what a heterosexual person had to put up with, and this sort of thing. . . . I was looking at the fact that a lot of the stereotypes about homosexual people are false, and second, that there's a lot of discrimination out there, and how would you feel if that was happening to you? So we did a lot of that sort of discussion. The book was generally well received across the board. . . . The thing that really blew me away was that there was a lot of willingness to talk about the feelings that were being thrown around in this book.

Like Anne, Jason highlights the limits imposed in terms of how homosexuality is defined, which is related to the constraints imposed by the school/community context in which he works. However, whereas Anne uses the text to deflect any attention away from discussing homosexuality as a moral issue, Jason, like Jane, attempts to personalize the issue by asking students if they know of anyone who is gay. He uses this technique to dismantle "false stereotypes" about gay people. He also uses his own "personal" experiences by making a point of sharing with his students that he has close friends who are gay:

> I don't give my students a total insight into my life, obviously, because you have to maintain a professional relationship with them, and you have to maintain privacy as well. Because you don't give away facts that are going to be used against you. . . . I think we have to contextualize where we're coming from, and I very much run on the philosophy that actions speak louder than words, so rather than just saying, give them something or show them something that proves what you're saying. And basically be as honest with the boys as possible. . . . So I tend to use my own personal life in the sense that if they can't trust in what I'm saying to be true for me, then they're not going to be able to trust in themselves. . . . It's sort of like, well, if Mr. X says he's got a couple of gay friends, and that they are all right for these reasons, and blah, blah, blah, then it might be okay for me to do it as well.

Jane, Anne, and Jason all find ways of helping students challenge problematic ways of thinking about gay issues and relationships albeit within the limits imposed by the dominant liberal ideology and school/community context that inform the way they address issues of sexuality in their classrooms. Although their practices appear to be grounded in attempts to encourage students to be more tolerant and accepting of gay people, they do not appear to move beyond the limits of merely "recover[ing] more authentic images of gays" in an attempt both to remedy the hostility experienced by those who cannot deal with such difference, and to restore self-esteem for those gay people who have been imagined as having no legitimate identity (Britzman 1995, 158). However, particularly in light of the students' responses to the text—which I discuss in the next section—such an approach, despite its limits, can serve as a platform for moving students beyond the limits of straight thinking.

READING *TWO WEEKS WITH THE QUEEN*

One hundred fifty students were asked to write extended responses to a series of questions that required them to record their thoughts and feelings about the novel and the characters. Although there was a tendency for more boys (n=35) than girls (n=5) to produce homophobic responses, there was an overall acceptance and acknowledgment of the need to learn more about gay issues. Although the students' responses are not entirely unproblematic, they signal the potentialities for using the text to interrogate and challenge familiar stereotypes about gay men and, hence, heteronormative ways of thinking.

Forty-five out of seventy boys, as opposed to only nine girls, rejected the novel outright on the basis that they didn't need "to know about homosexuals" and because reading about "homos" might make children think that "it is the right thing to be a poof."

> I would not recommend this novel to be given to young kids to read because they copy elders so if they read about homos they might think it is the right thing to be a poof but it's not. And I'm sure that their parents wouldn't like them reading it. I think that poofs should be mature enough to know it's the wrong thing to do, two people of the same sex trying to have sex. (Michael)

Other boys also referred to religion and claimed that "when God created people, they weren't meant to be gay"!

For some boys their responses were influenced by what they considered to be "appropriate" masculine behavior (see Martino 1995, 1998b). Sexuality, for these students, becomes the means by which they police and define "acceptable" heterosexual masculinity (Epstein 1997).

> I think Ted is a generous gay person but he sounds like a girl. He probably got bashed for being a gay. Who cares? I don't cause I hate gay people especially the ones that talk like girls. He deserved it. God didn't want us to be gay. (Greg)

> Well, quite frankly I thought it was a big load of rubbish. . . . I thought that the characters were pretty stupid and they acted really gay and it's about a bunch of homosexuals. . . . Ted sounds like he is gay cause he seems to have an interest in boys . . . he is also a bit of a pansy. (Damian)

Greg rejects gays on the basis of their association with girls and, hence, the "feminine." Here the link of homophobia to misogyny is important in highlighting how many boys learn to define their masculinity in opposition to femininity. He also refers to religion in his reference to God not "want[ing] us to be gay." Similarly, Damian labels Ted as a "pansy," and hence his rejection of this gay character is also caught up with his rejection of the "feminine" and the implication that he is a pedophile.

What was significant, however, was the overwhelming gay-affirmative responses to the novel that many of the boys and girls produced. One hundred ten students claimed that they had learned a lot from reading and studying the novel and were adamant in their assertion that other young people should read it. Many of their responses, in fact, tended to mirror those of their teachers in working with problematic liberal humanist notions of identity. For example, they tended to resort to discourses of sameness and difference to articulate their acceptance of Ted as a gay character who should be treated with respect and not discriminated against.

> I thought that this was really an interesting novel that really opened my eyes to certain issues in life like homosexuality and death. . . . I learnt that you must respect homosexual people and not make fun of or taunt them. They are normal average people like you and me. . . . They all had different but normal personalities and I felt like I had met them before, like they were familiar to me. . . . I think I related to Colin the most because of the way he acted. For example, being friends with a grown homosexual man who was crying isn't seen everyday. I think Colin is a shining example to boys everywhere. (Robert)

> Colin's friendship with Ted shows that *we're all the same* whether we're straight or homosexual. (Mark)

> I learnt that everybody is different in some way and that is what makes us unique. Somebody's differences are not to be held against them, it is part of what makes them themselves. Everybody is different and we have to learn that there is no such thing as sameness. (Annie)

Although these responses indicate that students are working with problematic liberal humanist notions of identity that slip into straight patterns of thinking, it is important to note the level of their engagement with the text and the possibilities that this engagement signals for interrupting heteronormativity (Sumara and Davis 1999). Teachers as classroom strategists (Patterson 1997) may very well find that dealing with the text in this way is a point of entry for them to engage with issues that they find difficult and potentially threatening, particularly if they are working in Catholic or religious schools. However, it is also important to reiterate that ways of moving beyond positions of mere acceptance and tolerance for the other need to be considered. Students need to be encouraged to think about what we take for granted as normal and natural. This becomes even more pertinent in light of one student's comment about the fact that the novel made her understand how lucky she was "to be normal." It is in this capacity that the novel can be used to problematize the whole idea of what is normal and natural and how we come to understand ourselves in these terms. For instance, "Who decides if someone is normal or not?" could be posed to students in the context of discussing the characters and their relationships in *Two Weeks with the Queen.*

It is important to stress that many of the students did not resort to producing homophobic readings of the text. In fact, student after student reiterated the need for young people to learn about "homosexuality so that they can understand it."

> I think Ted is a very caring person. . . . He must have really loved Griff because even the fact that Griff has AIDS and he got bashed for being gay hasn't put him off. Some selfish people might leave the other person because they have a serious problem and they are dying but Ted still stuck with Griff and supported him—this is a very good quality. . . . I would recommend this book to younger people as they can learn about the qualities of being gay, like in the show called South Park. A young eight-year-old boy Stan finds out his dog is gay and he can't accept that but when he learns about homosexuality he accepts that. All children should learn about homosexuality young so that they can understand it. (David)

This student's reference to *South Park* is interesting in light of the role that popular culture is playing in his education "about the qualities of being gay." Teachers need to consider the significant role that "everyday texts" play in children's lives and their educative value. It is also important to avoid problematic constructions of children as innocent and in need of protection from the evils of popular culture. Teachers could ask students about other texts they have read or viewed that include gay characters and, hence, draw on their already existing knowledge of these issues. Within this intertextual context, students could also be encouraged to reflect on how gay characters are constructed across a range of texts.

Furthermore, as I have argued elsewhere, it would appear that within English there already exists a requirement to encourage students to reflect critically on their worlds and to problematize themselves when reading texts (see Martino 1998a, 1998b). These reading practices or approaches to working with texts already require students to undertake a particular kind of work on themselves. Texts have been used in the English classroom for some time now to teach students particular lessons about life and to relate these kinds of lessons to their own lives (Hunter 1983, 1988; Mellor and Patterson 1991). For example, we see the following students using these techniques and ways of reading to problematize discriminatory practices against gays and in so doing move to an acceptance of gay sexuality as okay.

> If people read this novel they'll see that people get bashed up from being gay and that it's not alright to bash up people. (Alicia)

> [In reading the novel] I did realize that our parents don't instill enough knowledge of the world into their children. Why aren't children taught to be aware of AIDS or to understand homosexuals. . . . I relate to Ted as any other person. I don't see what's wrong with gay people! I serve them in my father's hardware shop. They are nice people. You can have

sensible conversations with them and you won't even realize they're gay. ... Parents should teach children about AIDS and homosexuality. Colin does not act differently around Ted or Griff. Children should be taught about homosexuals and how to understand them. Without proper knowledge or teaching they would start to ridicule them! (Joseph)

Other students were adamant in their assertion that it was "okay to be gay."

I liked the novel because it kind of said it was alright to be gay and there's nothing wrong with gay people. (Lynne)

I would recommend this novel to young people because homosexuality isn't that bad but some people hate it and want to bash the people who are gay and this story tells people that they are okay and you don't have to bash people up because they are different [from] you. (Jake)

On the basis of these responses it would appear that there exist possibilities for putting already available ways of reading to use in taking students beyond mere acceptance and tolerance of gay people to a position of interrogating the very basis of normality. This, I believe, is the task that must be addressed if we are serious about interrupting the limits imposed by the hetero/homo distinction.

CONCLUSION

The responses of the teachers and students presented in this chapter point to the very significant ways in which this novel could be used to assist teachers in their attempts to interrupt straight thinking or heteronormativity. It is possible to move beyond positions of mere acceptance and tolerance of the *other* to encourage students to think about what we take for granted as "normal" and "natural." However, in order for this critical practice to be realized, teachers need to move beyond a dominant liberal pedagogy to encourage students to interrogate issues of sexual identity outside the limits of fostering tolerance and understanding. It appears, though, that attempting to challenge one-dimensional stereotypes of gay characters may well serve effectively as a platform for taking students beyond the discourses of mere acceptance and tolerance of the *other* as caught within the hetero/homo divide. Texts such as *Two Weeks with the Queen* can be used to draw attention to the naturalization and normalization of sexual identity, and this can be achieved by encouraging our students to consider questions related to how we come to understand what is constructed as "normal" and who determines these norms.

Furthermore, as the students' responses have indicated, already existing practices of self-problematization can also be used in the English classroom to encourage students to think about such issues in relation to their own lives (Knobel and Healy 1998). It is in this way that attempts to interrupt straight thinking in the English classroom can be realized. In light of the way students responded to *Two Weeks with the Queen* and what teachers themselves said about their work with this text, it would appear that there are tremendous possibilities for teachers to engage students in this kind of critical work.

NOTES

1. The students were from lower-middle-class socioeconomic backgrounds. Many were second- and third-generation Australians. The six teachers interviewed were white; two were male.
2. *Poofter* and *poof* are the equivalent of *faggot*.
3. Girls and boys were separated for English classes at this school.

REFERENCES

Angelides, S. (1994). The queer intervention: Sexuality, identity, and cultural politics. *Melbourne Journal of Politics* 22: 66–88.

Britzman, D. (1995). Is there a queer pedagogy? Or stop reading straight. *Educational Theory* 45(2): 151–65.

Curran, G., M. Crowhurst, and L. Halliday. (1998). Being lesbian and gay in a Catholic school. *Campaign*, 26 March, 31–2.

Epstein, D. (1997). Boyz' own stories: Masculinities and sexualities in schools. *Gender and Education* 9(1): 105–15.

Epstein, D., and R. Johnson. (1998). *Schooling sexualities*. Philadelphia: Open University Press.

Gleitzman, M. (1996). *Two weeks with the queen*. Sydney: Pan Macmillan.

Hunter, I. (1983). Reading character. *Southern Review* 16: 226–43.

———. (1988). *Culture and government: The emergence of literary education*. London: Macmillan.

Knobel, M., and A. Healy. (1998). *Critical literacies in the primary classroom*. Sydney: Primary English Teaching Association.

Martino, W. (1995). Deconstructing masculinity in the English classroom: A site for reconstituting gendered subjectivity. *Gender and Education* 7(2): 205–20.

———. (1998a). "When you only have girls as friends, you got some serious problems": Interrogating masculinities in the literacy classroom. In *Critical Litera-*

cies in the Primary Classroom, ed. M. Knobel and A. Healy. Sydney: Primary English Teaching Association.

———. (1998b). "Dickheads," "poofs," "try hards," and "losers": Critical literacy for boys in the English classroom. *English in Aotearoa* (New Zealand Journal for the Teaching of English) 35: 31–57.

———. (1998c). "It's all a bit of a mess really": Addressing homophobia in schools. In *Everyone is special: A handbook for teachers on sexuality education*, ed. L. Beckett. Brisbane: Australian Women Educators.

Mellor, B., and A. Patterson. (1991). Reading character: Reading gender. *English in Australia* 95: 4–23.

Pallotta-Chiarolli, M. (1995). Can I use the word "gay"? In *Boys in Schools*, ed. R. Browne and R. Fletcher. Sydney: Finch.

———. (1998). When religious liberty is religious bigotry. *Campaign*, 26 March, 28–30.

Patterson, A. (1997). Setting limits to English. In *Constructing critical literacies*, ed. S. Muspratt, A. Luke, and P. Freebody. Sydney: Allen and Unwin.

Sumara, D., and B. Davis. (1999). Interrupting heteronormativity: Toward a queer curriculum theory. *Curriculum Inquiry.* 29(2), 191–208.

· 13 ·

HOW TEACHERS UNDERSTAND
GAY AND LESBIAN CONTENT IN THE
ELEMENTARY SOCIAL STUDIES CURRICULUM

Kevin P. Colleary

INTRODUCTION

Sister Mary Joel dressed up as Robin Hood when teaching about medieval England. Mr. Flora had the entire class repeat aloud over and over "SOL—ZHE—NEET—SIN" during current-events lessons on the Soviet Union. Ms. Anderson was the judge during mock trials involving heated topics explored at the time of the Constitutional Convention, the Dred Scott decision, and Watergate. These were three social-studies teachers who made strong impressions on my young mind about the importance of history, geography, and civics. These were the people who made me want to teach. As much as I loved them, however, throughout my entire elementary and high school career there was one important social issue that they never discussed. One topic that never made it into the social-studies lessons these teachers and their colleagues worked so hard to prepare. That was the issue of homosexuality.

As a young boy who was slowly coming to consciousness about his difference regarding sexual orientation, and later as a gay adult classroom teacher planning social-studies lessons of my own, this silence around homosexuality continued to rule. It was only years later, as a graduate student in education, that I began to ask the question, Why? While the world provided many obvious answers, I wanted to find out, through research, what teachers understood about including content on gays and lesbians[1] in their social-studies teaching.

Theorists agree that the social-studies curriculum, in order to live up to its goal of helping students develop a sense of human dignity for all persons, must include content about those groups who were ignored or underrepresented in past decades of social-studies teaching and learning (Armento 1993). A multiculturally sensitive understanding of social studies has helped some teachers integrate a wider variety of representatives from across the racial, religious, ethnic, and cultural spectrums in order to achieve this goal. However, with few exceptions, even multiculturalism as understood by many scholars and teachers in the United States still does not include discussion of gays and lesbians.

Gays and lesbians have historically been one of the most maligned and hated subgroups in U.S. society. Incidents of violence and prejudice, and negative portrayals of gays and lesbians, continue to diminish us all as the twentieth century ends. This has a direct impact on students in our schools. As long as schools and curricula fail to engage proactively with the realities of homosexuality and homophobia, we shall continue to see all students diminished in their understandings of history, culture, and democracy.

Citizenship education, and respect for our unique national diversity, are two major foci of elementary social-studies education (National Council for the Social Studies 1994). These issues cannot be fully addressed while one segment of the population is ignored or vilified in our schools. This silence and vilification affects every student who experiences it, but it especially affects those students, estimated at between 6 and 14 million (Patterson 1992), who are part of gay/lesbian families. It also may have crippling effect on those students who are experiencing a growing awareness of their own lesbian or gay feelings and desires.

HOMOPHOBIA AND SCHOOL SILENCE

Much research has been published in the last ten years focusing on the spread of homophobic activity against, and isolation of, gay/lesbian youth (Gibson 1989; Martin and Hetrick 1988; Remafedi, Farrow, and Deisher 1991; Rofes 1993; Sears 1991). A study by the Massachusetts Department of Education (1995) found that students who describe themselves as gay, lesbian, or bisexual are four times more likely to have attempted suicide, and five times more likely to miss school because of feeling unsafe, than other students. Herdt and Boxer (1993) studied over two hundred Chicago youth and found that most remembered their first same-sex attraction slightly before their tenth birthday, and that awareness of difference among gays and lesbians often occurs as early as age four or five. If teachers could integrate issues of homosexuality into their elementary social-studies curricula, it would give these students one further opportunity to participate more fully in their school community, thus increasing their own sense of self-worth and achievement and significantly decreasing their chances for isolation, academic failure, or suicide.

A school community that, through its silence, does not proactively attempt to dispel society's prejudice within the curriculum extends that prejudice against gays and lesbians. In the elementary social-studies curriculum students are introduced to various leaders in the struggle for political, civil, and human rights throughout U.S. and world history. One important goal of these introductions is the reduction of prejudicial and biased attitudes and an increase in student tolerance (Bullard 1996; Jarolimek and Parker 1993). But there is most often only silence regarding the existence of homosexuality in elementary classrooms, never mind the introduction of an active proponent of homosexual rights, either historical or current, to help combat negative attitudes in this area.

These realities, in concert with my own identity as a gay man and social-studies educator, led me to explore teacher understandings about gays and lesbians in the elementary social-studies curriculum for my doctoral dissertation. This chapter will discuss findings based on initial research with six classroom teachers. My focus will be on three areas: (1) the paradigm of "explict versus implicit" social studies as understood by the teachers; (2) the "waiting rather than creating" impulse of most of these teachers regarding gay and lesbian themes; and (3) the lack of teacher knowledge about lesbian and gay content in order to integrate it into social-studies curricula.

THE RESEARCH PROJECT

Six public- and private-school teachers from New York City's boroughs of Manhattan and Brooklyn agreed to take part in this project. At the time of the study, Brigid, Claire, John, Mary, Teresa, and Ursula taught across the grade levels from 1 to 6. They represent a variety of ages and teaching experiences, as well as religious, cultural, and ethnic backgrounds. As the names I've assigned them suggest, five are women and one is a man. Only John self-identified as gay. Teresa and Mary are married. Ursula, Brigid, John, and Claire are single. Their school settings are located in six different neighborhoods and represent a wide demographic spectrum of students. The project involved both group and individual interviews on the topic.

Explicit versus Implicit Social Studies

Hollins (1996) explains the explicit or planned curriculum as the content areas and topics to be studied that are overt or intentional, whereas the implicit is "indirect in that what is legitimated is culturally, socially, and institutionally embedded and may be incorporated into school practices without planning or thought" (1). Hollins also defines the null, or hidden, curriculum in the same vein as Apple (1975): content and/or values, taught by teachers and learned by students in schools, that are never discussed openly, written down, or acknowledged. The teachers had a clear understanding of and were able to discuss the differences in their own experiences between explicit and implicit social studies. John stated, "There's this explicit social-studies curriculum made up of 'topics,' but then there's this implicit piece that says we are dealing with issues in the community and the classroom." The teachers initially placed all discussion of gay and lesbian issues within the implicit rather than the explicit realm. They believed that gay and lesbian topics, though important to discuss, fell squarely outside their stated or explicit curriculum.

Teresa acknowledged that there was no official mention of gay/lesbian topics in her school's social-studies curriculum. While planning a unit on families, however, she used a trade book that worked very well with her explicit curriculum goal of family studies: *Anna Day and the O-Ring,* by Elaine Wickens (1994). Featured in the story was a boy with two moms. When discussing the integration of gay and lesbian topics, Teresa said, "I feel really strongly that for me, it is going to come up. I make it come up because I know it's there. I think that kids have already begun to learn about what it means to be a good boy and a good girl in school and in the world and what is okay to say and what is okay not to say."

Teresa's references to the silences her students are understanding about certain issues mirror Paulo Freire's (1985) conception of the culture of silence. Freire discusses how silence plays a key role in the relationship between dominators and the dominated. The concepts of silence and of the closet have often been associated with sexual difference and the desire to ignore and imprison those who exhibit any behaviors associated with this difference (Sedgwick 1990; Lipkin 1999). Teresa's willingness to bring gay/lesbian content to the attention of her first-graders and her appreciation of the political nature of her role as teacher illustrate her understanding of the power of complicity in the continuation of this method of oppression. She asks,

> What's our role going to be at this time in our lives with families and children? Are we really going to sit back and let people have their ideas

and opinions and pretend we don't hear, hope that people really don't come out in school, just sort of pretend it's not there? Or are we really going to come out and say: This is who we are, this is what we believe, and we are going to bring up these issues because we want to be part of a movement that transitions people and moves people to a different place and a different way of thinking?

Teresa's questions and challenges help her bridge the implicit and explicit within her social-studies classroom in a powerful and meaningful way, creating, rather than waiting for, opportunities.

Creating Opportunities

Teresa was unique in the group of teachers in her willingness to bring up, of her own accord, gay and lesbian topics as part of the explicit curriculum. The other teachers were clearly most comfortable with dealing with the issues if they arose as a part of "classroom life" (implicit social studies) but were reluctant to integrate them into content lessons (explicit social studies).

Second/third-grade teacher Ursula believed that the goal of talking about homosexuality and homophobia was important. She stated that, "It is absolutely important, in fact I don't think we have a choice about it. Just like we don't have a choice about addressing racism or prejudice or whatever, I think it needs to be in the curriculum. I think that it is the teacher's responsibility to bring that in, as part of the content." She, however, never "brought it up as a content piece" herself. This dissonance in Ursula's statements was discussed further. "I've not been able to really implement it explicitly in the curriculum. I'm still looking for opportunities in my social-studies curriculum to make it more of an explicit part since I'm not studying families per se, so I address it now implicitly."

Ursula's contradiction is evident in the use of her language. Her response to whether or not this should happen was emphatic—even stating that "we don't have a choice about it," and saying that it should be "part of the content"; yet her own inability to treat the subject as a content piece was evident. Rita Marinoble's (1997) work with teachers illuminates this constant challenge. Even after a professional-development seminar on the issue of homosexuality in the elementary-school curriculum, where over 90 percent of the teachers had stated that their comfort level was improved or substantially improved, Marinoble states, "Many teachers shared their continuing anxiety about directly discussing the topic of homosexuality with elementary school students" (258).

In examining this contradiction and uncertainty in Ursula's language, I was struck by the concern she (and other teachers) voiced about waiting for an opportunity, as opposed to meeting the challenge to create an opportunity to discuss gay/lesbian content. This "waiting for rather than creating" is an understandable strategy when the topic at hand is a difficult or sensitive one on which there may be many divergent opinions from parents, administrators, and community members. It is much more difficult to blame a teacher for responding to an issue when it arises than to blame the teacher for bringing the issue to the fore her- or himself.

When queried about integrating gay/lesbian content, Claire couldn't imagine a "natural fit anywhere." She stated, "It doesn't seem it can be done naturally in a sort of natural way in talking about a culture with this age group, in elementary school." Claire's multiple use of the word *natural* in this context seems to denote a strong desire for some acceptable or normative process for including this content. Although Claire, like the other teachers, stated that this topic was an important one to deal with, there is still the sense of challenge and danger in actualizing this belief, and a desire for natural opportunities at the elementary level. Like Ursula, Claire seems to be waiting for, rather than creating, those opportunities.

Lack of Teacher Knowledge Base

Although there might be many reasons that play into a teacher's sense of waiting for rather than creating opportunities, one issue that arose was the absence of a knowledge base of appropriate lesbian and gay social-studies topics. Most teachers currently have no background regarding historical or cultural content about gays, lesbians, or same-sex relations. There is a critical need in the teacher-education process, especially in social-studies education programs, for better preparation in this area. Walter Williams (1997) writes of the importance of the *berdache*, or two-spirited people, in various Native American cultures and the same-sex relationships that were accepted in parts of early Indian and Japanese culture. Native American cultures and the histories of India and Japan are all classic social-studies topics studied in the elementary school. However, few elementary classroom teachers know about the *berdache* or about the role of same-sex relations in ancient India and Japan. Few resources exist to help them. In the nation's most widely used elementary (grades K–6) social-studies textbook series, McGraw-Hill's *Adventures in Time and Place* (Banks et al. 2000), there are over three hundred pages in both pupil and teacher editions devoted to topics on Native American history, culture, religious beliefs, government, economic systems, health care, housing, clothing, diet, and family life. Never once is the *berdache* or any similar topic introduced for students or teachers. Yet Williams describes the *berdache* as a critical element of many Native American cultures. The *berdache* were "seen in many Native American religions as a gift from the spirit world, of great benefit to families, to friendships, and to society as a whole" (77).

As Teresa's work with her first-graders showed, there are many opportunities for integrating gay/lesbian content into the primary social-studies curriculum. Whenever a discussion of family or community occurs—both topics of great importance in almost all grade K–3 social-studies curriculum documents—there is an opportunity to talk about gay and lesbian families, and/or specific communities or neighborhoods where many gays and lesbians live in almost every major city. In fourth grade, when most curricula call for some sort of state, local, or regional study, the contributions of gays and lesbians to a particular state's history might be examined. In fifth grade, when most curricula call for a study of U.S. history, opportunities also exist for discussing gay and lesbian contributions to the civil and human-rights movements of the 1960s through 1990s.

Claire initially had a very hard time imagining what kind of "natural" fit gay and lesbian topics might make within an elementary social-studies curriculum. "I'm trying to think . . . most cultures—even a lot of African cultures—can talk about different formations of marriage and different formations of family in terms of who lives with who. You can go back to the Iroquois and see how they were matriarchal and that whole thing. But I can't think of any topic offhand where a gay/lesbian strand can be woven in." As the discussion continued, however, she had a number of ideas. During a discussion of her recent fourth/fifth-grade social-studies lessons on Plymouth Plantation, Claire had this to say:

> With that topic, I can't think of any . . .[*Pause*]. Except the idea of being discriminated against. But it didn't even occur to me. What one can do I guess is really talk about—take that springboard to discuss—other stuff, like discrimination. I think that could lead into a natural discussion about discrimination and then bring it from the 1620s to the 1990s. It's not about building houses in Plymouth Plantation, but it's certainly about the underlying issues of a group of people who were discriminated against so much that they had to flee their country.

Claire's sudden awareness that this kind of connection between explicit social-studies topics and gay/lesbian topics "didn't even occur" to her was critical to her growing realization of the possibilities of integrating gay/lesbian topics into social-studies teaching. This newfound discernment speaks to the typical lack of background knowledge among teachers about the potential that exists for instruction about gay and lesbian contributions to history and daily life.

Of all the complicated discourses that take place (or don't take place) each day in schools between teacher and teacher, teacher and student, student and student, teacher and parent, the rare discussion around sexuality of any kind or homosexuality in particular is usually a very uncomfortable and sometimes frightening one. It is, on one level, so much easier to remain silent rather than face the discomfort. Teresa understands this and faces the problem by daring to share the realities of gay and lesbian existence with her first-graders. She is also well aware of how difficult this decision can be. She says, "I'm very nervous about it and shaky about it because I feel that I am out on a limb by myself. So . . . I have to stand there and make my decisions about how brave am I going to be, and if the heat comes, be prepared to take it and respond appropriately. I don't know what the support's going to be like." Teresa's thoughtful and challenging view of teaching echoes the works of many educational philosophers such as Freire (1985) and Dewey (1916), as well as critical pedagogues like Giroux and McLaren (1986). Goodman's (1992) concept of educating for critical democracy, heavily influenced by Dewey, challenges teachers to understand their role in helping students develop a "connectivist perspective to move children towards values of social bonding, caring and responsibility" (110). Teresa's challenges to herself and her larger school community have begun such a task by introducing her first-graders to the realities and diversity of gay/lesbian people in their world.

CONCLUSION

The three themes discussed in this chapter—the explicit and implicit understandings of social studies curriculum, waiting for rather than creating opportunities for gay/lesbian content inclusion, and the lack of teacher knowledge about gay/lesbian social-studies content—are only some of the many complicated issues elementary teachers must deal with when including gay/lesbian topics within the framework of social studies. However, they speak to key issues that educators must face if we are going to begin to break the insidious cycle of silence that has existed throughout the history of elementary education in the United States.

The realities of including content about gays and lesbians within the context of the elementary social-studies curriculum are both profoundly complex and remarkably simple. As these teachers and others have noted, there is great fear and uncertainty as well as a great lack of knowledge regarding gay and lesbian topics. The political realities of both school and local communities often have a great impact on what teachers feel comfortable speaking about in a public forum. However, thoughtful and caring teachers must make decisions about what is taught every day. The many opportunities for inclusion of gay/lesbian topics within the social-studies curriculum should not be ignored. David Jenness (1990) writes, "Adaptation in society becomes impossible if we seek to limit freedom to invent and explore new social forms and attitudes, to rethink our own experience . . . the minimal goal for social studies here must be to make it socially realistic—not for the sake of the social studies per se, but for the sake of the people we are and the problems we face" (428). Much more research is needed on this topic, and many more discussions in faculty rooms, living rooms, and classrooms across the country. Incorporating gay/lesbian social-studies content for elementary students is one step toward Jenness's stated minimal goal.

The voices of these teachers, and mine, have helped break the silence in the educational research literature about a critical issue. This study should foreshadow others that also ask challenging questions about social-studies curricula, the role of gay/lesbian content and its impact on the intellectual and social life of elementary-school children, and the power of teachers' voices to increase our understanding.

NOTES

1. My choice in this chapter to employ the terms *gay* and *lesbian* reflects the use of the terms by the teachers with whom I worked. It is not meant to dismiss other terminology choices or to imply that the issues discussed are not relevant to the way that bisexuals or transsexuals might be understood in the elementary social-studies curriculum.

REFERENCES

Apple, M. (1975). The hidden curriculum and the nature of conflict. In *Curriculum theorizing: The reconceptualists*, ed. W. Pinar. Berkeley, Calif.: McCutchan.

Armento, B. (1993). Reform revisited: The story of elementary social studies at the crest of the twenty-first century. In *Teaching social studies: Handbook of trends, issues and implications for the future*, ed. V. Wilson, J. Litle, and G. L. Wilson. Westport, Conn.: Greenwood Press.

Banks, J., B. Beyer, G. Contreras, J. Craven, G. Ladson-Billings, M. McFarland, and W. Parker. (2000). *Adventures in time and place*. New York: McGraw-Hill.

Bullard, S. (1996). *Teaching tolerance*. New York: Doubleday.

Dewey, J. (1916). *Democracy and education: An introduction to the philosophy of education*. New York: Macmillan.

Freire, P. (1985). *The politics of education*. New York: Bergin and Garvey.

Gibson, P. (1989). Gay male and lesbian youth suicide. In *Report of the secretary's task force on youth suicide. Vol. 3, Prevention and interventions in youth suicide*, ed. M. Feinleib. Rockville, Md.: National Institute of Mental Health.

Giroux, H., and P. McLaren. (1986). Teacher education and the politics of engagement: The case for democratic schooling. *Harvard Educational Review* 56: 213–38.

Goodman, J. (1992). *Elementary schooling for critical democracy*. Albany, N.Y.: State University of New York Press.

Herdt, G., and A. Boxer. (1993). *Children of horizons*. Boston: Beacon Press.

Hollins, E. R. (1996). Introduction. In *Transforming curriculum for a culturally diverse society*, ed. E. R. Hollins. Mahway, N.J.: Erlbaum.

Jarolimek, J., and W. Parker. (1993). *Social studies in elementary education*. 9th ed. New York: Macmillan.

Jenness, D. (1990). *Making sense of social studies*. New York: Macmillan.

Lipkin, A. (1999). *Understanding homosexuality: Staff, curriculum, and student development*. Boulder, Colo.: Westview.

Marinoble, R. (1997). Elementary school teachers: Homophobia reduction in a staff development context. In *Overcoming heterosexism and homophobia*, ed. J. Sears and W. Williams. New York: Columbia University Press.

Martin, D., and E. S. Hetrick. (1988). The stigmatization of the gay and lesbian adolescent. *Journal of Homosexuality* 16: 163–83.

Massachusetts Department of Education. (1995). *Massachusetts high school students and sexual orientation* (Massachusetts Youth Risk Behavior Survey). Boston: Massachusetts Department of Education.

National Council for the Social Studies. (1994). *Challenges of excellence: Standards for social studies education in the next century*. Washington D.C.: National Council for the Social Studies.

Patterson, C. (1992). Children of lesbian and gay parents. *Child Development* 63: 1025–42.

Remafedi, G., J. Farrow, and R. Deisher. (1991). Risk factors for attempted suicide in gay and lesbian youth. *Pediatrics* 87(6): 869–76.

Rofes, E. (1993). *"I thought people like that killed themselves": Lesbians, gay men and suicide.* San Francisco: Grey Fox Press.

Sears, J. (1991). *Growing up gay in the south.* New York: Harrington Park Press.

Sedgwick, E. (1990). *Epistemology of the closet.* Berkeley: University of California Press.

Wickens, E. (1994). *Anna Day and the O-ring.* Boston: Alyson Press.

Williams, W. (1997). Multicultural perspectives on reducing heterosexism: Looking for strategies that work. In *Overcoming heterosexism and homophobia,* ed. J. Sears and W. Williams. New York: Columbia University Press.

• *Part 4* •

FAMILY

The chapters in section 4 problematize the conventional view of a certain type of nuclear family as "natural," and in the process they explore a variety of family configurations that today's schoolchildren come from. These four chapters focus on exploring the diversity of family structure from the perspectives of sexual minority parents, both biological and adoptive, rather than from the more commonly investigated vantage point of sexual minority children. What hopes do gay and lesbian parents have for their children in elementary schools? How do gay and lesbian parents engage with elementary schools? How do they understand and negotiate classroom expectations? And how can we better communicate to educators and the community about the diversity of families that today's schools really serve?

The first chapter in this section, by Rita Kissen, looks at how the presence of children of gay and lesbian parents "challenges teachers and administrators to rethink traditional assumptions about family and community, to examine their commitment to honor the safety and integrity of all students, and, at the deepest level, to confront their own homophobia." Through interviews with gay and lesbian couples who are "growing a family," in which she asks these parents about "their fears, their dreams, and their hopes for their children's school experience," Rita wants to "break the silence around sexual diversity in schools." Despite what appear to be complexities around these issues, "normalizing lesbian and gay families can be very simple," especially once, as these parents point out, we realize "that the children of the future age belong to all of us."

Gigi Kaeser's photo-essay in the next chapter draws on photographs from the *Love Makes a Family* photo-text exhibit and interlaces them with a narrative account of some of the controversies faced by two communities as they tried to bring this exhibit into their schools. The exhibit, which features photographs of gay, lesbian, bisexual, and transgender-headed families and some text interviews describing each family, challenges commonly held and often fiercely protected notions of what "normal families" are. The controversies around showing this exhibit have forced communities "to think about the significance of representing this very common family type," which is already a reality in the lives of many children who occupy our classrooms.

In chapter 16 Pat Hulsebosch, Mari E. Koerner, and Daniel P. Ryan write about how supporting all students means "responding to gay and lesbian parents." But it's not as simple as knowing whether a student has a gay or lesbian parent. For "even when school personnel know their students' parents are gay or lesbian, they may worry about the implications, for the parents, for the children, as well as the school, of including lesbian and gay issues in the curriculum." The authors used interviews with educators whom lesbian mothers had identified as "responsive" to look for any shared qualities of gay and lesbian family-friendly educators. What they found instead "were a broad range of definitions of 'responsiveness,' undergirded by varying views about what it means to support and educate children."

Educator and adoptive mother Barbara Danish writes about her daughter's experiences with "mutual presence"—placing kids with lesbian and gay parents in the same elementary classroom—in chapter 17. When curricular inclusion, for example, is not enough, parents and educators must take other steps. In an attempt to help remedy the isolation felt by these children, "who are obliged to develop sophisticated strategies for understanding their place in the world," Barbara and other parents lobbied the principal at their children's school to allow for "mutual presence" when placing their children. This chapter details the challenges and resistance, as well as the sense of belonging, of inclusion, and of community, that accompanied this bold experiment.

Because, as Pat Hulsebosch et al. point out, "families are the first and most important teachers of children," we must interrogate the relationships that schools have with gay- and lesbian-headed families and think deeply about strategies that work for inclusion and community building in our elementary schools.

· 14 ·

CHILDREN OF THE FUTURE AGE:
LESBIAN AND GAY PARENTS TALK ABOUT SCHOOL

Rita M. Kissen

Children of the future Age
Reading this indignant page
Know that in a former time
Love! Sweet Love! was thought a crime.

—William Blake
"A Little Girl Lost," 1794

A dozen years ago children of lesbian and gay parents were all but invisible to their teachers and classmates. Most were sons and daughters
of heterosexual marriages whose mothers or fathers had come out as lesbian or gay. In families with gay fathers, custody almost always went to the
mother, perhaps with a stepfather to complete the heterosexual picture.
Lesbian mothers often lost custody, or were forced to teach their children
to keep silent about their family, lest they be exposed as "unfit." At the
same time, homophobic adoption laws made nonbiological parenting virtually impossible for gay men and for lesbians who did not have an opposite sex partner available to participate in conception.

The greater visibility of lesbian and gay people during the past decade,
along with more sophisticated insemination technologies and slightly less
repressive custody and adoption laws, has led to a virtual gay and lesbian
population explosion. These children bring a new identity to the diversity
equation. Their presence challenges teachers and administrators to rethink
traditional assumptions about family and community, to examine their
commitment to honor the safety and integrity of all students, and, at the
deepest level, to confront their own homophobia. But the heterosexist assumptions implicit in most early childhood teacher education programs,
and in society at large, leave most teachers ill equipped to meet this chal-

lenge, and even the best intentioned may feel uneasy about having a child with two moms or two dads in the classroom.

Although there is a growing body of literature on lesbian and gay parents and their children, much less has been written about the presence of these children in classrooms and schools. Early researchers tended to focus on comparisons between children in families headed by gay or lesbian parents and those in heterosexual households, reaching the virtually unanimous conclusion that children in gay families met every established criterion for "normal" emotional, cognitive, and psychosocial development, including gender identity and sexual orientation (Flaks et al. 1995; Gates 1991; Golombok, Spencer, and Rutter 1983; Patterson, 1986, 1993, 1994; Ricketts 1991; Steckel 1987; van-Nijnatten and van-Nijnatten 1995). By the late 1980s this pathologizing model was being replaced by studies of how gay and lesbian families were coping with the stresses of institutionalized and cultural homophobia (Crawford 1987; McCandish 1987; Rafkin 1990; Reimann 1998); how children conceived in heterosexual marriages before a parent came out differed from children conceived or adopted by self-identified lesbians or gay men (Benkov 1998; Crawford 1987; Rafkin 1990); and how the challenges faced by children in gay families resembled or differed from those faced by racial and ethnic minority children (Greene 1990; Morales 1990). More recently researchers have begun to consider the presence of children from lesbian and gay families in schools and classrooms. Research in this crucial arena has addressed the importance of teacher attitudes toward homosexuality (Carter 1994; Casper et al. 1996; Casper and Schultz 1996; Clay 1990; Gelnaw et al. 1998; Maney and Cain 1997; Patterson 1986; Rubin 1995; Wickens 1993). Others have sought to advise lesbian and gay parents negotiating the terrain of school and society (Benkov 1994; Burke 1993; Carter 1994; Gelnaw et al. 1998; Guggenheim, Lowe, and Curtis 1996; Hanscombe and Forster 1987; Martin 1993; Pollack and Vaughn 1987; Schulenburg 1985; Weston 1991). Certainly, the presence of increasing numbers of "gayby boom" children in America's schools has enormous implications for teachers, administrators, and teacher educators (Coontz 1998), and will require a rethinking of how we talk about families, sexuality, and multiculturalism.

As a teacher educator committed to a broad vision of diversity, and as the parent of a lesbian daughter about to start her own family, I decided that the best way to break the silence around sexual diversity in schools was to talk to lesbian and gay parents themselves about their fears, their dreams, and their hopes for their children's school experience. Accordingly, I interviewed two gay male couples and four lesbian couples, all parents of young children or planning to have children in the near future. I asked them about the process of motherhood and fatherhood, about their memories of elementary school, their experiences with their children's schooling so far, and their advice for teachers working with their children.

Five of the couples live in New England and one on the West Coast; all are in their thirties and forties, and all brought children into their families after the couple had already established a permanent commitment to one another. Although all the couples are white, several have adopted children of color and talked eloquently about the interwoven threads of race and sexual identity in their children's lives.

GROWING A FAMILY

Becoming a lesbian or gay parent is always a deeply conscious decision. Family expectations, societal pressure, and images in the media do not tell these men and women that parenthood is their destiny, nor are "accidents" or birth-control failure part of their biological equation. On the contrary, same-sex couples choosing parenthood were until very recently stepping into unknown territory, defining an identity where none had existed before. Yet when they discuss their reasons for wanting children, these six couples sound like many heterosexual moms and dads. Louis, who with his partner Martin has three adopted children, says: "I think that we decided to have children the same way that any straight person decides to have children when you're ten, fifteen, twenty, twenty-five—you're going along and you either assume you're going to have children or you assume you're going to think about it, or you assume you're not."

Once they decide to become parents, lesbians and gay men face a unique set of logistical questions. Though some gay men form coparenting arrangements with lesbian friends, the two gay male couples I interviewed wanted to build their own families, and decided, in Louis's words, to "grow [a] family though adoption." Three of the lesbian couples chose biological motherhood through donor insemination, but the fourth, Rose and Ruth, chose adoption. For them, and for Louis and Martin, adoption meant building an interracial family. Rose and Ruth now have two daughters, eleven-year-old Rachel, who is of European American/African American heritage, and seven-year-old Maria, who is African American/Mexican American. Louis and Martin are the parents of five-year-old Annie and three-year-old Lisa, both African American, and sixteen-month-old Ronnie, a Vietnamese child who came into their family through international adoption.

Like all good parents, lesbian and gay parents worry about their children's welfare. For these six couples, the worries include societal attitudes toward homosexuality, a threat they know they cannot control. Despite their understanding that heterosexism is not their fault, they often feel responsible for the abuse their children might suffer. "Our kids didn't choose to have lesbian parents," Denise says. "I would hate to see something . . . horrible happen to them for something that had nothing to do with them directly."

Yet even as they struggle against heterosexual privilege, lesbian and gay couples find that the experience of parenthood creates a bond with heterosexual parents even stronger than their links to childless gay and lesbian friends. Lenore recalls an annual lesbian Valentine's Day dance that she and Helene attended when their son Eric was about a year old. "I felt very disconnected, and I said to Helene, I would feel much more at home in a group of parents of young kids. . . . You want to talk about sleep deprivation, and language acquisition, and potty training, and you just want somebody who's going through that same thing."

Lesbian and gay parents with adopted children feel an additional bond with other adoptive parents, whether straight or gay. Rose and Ruth are part of two networks, one made up of lesbian mothers with multiracial children, and the other, larger group, where "there are lots of other multiracial families, there are lots of other adoptive families."

Lenore, who is Eric's legal parent but not his biological mother, says she feels a "very immediate bond" with adoptive parents. "I connect with them immediately. . . . In some sense I am an adoptive parent, but also they know what it's like to have different families. They know what it's like . . . not to be biologically connected to the child."

Like the heterosexual adoptive parents with whom she feels a bond, Lenore's identity as a mother challenges the essentialist definition of the nuclear family as a unit consisting of one woman, one man, and their biological children. Traditionally, society has taught adopted children to think in terms of their "real" (that is, biological) parents and their adoptive (presumably not real) parents. The same assumption lies behind the question often asked of children with two moms or two dads: "Who's the real one?" Carried to its logical extreme, the assumption that every child must have one mother and one father suggests that the "real" father of a child of lesbian parents is the sperm donor, no matter how anonymous or removed from the process of conception he may be. Yet parents and children in gay families and adoptive families have always known that "real" parenthood is not an abstract identity but a relationship based on the commitment to love and care for a child over time.

Children of lesbian and gay parents live in a legal limbo arising from this patriarchal view of parenthood. For decades lesbians have helped raise the children of their partner's previous heterosexual unions, and in doing so have played the role of stepparent. But Lenore is not a stepparent: She is Eric's mother. And unlike the adoptive heterosexual parents with whom she feels a bond, her legal right to claim Eric as her son depends on where she lives and what a particular court in a particular county might decide. To date, no state statutes anywhere in the United States specifically permit second-parent adoption. Appellate and State Supreme Court rulings in five states and the District of Columbia support these adoptions, while rulings in three other states have specifically denied them, and two states, Florida and New Hampshire, bar lesbian and gay adoptions altogether. Everywhere else gay families are at the whim of county ordinances and local precedents.

The legal invisibility of gay and lesbian families is a matter for legislative reform, not the schools. Yet as Lenore points out, "A teacher can't change the laws . . . but the law . . . is a real signal that these are not equal families, these are not legitimate families, many of these moms are not real moms, many of these dads are not real dads. . . . It delegitimizes them."

And as Roberta reminds us, the assumption that lesbian and gay parents are not "real" moms and dads has difficult consequences for their children. "There are kids at school who can't get it in their head that he has two moms, and so they've tagged me Daddy—'Oh, look, it's your Daddy,' and he's like, 'That's not daddy, that's Mommy Roberta.' And he actually went through a period that he called me Daddy because there must be a Daddy, because that's what's in all the books."

TALKING ABOUT SCHOOL

Advocacy by groups like GLSEN (The Gay, Lesbian and Straight Education Network) and PFLAG (Parents, Families and Friends of Lesbians and Gays) have made lesbian and gay students more visible in schools and society, and have brought to public attention the suffering inflicted on many of these youth, from shame and invisibility to harassment and physical violence. Though some of the parents I spoke with recall friendly teachers, supportive classrooms, and strong friendships, many of these gay men and lesbians share painful memories of school. Roberta, who was "teased a lot, beaten up a lot," wonders whether her son will suffer as she did: "Would people protect him, will the teachers be there like they weren't there for us?"

Gay men, for whom same-sex attraction was the ultimate taboo, carry even harsher memories. Martin wants school for his children to be different from what it was for him: "As a little gay boy school meant taunting most of the time that I was there. . . . They know, even if you don't know yet, they know."

Lesbian and gay parents of adopted children of color have their own concerns about the double oppression their children face. All say they worry more about racism than about prejudice against lesbian and gay families. Rose explains: "You know, because her having lesbian mothers, it's not like we walk around with these signs, and if I drop her off people see, here's a black child with a white mom. The fact that I'm a lesbian isn't necessarily known. So to me the race thing is always visible."

Martin agrees, drawing a distinction between legal discrimination and cultural prejudice. "Maybe it's illegal to discriminate against blacks [and] it's legal to discriminate against gays, but blacks are terribly discriminated against, prejudice is awful in this country. And so they're going to get called niggers. That will happen to them for sure."

As white parents of children of color, these two couples know that their children bear an additional burden. Unlike their counterparts in Asian or African American families, these boys and girls do not return to a home that mirrors their ethnic identity. In this they are like gay youth in heterosexual families, who may feel "different" at home as well as in the outside world. And just as supportive heterosexual parents understand the role that lesbian and gay youth groups can play in affirming their children's identity, so white lesbian and gay parents seek out support groups wherein their multiracial children can find others who look like them. This quest to affirm their children's racial and ethnic identity provides an additional bond with white heterosexual parents in multiracial families.

When lesbian and gay parents talk about school, one of the first issues to arise is the choice between private and public school. Heterosexual parents for whom private school is an option may base their decisions on the quality of the curriculum, or the smaller classes that private school can provide. But for lesbian and gay parents, regardless of income, the decision is all about safety. Louis says ruefully: "If you know that your children are safe from bigotry for this year, or it seems that way, or there's a better chance that they're safe, it's probably worth seven thousand bucks to keep them safe and innocent as long as you can."

Yet Rose and Ruth, who live in Massachusetts, have not regretted their decision to send Rachel and Maria to public school. Rose says that many of their lesbian and gay friends "made assumptions that these environments would be way more hostile than they are turning out to be. . . . I think some has to do with how much as adults we've had to deal with coming-out issues in non-gay/lesbian environments."

TALKING TO TEACHERS

Whether their children attend public or private school, gay and lesbian parents have plenty of advice for those seeking to make schools better for gay families. For Laurence the key is the administration: "If there's good people at the top that say, 'These are our policies and we will tolerate nothing but this,' I think it works its way down."

Like other parents, especially those in multiracial families, Rose considers gay families part of the "big picture" of diversity and wants to see sexual diversity addressed that way in staff development: "The teachers all have to undergo antiracism training, [but] they don't all have to undergo, at least at this level, training around homophobia. So I'd like to see that folded in more."

Within the curriculum parents want to see their children's lives validated and valued. Michelle encourages the inclusion of "all kinds of families, including our child," in classroom discussions, so that "our kid doesn't start feeling like there's something wrong with them because we're all celebrating father's day and I don't have a father. . . . So the first thing that comes to my mind is that our child feel that their family is one of many normal families."

The theme of normality emerges often in these discussions. Lenore says, "Our message to him is always that we're normal, that we're a family like every other family, and we can say that all we want, but if it doesn't get represented, he really will feel that somehow the situation is not just different but is inferior."

Normalizing the discussion of alternative families may become difficult for teachers when they encounter children conceived through donor insemination. Michelle and Denise want their child to be able to discuss these issues with teachers and classmates: "Teachers who could be generally comfortable with gay and lesbian people may get kind of weird about talking about this, you know, the insemination thing. . . . And if they feel like things are going past the scope of what they need to address, that's okay, but they need to limit the conversation in a way that feels respectful and not weird."

Denise's words are an interesting reminder of the ways that talking about nonheterosexual identities get labeled as talking about sex. Because our society assumes heterosexuality, discussing one's husband or wife does not carry a sexual connotation; yet lesbians and gay men who mention their partners (or worse, are openly affectionate with them) are often accused of "flaunting it," as if their relationships were about nothing but sex. In the same way, normative heterosexuality means that talking about families in elementary-school classrooms does not convey a sexual connotation as long as those families are heterosexual. Though teachers may avoid answering young children's questions about how they were made, most of these children live in a world where heterosexual conception is taken for granted and the "facts of life," however emotionally charged, are assumed to apply to them. On the other hand, children of lesbian couples in a society where everyone seems to have a dad may need to know very early in life how they were made, and their presence in the classroom may introduce the subject of "sex" long before a teacher thinks it is appropriate.

Despite these complexities, normalizing lesbian and gay families can be very simple. Laurence draws on his experience as an adult advisor to a support group for lesbian and gay teens to formulate some advice for teachers. "Make yourself visible, and then make yourself available on a one-to-one basis and you will be found. . . . It doesn't take much, it takes, 'I have a gay brother and he's coming for Thanksgiving.'"

Gay parents also encourage teachers and administrators to ask questions if they are unsure how to respond to the presence of a child from a gay family. They agree with Denise: "A lot of times straight people who might be a little well meaning but aren't around gay people, they're just afraid to ask some basic questions. I would want our teachers to feel that they could call us up and ask us questions that sounded stupid to them, so that they could start feeling more comfortable with us and our family."

Finally, lesbian and gay parents urge teachers to work at becoming comfortable with diversity in their own lives. Beth explains, "We bring our personal life to everybody, and I would encourage [teachers] to try and be as comfortable with diversity personally as they can be and then it doesn't become diversity, it becomes interest, or interesting, you know, it becomes the fabric of life."

Lesbian mothers and gay fathers, through their willingness to defy stereotypes and limitations, have much to teach us about courage, about love, and about families. Like all the students in our classrooms, their children belong first to the parents who love and nurture them. But as the adults to whom these children are entrusted every single day, teachers and teacher educators cannot turn away from our responsibility to them and their parents. Ultimately, gay and lesbian families teach us that the children of the future age belong to all of us.

REFERENCES

Benkov, L. (1994). *Reinventing the family: Lesbian and gay parents.* New York: Crown.
———. (1998). Yes, I am a swan: Reflections on families headed by lesbians and gay men. In *Mothering against the odds: Diverse voices of contemporary mothers,* ed. C. Garcia Coll, J. L. Surrey, and K. Weingarten. New York: Guilford Press.
Burke, P. (1993). *Family values: Two moms and their son.* New York: Random House.
Carter, M. (1994). Supporting the growing identity and self-esteem of children in gay and lesbian families. Paper presented at the meeting of the National Association for the Education of Young Children, Anaheim, California.
Casper, V., H. K. Cuffaro, S. Schultz, J. G. Silin, and E. Wickens. (1996). Toward a most thorough understanding of the world: Sexual orientation and early childhood education. *Harvard Educational Review* 96(2): 271–93.
Casper, V., and S. Schultz. (1996). Lesbian and gay parents encounter educators: Initiating conversations. In *The lives of lesbians, gays, and bisexuals,* ed. R. C. Savin-Williams and K. M. Cohen. New York: Harcourt Brace.
Clay, J. W. (1990). Working with lesbian and gay parents and their children. *Young Children* 45(3): 31–35.
Coontz, S. (1998). *The way we really are: Coming to terms with America's changing families.* New York: Basic Books.
Crawford, S. (1987). Lesbian families: Psychosocial stress and the family-building process. In *Lesbian psychologies.* Urbana, Ill.: University of Illinois Press.
Flaks, D. K., I. Ficher, F. Masterpasqua, and G. Joseph. (1995). Lesbians choosing motherhood: A comparative study of lesbian and heterosexual parents and their children. *Developmental Psychology* 31: 105–14.
Gates, S. (1991). Children from lesbian-mother families: A review of the literature and implications for therapists and counselors. Unpublished manuscript, College of Education, University of Southern Maine, Gorham, Maine.
Gelnaw, A., M. Grickley, D. Ryan, and H. Marsh. (1998). *Opening doors: Lesbian and gay parents and schools.* San Diego: Family Pride Coalition.
Golombok, S., A. Spencer, and M. Rutter. (1983). Children in lesbian and single-parent households: Psychosexual and psychiatric appraisal. *Journal of Child Psychology and Psychiatry* 24: 551–72.

Greene, B. (1990). Sturdy bridges: The role of African-American mothers in the socialization of African-American children. *Women and Therapy* 10(1/2): 205–25.

Guggenheim, M., A. D. Lowe, and D. Curtis. (1996). *The rights of families: The authoritative ACLU guide to the rights of family members today.* Carbondale, Ill.: Southern Illinois University Press.

Hanscombe, G. E., and J. Forster. (1987). *Rocking the cradle: Lesbian mothers, a challenge in family living.* Boston: Alyson.

Maney, D. W., and R. E. Cain. (1997). Preservice elementary teachers' attitudes toward gay and lesbian parenting. *Journal of School Health* 67(6): 236–42.

Martin, A. (1993). The lesbian and gay parenting handbook: Creating and raising our families. New York: HarperCollins.

McCandish, B. M. (1987). Against all odds: Lesbian mother family dynamics. In *Gay and lesbian parents,* ed. F. W. Bozett. New York: Praeger.

Morales, E. S. (1990). Ethnic minority families and minority gays and lesbians. *Marriage and Family Review* 14(3/4): 217–39.

Patterson, C. J. (1986). Contributions of lesbian and gay parents and their children to the prevention of heterosexism. In *Relationships and development,* ed. W. W. Hartup and Z. Rubin. Hillsdale, N.J.: Erlbaum.

———. (1993). *Lesbian and gay parenting: A resource for psychologists.* A joint publication of the American Psychological Association's Committee on Women in Psychology, Committee on Lesbian and Gay Concerns, and Committee on Children, Youth and Families.

———. (1994). Children of the lesbian baby boom: Behavioral adjustment, self-concepts, and sex-role identity. In *Contemporary perspectives of gay and lesbian psychology: Theory, research and applications,* ed. B. Greene and G. Herek. Beverly Hills: Sage.

Pollack, S., and J. Vaughn, ed. (1987). *Politics of the heart: A lesbian parenting anthology.* Ithaca, N.Y.: Firebrand.

Rafkin, L., ed. (1990). *Different mothers: Sons and daughters of lesbians talk about their lives.* Pittsburgh: Cleis Press.

Reimann, R. (1998). All in the family: Lesbian mothers' involvement with friends and kin. Paper presented at the meeting of the International Sociological Association, Montreal.

Ricketts, W. (1991). *Lesbians and gay men as fosterparents.* Portland: Muskie Institute of Public Affairs, University of Southern Maine.

Rubin, S. (1995). Children who grow up with gay or lesbian parents: How are today's schools meeting this "invisible" group's needs? Master's thesis, University of Wisconsin, Madison.

Schulenburg, J. (1985). *Gay parenting: A complete guide for gay men and lesbians with children.* New York: Anchor/Doubleday.

Steckel, A. (1987). Psychosocial development of children of lesbian mothers. In *Gay and lesbian parents*, ed. F. W. Bozett. New York: Praeger.

van-Nijnatten, C. H., and C. J. van-Nijnatten. (1995). Sexual orientation of parents and Dutch family law. *Medicine and Law* 14(5–6): 359–68.

Weston, K. (1991). *Families we choose: Lesbians, gays, kinship*. New York: Columbia University Press.

Wickens, E. (1993). Penny's question: "I will have a child in my class with two moms—what do you know about this?" *Young Children* 48(3): 25–28.

· 15 ·

LOVE MAKES A FAMILY:
CONTROVERSY IN TWO MASSACHUSETTS TOWNS

Gigi Kaeser

Photographs by Gigi Kaeser

In the summer and fall of 1992, the writer Peggy Gillespie and I interviewed and photographed people in our immediate area of western Massachusetts who had come together in multiracial families through adoption or marriage. The subject was germane, and the resulting exhibit drew favorable comment when it appeared in local schools. We wanted to follow up with something equally interesting. In the course of our work on *Of Many Colors*, we had included a number of families that were both multiracial and headed by gay or lesbian parents. With little more incentive than a desire to continue what seemed to be important work, we started on *Love Makes a Family*. We were relatively innocent and unaware of the politics of gay and lesbian struggles, and we knew nothing of the efforts among schoolteachers, administrators, and parents at bringing up the subject in schools to counter homophobia among schoolchildren.

In the spring of 1994, funded by a small grant, we set about finding, photographing, and interviewing local families for the lesbian–gay project. It was easy to do. In our area there was a ready congregation of lesbian and gay people who were proud of the families they had created and who wanted to tell their stories.

At the same time, our other exhibit was showing in local schools. When we asked these schools' principals if they might be interested in hosting our new project, all of them, with enthusiasm, agreed. The parents of the elementary-school children questioned the rightness of their schools' putting up queer families as objects of study. Invariably, these parents had to be educated first—a process that was sometimes painful and chaotic, but which proved to be the most important step in bringing *Love*

Makes a Family into schools. If parents were not behind this kind of curriculum, they would undermine it. Schoolchildren listen to their teachers, but their families are still more influential.

Al Ferreira, a gay teacher at Cambridge Rindge and Latin who had started Project 10 East (a very effective program for gay high school kids), suggested that we open our exhibit at the Peabody Elementary School in Cambridge. The school's principal, Ellen Varella, was an experienced administrator. She was committed to bringing gay and lesbian awareness into the school, and Ferreira had already trained her teachers.

In preparation for the June 1995 exhibit, local gay and lesbian parents and organizations set events in motion to make the exhibit a success. The parents of the Peabody School children received mailings from the administration explaining the exhibit. The parents' calls and complaints to Ms. Varella were brought before a meeting of the school community, where there was a clash between the parents belonging to the Lavender Alliance and opposition parents. Ellen Varella was unsettled by the anger of the parents who attended the meeting, but she believed that it was important to bring the show to her school. She compromised and showed the exhibit to the third- through eighth-grade children. In addition, any child could be excused from seeing the exhibit, if her parents so desired.

On the night of the show's opening, and for several days afterward, two filmmakers from California came to film the presentation. Their presence resulted in the controversy's being featured in a segment of *It's Elementary*, a film by Debra Chasnoff and Helen Cohen (1996). The cameras, cables, and microphones made the event seem important to everyone there. At the end of the evening, Ellen Varella delivered a heartening speech about the importance of respecting all families in the school community. The Cambridge showing of the exhibit, which was guarded by a police officer, ran smoothly for two weeks.

Love Makes a Family found its way into elementary schools in Massachusetts partly because the governor had commissioned a report on gay and lesbian youth. Gay and lesbian teenagers told their stories of harassment in schools to the state legislators. They spoke about how dangerous the schools were for queer kids, explaining how their suffering led to drug abuse, homelessness, and suicide. As a result of the hearings that led to the report, a new law was passed—the Massachusetts Gay and Lesbian Student Rights Law—which stated specifically that no student shall be discriminated against because of race, color, sex, national origin, or sexual orientation. In the face of shocking statistics of suicide among gay and lesbian teenagers, and with the passage of this law, school administrators found themselves encouraged to take a forward, active position toward educating all kids in school about gay and lesbian people.

The Fleishman/Krieger/Tabachnick/Mayer Family

"When we decided to bring a child into a lesbian and gay family, we made a choice. As Jews, interracial couples, or any other oppressed group, we could have said 'This is going to be too hard to deal with.' But, there wouldn't be any Jews left in the world if Jews decided that it was just too hard. That's not our spirit. It's going to be tough to deal with homophobia. And it's a very rich tradition that our son, Ezra is coming into. So, yes, it's going to be hard, and yes, he's going to be lucky. Both are true."

—Jane Fleishman

The Bellavance-Grace Family

"I am not trying to say that we are 'normal,' as in, 'just like straight people.' I mean we are normal, lesbian parents. We have a lot to offer our son, our foster children, their schools and our community. When are people ever going to get over the belief that difference is negative?"

—Beth Bellavance-Grace

The Watson/Hutchins Family

"I think it's important that people know that being a gay parent is no different than being a parent in a traditional family. We have the same feeling of love for our children, the same feeling of sadness when our children have problems, and the same feeling of pride when our children do well."

—Ken Watson

The Stokes/Dupree Family

"Don't be ashamed of who your parents are."
—Nabowire Stokes

The Cooper Family

"It's very important for people to understand that love makes a family. Without love, there's no family. Gay families do the same thing straight families do, which is to love. Gay parents have the same power of love as anyone else."

—Rob Cooper

Students interacting with the exhibit at the Hawthorne School in Madison, Wisconsin

The argument most frequently made in favor of showing the exhibit is that it will validate the families of gay and lesbian parents, but it is clear to me that these are not the most vulnerable viewers. Children who are growing up in lesbian and gay households usually already have a sense of family validation and worthiness, provided by the lesbian and gay community around them. The children with straight parents who will grow up to become gay or lesbian adults have no positive images of gay people in their schools. Their parents usually accept and breathe the homophobic atmosphere that stifles gay teenagers. These kids need the support of out gay adults, rarely found in schools, and examples of dignified lesbian and gay people living ordinary, happy lives, a reality that never surfaces in the schools. A third group are the kids who will grow up to be straight, who need to be educated to respect gay people. These kids are crucial in the effort to fight teen suicide, because they will be the best friends of the gay kids. When the gay teenagers tell their straight friends that they think they might be gay, it is very important that the friends be able to respond in a respectful way. Rejection at this moment by a close friend often leads to a suicide attempt by the gay or lesbian teenager.

The following spring, in Amherst, Massachusetts, the home base of the exhibit's creators, the school superintendent denied the need to have the exhibit in the elementary schools. A group of gay and lesbian parents and kids from the high school's Gay Straight Alliance came to his office to protest. They made it clear to him that they had suffered from homophobic treatment in school, and that they wanted *Love Makes a Family* to be shown throughout the school system. The superintendent decided that individual principals could choose whether or not to show the exhibit in their schools. This decision initiated a seven-month debate in this small academic town, as each school community took up the matter. Nick Grabbe, editor of the *Amherst Bulletin*, said that in the entire history of the paper there had never been so many letters to the editor on one subject.

One type of letter came from a group of people, some of them gay, who favored showing the exhibit because it represented families never before validated formally as families. Other writers held a not-so-sure middle ground; they feared that the content of the show was sexual, but they were reassured once they previewed it and heard advocates from the local lesbian and gay community speak about their families. Some of the people in this group also believed that the subject did not belong in schools or that homosexuality was not something they wanted their children to know about at all. There was also a very vocal and organized group who were profoundly opposed to the notion of gay and lesbian people being represented as living in "normal families."

In March 1996, as the debate in town continued, a local attorney, Gregory Hession, who claimed to represent ten unidentified local families, wrote a public letter to the superintendent. "The parents wish me to be quite clear about their willingness to oppose you politically, legally, and at the voting booth. This will not go away quietly, and your very future with Amherst schools may be tied in with your decision on this matter," he said. He wrote that "artificial insemination, transient relationships, same-sex marriages, and tangled family structures are not issues children should have to confront in kindergarten." And citing laws against sodomy, he wrote, "This exhibit exalts vice as virtue, encourages infidelity, not chastity, and in the text literally mocks the moral principles that this law requires instructors to encourage in school children" (*Amherst Bulletin*, March 15, 1996).

Hession also filed suit on behalf of five of these Amherst families to stop the exhibit from being shown. On May 15 the request for an injunction to stop the showing of *Love Makes a Family* in Amherst schools was denied by U.S. District judge Frank H. Freedman. The attorney for the schools, Alan Seewald, argued that "There is nothing sexual about this exhibit, it simply shows families, many of whom live in the immediate area, and discusses their family life." When Freedman asked what the educational goal of the exhibit was, Seewald replied: "It is part of a larger effort to teach respect for differences." Hession said that his clients find the exhibit offensive because it "violates their deeply held religious and moral beliefs." The judge said that as long as both sides have the freedom to express themselves—one to see the exhibit and the other to avoid it in protest—he could see no reason to halt its showing (*Daily Hampshire Gazette,* May 16, 1996).

The controversy forced the townspeople to think about the significance of representing this very common family type, which was already exemplified by students in most classrooms. Many of the subjects in the exhibit were local people. A local first-grade teacher came out to his school community through his inclusion in the exhibit, which added personal drama to the already piquant panorama. The teachers all got training in the use of the exhibit by the State Department of Education's Safe Schools Coordinator. In the end, all four of Amherst's elementary-school communities chose to show the exhibit.

The book, *Love Makes a Family: Lesbian, Gay, Bisexual and Transgender People and Their Families* (Kaeser and Gillespie 1999), was taken in part from the photo-text exhibit depicting these sorts of families in photographs and interviews. The exhibit has been touring the country since 1995, appearing most often in colleges but also in churches, libraries, and schools. Peggy and I have always believed that the show would have the greatest impact in elementary schools, toward which we directed our first efforts. The attention that the show generated was often hostile, but led to the education of many more people than we could have foreseen. In Amherst the ambivalent position taken by administrators, combined with the hostile imprecations of antigay people, worked to draw attention to the ordinary and admirable lives of gay and lesbian people and their family members, thus moving the undecided citizens to support the showing of *Love Makes a Family*. In this drama the rabid and self-appointed moral police are the unknowing foot soldiers in the battle to bring equality to gay, lesbian, bisexual, and transgender people.

To bring *Love Makes a Family* to your site, contact Family Diversity Projects, P.O. Box 1209, Amherst, MA 01002-1209. E-mail: *famphoto@aol.com*.

References

Chasnoff, D., director/producer, and H. Cohen, producer. (1996). *It's elementary: Talking about gay issues in school.* San Francisco: Women's Educational Media. Film.

Kaeser, G., and P. Gillespie. (1999). *Love makes a family: Lesbian, gay, bisexual and transgender people and their families.* Amherst: University of Massachusetts Press.

· 16 ·

SUPPORTING STUDENTS/RESPONDING
TO GAY AND LESBIAN PARENTS

Pat Hulsebosch, Mari E. Koerner, and Daniel P. Ryan

INTRODUCTION

Elementary teachers have become increasingly aware of the need to respond to the diversity of their students. However, teachers, especially
those in elementary schools, do not necessarily consider sexual orientation
as part of that diversity. Although there are currently an estimated 6 to 14
million children who have gay or lesbian parents (Harvard Law Review
1990), even teachers who are passionately committed to issues of inclusion
and social justice in elementary classrooms are uncertain when encounter-
ing lesbian- or gay-headed families in their classrooms.

There are many reasons for this uncertainty: heterosexism, religious
beliefs, and lack of knowledge, as well as the social stigma, legal restrictions,
and threat of physical danger associated with gay and lesbian identities. Oftentimes lesbian and gay parents and their children must decide whether
or not they will describe themselves as such. Even when school personnel
know their student's parents are gay or lesbian, they may worry about the
implications for the parents, for the children, and even for the school, of
including lesbian and gay issues in the curriculum. Yet there are classrooms
in which teachers and parents find ways to respond to all families, as well
as to incorporate relevant issues into their curriculum (U.S. Department of
Education 1994).

A few years ago we attempted to understand ways in which schools
might become places for all children to feel safe to learn and grow. Our
interests became more focused as each of us realized, perhaps because of
our personal life experiences as parents, that families are the first and most
important teachers of children, and that good teachers learn ways to ally
themselves with the people who love and care about their students the

most. In addition, our commitment to inclusion and diversity led us to look at how students and their families who may be left out are brought into the parent/school relationship. Particularly important to us is the visibility of gay and lesbian families, and what this means in the culture of the school. This research "stems from and [is] a part of our own lives" (Reinharz 1992, 258).

All three of us are scholars and parents (heterosexual, gay, and lesbian) who have done previous inquiry work related to gay/lesbian parents, teachers, and students in varying relationships (Hulsebosch and Koerner 1997, Koerner and Hulsebosch 1996, Ryan 1998). We believed we might learn from teachers who had been recommended by gay or lesbian parents as having been responsive to their desire to become visible parts of their child's school life. This chapter looks at ways in which families who identify as lesbians, and the teachers of their children, negotiate the public space of elementary schools in order to address the needs of lesbian-headed families in schools.[1]

CONSIDERATIONS

When educators look at the lesbian women or gay men who bring children to the school doorstep, what they are likely to see first is parents. This is true not only because of the invisibility of sexual orientation, but also because, for most teachers, their relationships with parents are complex and often provocative (Lightfoot 1975). Teacher-parent interactions carry with them expectations, perceptions, and assumptions influenced by history, power, and context. Educators' perceptions of the value of social and cultural resources that students bring from home are a major influence on their response to the children and their parents (Lareau 1989). Teachers sometimes see parents as potential allies and support systems for learning. But just as often educators view families and the "curriculum of the home" as problematic for learning (Hulsebosch 1991). Thus, while politicians, researchers, and community activists call for greater parent-teacher partnership (Epstein 1995), parent involvement in schools is more often fraught with doubt, distrust, and frustration (Hulsebosch 1992).

Whereas parents are a provocative topic for some teachers, gay and lesbian issues in elementary schools remain controversial for most. *Faggot* continues to be a common but unreproved slur, and teachers fear that discussing lesbian and gay issues in the classroom means talking about sex (a fear that is challenged in *It's Elementary*'s portrayal of teaching gay issues [Chasnoff and Cohen 1996]).

On the other hand, teachers are also more aware of the need to provide a curriculum that is both a window into other peoples' experience and a mirror of the students' own lives (Style and McIntosh 1988). However, a looming challenge for teachers who seldom live in the same neighborhoods as their students is to find ways to learn about their students' lives and the important people in them. One way of doing this is to engage and talk to the adults who are most likely to be able to provide insights into their child's learning: parents and caregivers (Delpit 1995, Moll 1992). We used the word *responsive* to connote this kind of engagement between lesbian parents and teachers.

TALKING TO EDUCATORS

In this study we used open-ended interviews with educators who had been "responsive" to lesbian mothers to understand what this meant in different contexts. We interviewed six elementary-school educators (five teachers and one principal) in kindergarten through fourth grade who had either been recommended by lesbian parents as having been responsive to them, or were teachers who by reputation were committed to inclusion and respect for diversity. These six educators worked in public and private schools in both urban and suburban settings in the Chicago area. Two identified as African American, four as white. Arlene, Julia, and their principal, Roger, all work in the same school, which they describe as having a highly diverse student population.[2] Tasha and Kara also both teach at the same school and in the same classroom, while Charles teaches at a Chicago public school.

What does it mean for educators to be responsive to children with gay or lesbian parents? As we planned this research, we envisioned a variety of practices ranging from teachers changing the language they used to describe families, to incorporating gay- and lesbian-friendly books, such as *Asha's Mums* (Elwin and Paulse 1990) into the curriculum, to critical pedagogy that encouraged children to analyze media for heterosexism. In our research we left *responsiveness* to the parents to define. We asked, "Had they felt responded to? What was it the teacher said or did that supported this?" It was often a difficult question for parents to answer. One couple, for instance (ultimately not interviewed), disagreed with each other. Myra said teachers had been responsive, while Evelyn said, "They could be doing a lot better." When asked, their intermediate-grade daughter, Yolanda, told them the teachers had "never made a big deal of it." Like this child, the lesbian parents we talked to were often appreciative when teachers "were nice to them" and "didn't treat them any different from other parents."

When we looked at those teachers who were deemed responsive, we were surprised at how seemingly little it took for these mothers to feel responded to. We wondered how much of this might be due to fears of exposing themselves in the public space of schools. We're reminded that others have described the vulnerability many parents feel when entering schools, uncomfortable with their ambiguous role, and aware that they are engaging in a relationship that can have a lingering effect on their child (Lightfoot 1975). Although sexual orientation is "only one of many identity issues negotiated in the school context" (Silin 1995, 163), it is one that, in this age of civil rights and gay pride—and a resurgence of family values—might give gay parents pause for thought in coming out and coming into their local school.

CHILDREN FIRST

When we asked the teachers why they thought they had been named responsive to a particular child who had lesbian parents, most were surprised at having been recommended. One said she was "floored" because she "treat[s] everyone the same," while another said "I made them feel comfortable by just not making a big issue out of it." When we asked more questions about what enabled them to interact comfortably with parents, all said it was because they believed effective interaction was necessary *for the student*. Teachers talked repeatedly about making the child feel comfortable and said supporting the child was a goal they had, and something they looked for signs of, when working with parents. Charles, for example, who teaches first grade, observes: "If that is your ultimate goal as an educator to help kids, then you need to find a way to bridge the gap between the parents and the teacher with communication, and whether that communication means being open to parents or people who are maybe different than you are, that is what it is all about."

According to the educators, their professional commitment to relationships with parents in the interest of the child superseded any personal responses to family identities. However, as we looked a little further and talked a little more, we began to see variations among these educators in the meaning they gave to supporting a child.

Kara, a kindergarten teacher, says:

> Because if there's a family . . . whatever their heritage is, or [whatever] their family's like . . . if they are perceived as different by the community, I can use them to help educate the people in my room. But if they

don't want to be used that way, I have to respect that. Because that's when my agenda stops. But if they want to help, then let's do it. . . . I'm committed to it because I've seen the difference in my teaching from when I don't teach about diversity, or anything much outside of the classroom, and when I bring it all in. I get to a much deeper level of understanding. It creates a much bigger comfort zone. Children will learn a great deal more in the classroom. . . . And then everybody settles down.

Kara talks about comfort and support for the individual child, as well as the education of the entire class. Like Kara, Tasha believes visible differences in the classroom are a resource for curriculum—as windows into others' worlds, or as a way of mirroring a child's life: "I always commented on how fortunate our class was because we were the first class, that we knew of, anyway, that had a gay or lesbian family. Anytime something is different or something is new, I always count it a plus to be able to have it first to deal with. Because it is another opportunity to prepare children for the world and for life."

Arlene, a fourth-grade teacher, presents a different view of support when she describes her focus on "teaching the child" by, as much as possible, personally and professionally disregarding family characteristics: "That's how these people are. It's none of my business. Now, maybe that's something I don't personally believe [is] right. But, you know, I don't believe that Judaism is right either. But am I not going to teach the child, or hold it against the parent? You're just teaching the child. Just because I'm teaching Carl doesn't mean I am condoning what his parents do."

For Julia, as well as for Arlene, who teaches at the same school with a population they describe as extremely diverse, supporting Carl, the son of lesbian moms, does not usually mean modifying classroom practice. "So I guess what I am trying to say is that while I didn't make it any sort of an issue, or we didn't talk about different family styles at home or anything in here, I think [Carl] felt comfortable to talk about it should he have needed to. It's just that it really didn't come up."

Similarly, Julia notes:

You know, if I had [included family diversity in the curriculum], it might have brought more attention to it. And I don't know if that would have been good to make [Carl] feel comfortable. I don't know that I did it to hide anything, it was just something that just didn't come up. . . . Maybe if he had brought up wanting two [Mother's Day cards], I would have done something, but he didn't. . . . and as long as he was comfortable with what we did, then I had no problem.

For Julia and Arlene difference has the potential for danger. Thus, surfacing difference is seen as something to avoid because, they believe, it has the potential to harm the child who differs from the norm. Arlene asserts:

> I purposely did not do anything connected to Mother's Day especially because I had [a student], who oddly enough was Carl's best friend, whose mother had passed away a few years ago, and it's been really, really hard on this girl. She lives with Grandma. So I didn't think it was appropriate to do a Mother's Day kind of a thing in class. Obviously the kids probably mentioned it, but especially in fourth grade they don't make cards or do some kind of Mother's Day gift, so I just kind of steered clear of it all the way around.

Julia, who taught Carl in first and third grades, says he mentioned his two moms periodically throughout the year, while Arlene, who was Carl's fourth-grade teacher, says:

> It was never "my moms." I think it was pretty much common knowledge among the kids, but, no, he never did mention it. And I was kind of conscious of that—like, for instance, when I was addressing the awards invitation. I made sure to do it when the kids were all working on a project. . . . I didn't want to single him out and ask him, "What's your other mom's name?" Even though, like I said, I don't think anyone in here would have even cared, but I knew it was a sensitive subject with him.

As we read and discussed this interview, we wondered: How did Arlene know Carl's two mothers were a sensitive subject with him? And why the change in Carl from first to fourth grade, from a child who freely talks of "my moms" to one for whom it has become a "sensitive subject." And we remember the child in the video *Both of My Moms' Names Are Judy* (Lesbian and Gay Parents Association 1995) who says, "I just wish the teachers had brought up gay families, because then I would have known that it was okay to talk about my family."

As these teachers talk about their strongly held value of "children first," they sift through the ways in which they make decisions regarding how to acknowledge, at least personally, one-on-one, the child's family identity. They balance this against their belief that this was "a sensitive subject" for the child, and their fear that to draw attention to an identity that has been stigmatized in our society (such as that of having two lesbian mothers) might be harmful to the child.

Yet we know that what is *not* studied and talked about in school also teaches—the omissions, gaps, and silences also take their toll. Psychologists and cultural theorists have shown us the negative impact on children of not seeing themselves represented in the curriculum (Casper, Schultz, and Wickens 1992; Clark 1955/1970). Helen Cohen, who with Debra Chasnoff produced the video *It's Elementary,* on gay and lesbian curricular issues, observes, "The youngest kids have a sense of fairness and a kind of instinctual philosophy about gay people. As they grow older, they become more difficult to reach because of the negative things they've picked up" (Walters 1996). We wonder if at least some of the "negative things" picked up are as much about what's not talked about in the public space of classrooms as what *is* talked about on playgrounds and in the media. These educators say they do not include gay and lesbian families in their curriculum, even at times when there might be an opening to do so, such as Mother's Day cards or addressing invitations to parent night. We wonder to what extent the purposeful omission of references to Carl's two moms has been a part of the "null" curriculum (Apple 1993), teaching Carl, as well as his classmates, that this particular part of identity is not acceptable.

For educators, activists, and parents who might hope that the presence of diverse identities in schools will cause changes in school curriculum, the ways in which these teachers have negotiated the presence of lesbian mothers may be discouraging. For Arlene, Julia, and their principal, diversity means accommodating differences so that the child can go unnoticed and, therefore, unharmed. Most of these educators boast of the way they "treat everyone the same" while in the same breath adding, "diversity is the hallmark of this school." This approach to diversity is in sharp contrast to one in which differences are surfaced, and privilege is imbalanced (Fine, Weis, and Powell 1997; Smrekar 1992).

GOOD PARENTS

Although there was variation among these educators in the meaning of family diversity for the curriculum, we found more homogeneity when it came to the perception of a "good" parent in relation to schools. Good parents were defined by their involvement in their child's education, and we found "a clear and narrowly defined standard for parent involvement in education" (Lareau 1992, 3). These educators say they responded to the lesbian parents with whom they'd had contact, at least in part, because they fit their standard for good parents. This standard was often made clear when they talked about who didn't fit this norm. Roger's comment is illustrative: "The case with children of gay/lesbian parents is that, for the most part, they are middle class. They and schools have the same values:

hard work, study, education [are] important. I would welcome gay/lesbian parents into the school because they would work with the school to educate their children."

The definition of *parent involvement* used by these educators was a consistent one: parents showing up at the school and supporting what the teachers are trying to do in the classroom. Excluded from this picture of "good parents" are those who support the education of their child by explicitly challenging the norms and assumptions of the school and providing information about the strengths and needs of their child that conflicts with what the school "sees." We heard from these educators about their displeasure with parents "who don't even bother to show up," and about the parents they worry about, those who "come here from city schools."

The relationships between educators and lesbian mothers described in this chapter appeared to have more to do with how the educator viewed the cultural resources that the couple brought to the interaction than with the couple's sexual orientation. When Julia says, "they were responsible enough to come" and "they are concerned about Carl's education," she is interpreting the ways in which these mothers interact with the school as indicative of the importance they place on education. Like many schools, theirs is one that emphasizes the importance of parents' being positive and supportive, demonstrated at least in part through their presence at the school for key formal events. The principal says, "I don't care if they're gay, but please be involved." Among the parents we interviewed, all fit the standard for what the principal described as "good parents." Most of the educators we interviewed are in schools that are "extraordinarily diverse" with "all different kinds of families." Kara's school, which is more homogeneous and elite, is one in which antibias curriculum is prevalent, and which has a self-identified gay male principal.

The educators we interviewed all spoke with high regard about the lesbian mothers we interviewed, some of whom had been "cheerleaders" for the classroom, and had "at least come in for conferences." Perhaps that is not surprising, since all of the lesbian parents with whom these educators had contact were middle class. All but one mother was European American, and all spoke English as their first language. None of the parents were distrustful or critical of the school, and all of their children were successful in school and well liked by the educators. We wondered what the responses of the educators might have been had the parents been recent immigrants or working poor, as well as lesbian. We also wondered about the responses of educators working in schools in which diversity, whether it be through demographics or curricula, was less prevalent.

CONCLUSION

What we found were engaged and committed parents and teachers who wanted to do what was best for the children in their lives and in their classrooms. We found what we already knew, that classrooms are complex places where a lot goes on at once. We found that often the same words have different meanings to different people. "Good" parent is not only a way of identifying who is acceptable, it is also a way of affirming the teacher's own belief and values. We went into this study believing that there were shared qualities of gay/lesbian family–friendly educators, and we structured our questions to find out when and how teachers realized the value of responding to gay/lesbian parents in the interests of a pluralistic society. What we found, instead, was a broad range of definitions of "responsiveness," undergirded by varying views of what it means to support and educate children. We saw this, initially, as a study of teachers and lesbian parents negotiating public space in the classroom. What we found was less a negotiation, implying discussion and compromise, than a filtering of new elements of identity through preestablished paradigms regarding norms of parental involvement, student support, and classroom community.

NOTES

1. Although gay- and lesbian-headed families have become more visible in the last few years, this is more often true for lesbians than gay men. All of the parents we located were lesbians. Therefore, all of the teachers with whom we spoke had had children of lesbians in their classroom.

2. All names used in this paper are pseudonyms.

REFERENCES

Apple, M. (1993). *Official knowledge: Democratic education in a conservative age*. New York: Routledge.

Casper, V., S. Schultz, and E. Wickens. (1992). Breaking the silences: Lesbian and gay parents and schools. *Teachers College Record* 9: 109–38.

Chasnoff, D., director/producer, and H. Cohen, producer. (1996). *It's elementary: Talking about gay issues in school*. San Francisco: Women's Educational Media. Film.

Clark, K. B. (1955/1970). *Prejudice and your child*. Boston: Beacon.

Delpit, L. (1995). *Other people's children.* New York: New Press.

Elwin, R., and M. Paulsee. (1990). *Asha's mums.* Toronto: Women's Press.

Epstein, J. L. (1995). School/family/community partnerships: Caring for the children we share. *Phi Delta Kappan,* 701–12.

Fine, M., L. Weis, and L. Powell. (1997). Communities of difference: A critical look at desegregated spaces created for and by youth. *Harvard Educational Review* 67(2): 247–84.

Harvard Law Review. (1990). *Sexual orientation and the law.* Cambridge, Mass.: Harvard University Press.

Hulsebosch, P., and M. Koerner. (1997). You can't be for children and against their families: Family diversity workshops for elementary school teachers. In *Overcoming heterosexism and homophobia: Strategies that work!* ed. J. T. Sears and W. L. Williams. New York: Columbia University Press.

Hulsebosch, P. L. (1991). Beauty in the eye of the beholder: How and why teachers involve parents. *International Journal of Educational Research* 15(2): 183–200.

———. (1992). Significant others: Teachers' perspectives on relationships with parents. In *Teacher lore,* ed. W. Schubert and W. Ayers. New York: Teachers College Press.

Koerner, M., and P. Hulsebosch. (1996). Preparing teachers for family diversity: Supporting gay and lesbian families. *Journal of Teacher Education* 47(5): 347–54.

Lareau, A. (1989). *Home advantage: Social class and parental intervention in elementary education.* Philadelphia: Falmer Press.

———. (1992). "It's more covert today": The importance of race in shaping parents' views of the school. Paper presented at the Annual Meeting of the American Anthropological Association.

Lesbian and Gay Parents Association. (1995). *Both of my moms' mames are Judy.* San Francisco: Lesbian and Gay Parents Association. Video.

Lightfoot, S. L. (1975). *Worlds apart: Relationships between families and schools.* New York: Basic Books.

Moll, L. (1992). Bilingual classroom studies and community analysis: Some recent trends. *Educational Researcher* 21(2): 20–24.

Reinharz, S. (1992). *Feminist methods in social research.* Oxford: Oxford University Press.

Ryan, D. P. (1998). Gay/lesbian parents and school personnel: The contexts that inhibit or support the home/school partnership. Ph.D. diss., Teachers College, Columbia University, New York.

Silin, J. (1995). *Sex, death and the education of children: Our passion for ignorance in the age of AIDS.* New York: Teachers College Press.

Smrekar, C. (1992). Building community: The influence of school organization on patterns of parent participation. Paper presented at the Annual Meeting of the American Educational Research Association, San Francisco.

Style, E., and P. McIntosh. (1988). *Curriculum as window and mirror* (monograph). Summit, N.J.: Oakknoll School.

U.S. Department of Education. (1994). *Strong families, strong schools: Building community partnerships for learning* . Washington D.C.: U.S. Department of Education.

Walters, B. (1996). Taking gay issues into the classroom. *San Francisco Examiner*, 4 June.

· 17 ·

PLACING CHILDREN FIRST: THE IMPORTANCE OF MUTUAL PRESENCE IN THE ELEMENTARY CLASSROOM

Barbara Danish

> I would feel worse if there were no other two-mom families. What if I wanted to feel like other kids and nobody was like me?
>
> —Jake, age 6

> This is something I really don't like. First they ask me what's it like to have two moms. And then they ask me are you Jewish or Christian. And then they ask me where are you from. I especially don't like that. And then— they've never asked this before, but I have to beware of this in the future— what's your life like?
>
> —Katie, age 7

Those of us lesbians and gay men who have created families—in our case, a two-mom, adoptive family—know that our children often do not see others like themselves as they look around their classroom, school, or neighborhood. Often the only ones with lesbian or gay parents, they are obliged to develop sophisticated strategies for understanding their place in the world and for explaining that place to others, especially to their naively curious, but relentlessly questioning, classmates and friends. They are obliged as well to cope with the homophobia that is rampant in the schools and on the streets. What can we do to help our children? Some thought has been given to the kinds of curricular activities that may be important, but almost no attention has been given to the question of whether the isolation that our children experience is, at least in part, remediable by placing them in classes with others from a similar family structure—by arranging for that mutual presence. Let me begin to consider that possibility by telling our family story.

195

We chose the preschool we did for our daughter because it had just the kind of loving, creative environment we believe helps children to learn. When we first saw the director of this small parent cooperative, she had a pair of shorts on her head, was beating a drum, and marching in a parade that a four-year-old had concocted. We would have preferred a preschool with other lesbian and gay families, but the director followed the children's interests and needs and was comfortable with our two-mom family. It seemed the perfect place.

But early on, the consequences of there being no other lesbian or gay families became apparent to us. In the second week of school, our daughter, just three, returned home to tell us she had a father who had died.

In tracking down the origin of this made-up story, we discovered that the teacher had asked the children to take turns telling with whom they lived. I can imagine Katie, an observant child, interested in making sense of things through language even at three, listening as she heard each child say: "I live with my mommy and daddy." When it came her turn, she must have assumed, despite the stories we had told her of her birth and adoption, that she, too, would have had a father if something tragic had not happened. This experience convinced us that even a school comfortable with us as lesbians did not know *enough* about how to imagine the world for our daughter.

Looking back now, I see how the director/teacher did try to address Katie's world. She read books that referred to adoption and that had two moms. During a study of families, she hung a poster that showed a two-mom family. When she planned Mother's and Father's Day activities, she invited the children to make a gift for any woman or man important in their lives. Despite all of this, there was something missing. Could anything have prevented Katie's first experience of *otherness* until she was older? Would another child with two moms in her class have helped Katie confirm her family as the other children were continually confirmed? Though I could find little written on the subject, my hunch was supported by Vivian Gussin Paley's observations in *Kwanzaa and Me* (1995), in which African American parents discuss their reluctance to send their children to the primarily white teacher/white student lab school at the University of Chicago. When we asked Katie if she would like to be in school with other children who had two moms, she said yes.

In planning for kindergarten, my partner and I decided to follow this hunch. We had heard that the principal of the local elementary school wanted his school to be a safe place for lesbian and gay families. A number of children from such families already attended, but from what I heard, none had ever been in a class together.

So one November night, almost a year before kindergarten was to begin, I called the principal. Would he be willing to place two or more children from lesbian/gay families in the same kindergarten class? A week later he called with the following plan: If I could find other families, if they identified themselves and requested such placement, he would place our children in the same class. I spoke to two families; one forwarded its child's name to the administrators. The next September, Katie entered a kindergarten class with Richard, a rambunctious, friendly boy from an adoptive two-dad family.

Interestingly, at the beginning of kindergarten, a two-dad family did not strike Katie as similar to ours. Comfortable with telling us about her life and thoughts, she came home one day and said, "Richard has two dads. Nobody has two *dads!*" She was too young to understand the irony of her surprise; she would come to hear that exclamation many times in reference to our family. Over time we discovered a third adoptive family with a daughter, Gabriella. The mutual presence of these children, Katie, Gabriella, and Richard, and their parents would become important during the two years the class spent together.

Those years were relatively uneventful in terms of family structure, at least as it appeared to me. The children quickly became familiar with each other's parents. The teacher posted photographs of our families. As in preschool there was a general comfort with our family. Katie and Richard went in and out of being good friends but always seemed attached by the knowledge that they came from similar family structures. As for the teacher, she did not celebrate Mother's Day or Father's Day, a relief for us and some other parents in the class's nontraditional families. She referred to us by our mother names: Mommy and Mama. Most important, she insisted—of children and parents alike—that the class be a caring community, and she taught the children how to appreciate each other's strengths and weaknesses through activities and discussions.

There were, however, several moments, precursors of the future, when the mutual presence of our families was more than reassuring. Once, for example, I was helping four children make collages when one asked the others, "Does Richard really have two dads?" Then they asked me, "Does Katie really have two moms?" Theirs were curious questions, and I was glad to answer, not only to take this little bit of pressure off of Richard and Katie but to experience the questions that Katie had complained about. In another example, the other adoptive mother in the class reported an incident from a class trip. She heard Jerome call across swampy Jamaica Bay, "Katie why don't you have a father?" Katie ignored him, she said. Jerome called out again, "Katie, why don't you have a father?" The mom began to step in when Katie responded on her own.

Looking back at these stories now, I begin to realize that kindergarten and first grade looked uneventful to me, but Katie, at the same time a physically energetic and philosophical, meditative child, was already under pressure to explain her family. Moreover, where I was comfortable making such explanations, Katie was not.

There were other problems, too. A child from a biological family said to Gabriella, "That's not your real mother and she doesn't really love you." This mean-spirited comment no doubt came from the child's own home difficulties, but Gabriella understandably felt it as a blow. A private person, she didn't report this incident to her parents or teacher; rather, Katie did. Gabriella later told her mother that Katie's presence was a help to her then. Katie, too, found support in Gabriella's presence, for example, when the teacher introduced memoir—the foundation of much writing instruction in elementary schools. For many of the children, early memories were exciting to retell, but for Katie and Gabriella, whose early lives involved profound separation from their biological parents, an assignment to write about an early moment in their lives was disturbing. Katie wrote, "I don't want to tell you about an early experience in my life, but I'll tell you something else." Gabriella chose to write about a favorite singing group. We were lucky that the teacher—highly experienced, intelligent, and thoughtful—understood our daughters' responses when we explained them and welcomed the children's variations on her assignment, even apologizing for not anticipating their discomfort.

Looking back, I see how much the children's mutual presence provided support for each other and how the parents' mutual presence provided support as well. Katie recognized this, too, and expressed her wish that there be children from adoptive and lesbian/gay families in her second-grade class.

Still, in the spring of first grade, I wasn't sure what to do about Katie's second-grade placement. The teacher said to count on her and the coordinator for placement, but I wondered. Would they think of Katie's need for mutual presence? Richard was remaining in first grade, but could I ask that Katie be placed specifically with Gabriella? Or did I need to make a general request? Would I be seen as meddling, as some parents suggested? In the face of this uncertainty, I requested nothing.

As it turned out, the teacher and coordinator did not think of Katie's need for mutual presence. Her second-grade class had no other children from lesbian/gay or adoptive families, and she felt her uniqueness keenly. The children asked about her family life. She said of one boy: "I don't like him. He asks too many questions about private things."

"Why do you think the children ask?" I questioned her.

"They're interested 'cause it didn't happen to them," she answered, "but to the people who are being asked questions, it's an insult." She wished that Richard were still in her class: "They would be asking him questions, so it's sort of easier for me."

Her second-grade teacher, warm and caring, dealt with Katie in the same way he dealt with the other children in his classroom—by committed inclusion. He wanted no child to feel different. The children's similarities rather than their differences were important to him. He was adamant that he would read no book with lesbian or gay parents unless Katie agreed to it, and though I doubted him, his concern turned out to be right—Katie was "horrified" that he might read such a book when I suggested it to her. Administrators had not told this teacher that he would have a student from a two-mom household. They had no written material or staff meeting to help him think about particular needs she might have. In a parent-teacher conference I discovered that he was unaware of the questions Katie was being asked or of the jokes a classmate was telling that started, "Say you're gay." At the age of seven, Katie protected herself primarily through privacy. My partner and I needed to help Katie cope with these questions and "jokes," but the school had some work to do, too.

Tom Roderick, director of Educators for Social Responsibility, would call this work that the school faced the responsibility to create a broad context in which children are respectful of difference. "Within such a context, you can have discussions with kids," Roderick says. "The kids build a common vocabulary that they can bring into any discussion. They learn to communicate, deal with anger, confirm difference, and mediate. They look at similarities and differences. They see that name-calling really affects people" (personal communication, December 2, 1998). Within such a context perhaps Katie would feel comfortable if a teacher read a book with two moms or two dads. Maybe the children would have fewer questions. I continued to think that the presence of another child in a lesbian/gay or adoptive family would help, although I saw that that, alone, was insufficient.

During the previous year I had suggested to the lesbian and gay families I knew that they talk to school administrators about their child's placement. Thus, the following year, when five children from lesbian/gay families appeared in a kindergarten class, it seemed the principal's informal policy had worked again. As it turned out, most of the parents had never thought of such placement; rather, they had requested placement with their child's friends, also children from lesbian/gay families. If they had not considered it previously, however, they considered it "absolutely a value" when I spoke to them at the beginning of the children's second year together. One parent explained:

> When Jonah talks about his own and others' families, it's his average experience that there are all these different configurations. Not everyone

has a mother and a father. His self-esteem is great. In his class there is even another child who calls one of his mothers Imah (Hebrew for mother). It makes it so normal. He doesn't feel stigmatized. He'll come to see that his family isn't normal, but he'll have a core value, your notion of yourself. He won't have been attacked at so vulnerable an age.

While the parents were pleased in general, two were afraid that such a large group "ghettoized" their children and deprived children in other classes from knowing lesbian/gay families. The coordinator of early-childhood education who placed the children also was unhappy with the placement. "We put so much emphasis on equity," she said, "it looked like we were doing something different. If I had known these were all lesbian/gay families, I would have put them into two classes." I am not sure I agree with the coordinator or the parents. If such placement is of value to the children, might it not be positive to have the equivalent of a critical mass? With such a group, wouldn't the questions of other children be more likely to be raised with the teacher? Wouldn't the children's family lives be normal enough that secrecy could wait a while longer?

Three of the five children continued together to the first grade. With the attention of this "loving community," as one parent described it, focused more on academics and less on the caring of kindergarten, perhaps the mutual presence of these children is the central way their family structures are confirmed. One of the children, asked whether the presence of his two companions was important to him, answered, "I would feel worse if there were no other two-mom families. What if I wanted to feel like other kids and nobody was like me?"

But as interested as these families are in holding on to this mutual presence, at the end of first grade what will happen? Other needs of the children may well take priority—close friends, academic needs, the absence of compatible children. Daniel is a thoughtful and articulate fourth-grader in the school, the child of two moms. He explained,

> It would be nicer than not [to be in a class with a child from a similar family], but it wouldn't make a million-dollar difference. Because right now I don't tell everyone, so they don't know and don't question. I don't go blabbing around like I did in younger grades. [Now] when people ask me, it feels like the whole world doesn't know, so it makes me feel like that kid [in preschool] who said I was an alien. I'd rather be able to say freely I have two moms.

But that freedom is not easy to attain. One of his mothers says that Daniel finds himself on a playground "exploding with homophobia." She continues, "[Gay] is clearly something you don't want to be. He can deal with the question 'How do you have two moms?' But it's too big a burden to hear all these taunts that he knows are about his mothers, to out himself and his family, and to defend himself." She continues:

> When Daniel was in preschool, an older child who didn't know him said, "How can you have two moms? You can't be real." He answered, "Well, I am real and I have two moms." One of his peers added, "I know Anna. She has two moms." A third child said, "I have two moms." Those kids went on to elementary school with him, and he knows they're there. As the kids get older, there are more pressing social issues. There are children whose parents are divorcing. He feels secure in his family. More damaging than not having someone else in the classroom is the stuff that goes on outside the classroom.

Daniel agrees. At this age "the only thing I don't like, in every class they say [to each other], 'You're gay!' or 'You're lesbian!' That makes me feel like they're insulting my moms." He's critical of those parts of the curriculum that confirm his isolation.

> Sometimes I find in the class something which is disturbing. The teacher reads a book and it's, what's the word . . . racist? sexist? It's when the book starts, "You're like me, with a Mom and a Dad." It makes me feel like everyone in the world has a mom and dad, even though I know it's not true.

A pattern begins to emerge. It is the questions, the incredulity, the insults, the books that unconsciously exclude—the profound isolation—that our children experience.

What is so difficult about building a context that might reduce this isolation? For one thing, the important work of kindergarten—building a loving community—is set aside for academics as the children grow older. Second, the attitude of general acceptance, on one level comforting, masks a deeper level of indifference, or worse, a fear of difference. Third, there is outright homophobia—this is the district in which the infamous Rainbow Curriculum fight took place in 1992. The confrontation revolved largely around a column of text in the curriculum, "Fostering Positive Attitudes toward Sexuality" (Children of the Rainbow 1991) and the inclusion of several books about lesbian and gay families in the "Multicultural Bibliography." In the text teachers are told, "It is important for teachers of first graders to be aware of the changing concept of family in today's society." They are asked to include "actual experiences via creative play, books, visitors, etc. in order for them to view lesbians/gays as real people to be respected and appreciated" (372).

The outcome of the curriculum fight was an order to tear out these offending paragraphs and an informal "Don't Ask, Don't Tell" policy. A *public* placement option for children of lesbian/gay families, a collection of books about lesbian and gay families available for teachers to use in their classes, staff development for teachers, and sustained education for students about respect for and appreciation of diversity of all kinds, all run the risk of violating district policy and endangering the extensive freedom the school does have.

When people object to my idea of mutual placement, they make comments like, "Why do you harp so much on difference?" or "Don't worry about who's in the class; worry about what's taught." I wonder. Where possible, don't we all tend to live and work with people who confirm our identity in some way? My friend, an adoptive mother with a biracial child, looked for an elementary school with a population of African American and biracial children large enough for her daughter to confirm her place in the school, if not the world. In our school, administrators work hard to balance classes in terms of race and gender so that children have classmates from similar (and different) backgrounds. I want the same for Katie with regard to her family.

Still, this kind of advocacy is fraught with questions. Is such a presence actually useful to children? Is there another child from a lesbian/gay family on grade level? If so, does the child need to be a friend, or is presence sufficient? What kinds of privacy issues for the child and the family are involved? Is the school a safe place to come out? As Elaine Wickens, Director of the Bank Street/Parsons School of Design Collaborative Masters Program, points out, placement has to focus on the individual (personal communication, November 21, 1998) and is supported, not solved, with a policy. Still, we don't have to have all the answers before we act on behalf of our children.

Part of our advocacy has to be with administrators. In their book *Gay Parents/Straight Schools: Building Communication and Trust*, Virginia Casper and Steven Schultz (1999) found that administrators would do nothing to harm a child, no matter their values. What they would do, however, ranged widely according to those values, the willingness of the administrator to be proactive, the philosophy of the schools, the parent body, and other considerations.

The administrators of our school are on the right track, supported by the school's philosophy and their own convictions. They are also the victims of social fear and hostility toward lesbian and gay people. Within that they have had the courage to welcome our families and agree to our children's mutual presence. Now, how can they welcome our participation in our children's placement? How can they, with our help, build a school community that helps all children understand and appreciate the school's diversity?

Having written this essay, I see Katie's perspective with a clarity I didn't have before. Teachers and schools have great power in our children's lives. In the classroom and on the schoolyard much socializing and identity development occurs. "Mama," Katie says, "I'm trying to figure out whether I should be like everyone else or whether I should think for myself." The double-edged sword of difference pushes some of our children to be sensitive to boundaries, sharp readers of certain social situations, and thoughtful about identity issues that other children may come to later. That is a powerful search that we parents can help with. On the other hand, our children are too young to have to spend so much energy maneuvering their classmates' questions and insults. There we must look to the schools, districts, and schools of education for help.

Writing this essay, I realize I have work to do in the school. I need to talk with the administrator yearly about Katie's placement and help other lesbian and gay families know their options. I understand that Katie's teacher is a second-year teacher overwhelmed by numerous expectations and trying to teach all of his students responsibly. I understand, too, that teachers have various values, some of which don't include Katie. But believing that a broad context of understanding is essential for Katie and all of her schoolmates, I can ask that the school develop curricular structures that help and even oblige teachers to work with *difference*—their own attitudes and their students'. I can strongly urge our PTA to research and support such a curriculum and then do the tedious business of helping to raise money for that program.

All of this will take courage—as much courage as it takes Katie to face her questioners. I am not sure I have that much courage—to push and prod and argue with school administrators who have responsibilities to so many students, and with parents who have their own priorities. It is one thing to say "place children first" and quite another to face what that actually demands of us. I can only imagine that such courage will have its rewards. As children see all of us, gay and straight, parents, teachers, and administrators, fight for a schooling that allows everyone to be visible in their similarities and differences, they, too, may develop a commitment to that worldview and understand the benefits of courage so well spent. As for our children, our acts, I hope, will confirm the great courage we already require of them and that they call on daily with hardly a complaint.

REFERENCES

Casper, V., and S. Schultz. (1999). *Gay parents/straight schools: Building communication and trust.* New York: Teachers College Press.

Children of the Rainbow, First Grade. (1991). New York: New York City Public Schools.

Paley, V. G. (1995). *Kwanzaa and me.* Cambridge, Mass.: Harvard University Press.

• *Part 5* •

EDUCATORS AND THEIR ALLIES

This final cluster of chapters focuses on the essential roles that teachers, administrators, and other school professionals, in conjunction with parents and students themselves, play in envisioning and configuring our schools to address issues of sexual diversity and to create safe and welcoming spaces for people to learn, to work, and to experience a sense of community. Here the experiences of both practicing educators and teacher educators are represented, highlighting the many ways in which these issues play out in a variety of classrooms, for preschool-aged students all the way up to the undergraduate experience in teacher education programs.

Greg Curran's chapter leads off the section with a look at activism in the elementary school. Drawing on his own experiences as an elementary teacher, Greg comes to realize that activism on behalf of lesbian and gay students (and even students thought to be lesbian or gay) means "facing up to and working with my fears and tensions." Through a variety of school contexts, and across a range of issues, this chapter acknowledges the pain sometimes involved in "being so public and so challenging" on behalf of lesbian and gay issues as they affect children. But in the end the payoff is great, as activism means ending silencing, listening to and engaging with others, and becoming an effective and respected advocate for these issues in an elementary school context.

Describing the ways in which a myriad of identity categories "play themselves out" on a day-to-day basis in the life of an assistant principal, Karen Glasgow, forms the heart of chapter 19. In it Karen and her partner and coauthor, Sharon Murphy, write about how Karen has "struggled to increase my school community's awareness and assist them in acquiring the tools to combat homophobia effectively." The authors delineate four strategies for addressing these issues in elementary schools and with prospective elementary teachers, concluding that "by challenging the hearts and minds of the individuals and audience with whom we work, we have witnessed growth."

In chapter 20, by "integrating the two perspectives of mother and educator," Rita Marinoble writes about "the many dimensions of awareness

205

I have experienced around affirming sexual diversity in elementary schools." Reflecting on the salience of sexual diversity issues, first from the standpoint of an elementary school counselor, and next as a single adoptive mother of two young daughters, Rita realizes that "affirming sexual diversity in elementary schools amounts to nothing less than a paradigm shift in the school culture." To transcend the controversy that often accompanies such a shift, she writes about how hopefulness, survival, and generativity might help elementary schools "better respond to those challenges."

Chapter 21 explores "how historically imbued stereotypes about sexual minorities surface in language, and how they provide particular sites of tension for those who are becoming teachers." Examinig the cases of three preservice teachers, Kate Evans uses their words to examine critically the equation of "Queer + Children = Danger." She advocates thinking through the metaphor of "bridging the gap," because it "emphasizes how bringing together 'queer' and 'teacher' is a complicated endeavor." Further, she recommends "a reflective stance in which the multiple effects of language are considered as crucial to attend to in educational endeavors."

Margaret Mulhern and Gregory Martinez, in the final chapter in the book, share their "journey of teaching about sexual diversity issues to undergraduate elementary preservice teachers." The chapter takes the form of a dialogue between these two heterosexual partners, as they confront their own homophobia and deal with students' varying levels of engagement with these issues. They note how "teaching queerly required more than conviction" on their part—it required reading, preparation, really listening to others, and self-examination. But as teacher educators, "the decision to include sexual orientation in our multicultural education courses was easy."

Across the spectrum, from teacher preparation to in-service opportunities for practicing teachers, issues of sexual diversity are pervasive, albeit often in hidden and silent ways. These five chapters offer a variety of perspectives to help us think more deeply about the question, How do these issues impact and play out in the lives of gay and lesbian teachers and their allies?

· 18 ·

ACTIVISM WITHIN: WORKING WITH TENSION

Greg Curran

A ctivism has come to mean many things to me. As a union representative early in my elementary teaching career, I had come to associate
the term with questioning and challenging, standing up, speaking out, and
posing differing viewpoints.

Activism in support of gay and lesbian students came to be more
about a focusing on myself, learning to trust in my own skills, knowledge,
and what I knew was right regardless of the situation. It was about working with rather than against myself, and a critical part of that was truly accepting my sexuality.

Ultimately to achieve any of these things meant facing up to and
working with my fears and tensions. It also necessitated a change in how I
viewed people. Rather than seeing opponents all around me, I began to realize that by getting to know people and where they were coming from, I
could develop a support base. Others could then take up issues relating to
gay and lesbian students.

THE TENSION OF SPEAKING OUT AT STAFF MEETINGS

Most of my elementary teaching career was spent working in Catholic
elementary schools, where recognition of sexual diversity was rare or
nonexistent. I never heard anyone talk about lesbians or gays in my work
environment.

At staff meetings I was often tense, knowing that talking about homosexuality would usually mean standing up by myself. And so, as the
moment drew closer, the negative comments I presumed I would hear
would echo in my mind. Around and around they would reverberate. Inside I was twisting and turning, thinking, "Just once why can't someone

207

else stand up first?" In a school environment where homosexuality or gay and lesbian students were never mentioned, I was acutely aware that these words tumbling out of my mouth would sharply focus attention on me.

This scenario was so familiar to me, though. Throughout my teaching career I'd had numerous experiences of being cut down to size after taking a stand on various justice topics.

> *They'll pull me apart.*
> *The spotlight will be on ME,*
> *as though there's something wrong with me for talking about this.*
> *To stand still, to creep back, to retreat.*
> *That was too much like self-betrayal.*
> *Continually on alert to the absences of homosexuality in discussion,*
> *to the assumptions of heterosexuality.*
> *My mind wouldn't take a break.*
> *Move forward, just keep moving,*
> *take the steps into the unknown.*
> *Resist, refuse,*
> *fight the cage they seek to put me in,*
> *along with that oh so taboo topic.*
> *Keep chipping, keep chipping away.*

And so I did. The more my confidence grew, the more I raised issues relating to gays and lesbians. In those moments I was hypersensitive to the reactions of the people around me. Was it just I who noticed the groans, the muttering, the familiar "Oh, Greg's going on about *it* again" and the rolling of their eyes. It was as if the issue had relevance only to me, that I was a single-issue person who just kept shoving this same old issue in people's faces.

> *Amid all the negatives never lose sight of the emerging positives, the sparks that provide ways forward, knowing that you have set about creating these possibilities.*

Scenario #1: Speaking Out to Silence—A Staff Meeting about Bullying

The two facilitators have been presenting reasons why students are bullied. But there is no mention of gay or lesbian students as potential targets of bullies.

It was one of those moments: "Do I or don't I?" "It's going to be really obvious if I do speak up." One fear after another was going through my mind. I had to take a stand with my own insecurities. To allow the gaps and silences to continue was to be complicit. All the while a voice within questioned over and over, "Why do you have to stand up to this all the time? It's not just *your* responsibility." All of this internal bickering and questioning told me that I hadn't resolved my tensions. I needed to keep feeling this scared, unsure, and challenged in order to find greater confidence and alternative means of working to bring about change. Trusting myself and my own intuition was a real struggle, yet it was paramount.

As I spoke to the absence of sexuality in their presentation, the facilitators replied that the subject was covered under gender. I questioned this since they hadn't spoken about any of the issues that face students who are thought or known to be gay or lesbian. It was as if "it's covered but we won't talk about it." And so the silencing continues, I thought.

> *The clouds of negativity were forming in my head.*
> *They're going to be thinking, "He's going on about IT again."*
> *I felt this,*
> *sat with it,*
> *but I needed to walk to the edge and jump off, to see whether I could truly fly.*

I spoke of my own experiences of bullying throughout my school years. Interestingly, to this point the presentation had been totally detached from the personal experiences of staff. To me it was like "How is this presentation touching people?" So I revealed aspects about my own life, which until this time only close friends knew about. It absolutely terrified me to be this exposed, knowing that someone could come in at any time and challenge me. Yet this topic needed a human face that was quite distinct from the "made for staff consumption" accounts that were being played out for us. Staff could remain detached and distant from that, since it didn't require them to examine their own personal experiences of bullying.

> *My voice wavered.*
> *I felt the tears from long ago,*
> *the anger and nausea within me,*
> *taking me close to the edge but never over it.*

From outside my body I watched myself, thinking, "What the hell are you doing, Greg?" That phrase had increasingly served to mark significant moments of honesty and truth about who I was. When I stopped speaking, a silence, an incredible nothingness, filled the room. The session moved on. It was as if I hadn't spoken.

> *What did I expect?*
> *A response, I guess, some sort of response.*
> *But what was I after?*
> *Validation?*
> *Maybe people were just trying to process it.*
> *Maybe they didn't feel it to be appropriate to say anything.*

Secretly I hoped that my speaking up would initiate some discussion, if not in the public spotlight of the staff meeting, then afterward in one-to-one conversations. I needed to go beyond a mere hoping, though, and make it happen. Situations such as this were never solely negative if I took ownership of them. After the meeting I asked other staff who I knew were privately supportive for more public support in future meetings. Some staff took this on board lending support in a variety of ways.

There was going to be pain in this, in being so public and so challenging. Losses were to a certain extent inevitable as I found out who would and wouldn't stand with me on these issues, but at least I had some clarity on that. Connections were then made with people who had the courage to discuss issues relating to homosexuality and schools.

Support through Connection

> *It was people being prepared to hear me,*
> *being honest and willing to learn.*
> *They were there, I knew it, I felt it.*
> *The smiles between us when someone's ignorance showed,*
> *the looks of "I'm with you,"*
> *their readiness to delve into resources I provided,*
> *their speaking up in different forums, and*
> *their work behind the scenes educating others.*
> *Support happened in a myriad of ways.*
> *It was about people moving from where they*
>   *were.*

The school may not have changed (in a substantive sense) through these supportive relationships. But these people had engaged, contemplated, and reflected on an area that otherwise might not have touched them. My relationships with them certainly taught me a great deal. I had to shift my focus from my own perspective and begin to listen to and engage with others from where they were. It was about patience, being okay with feeling frustrated, and learning to hold myself in check when I wanted to push things along at a faster pace. I learned how to remain focused on the other person, constantly adjusting how I related based on what I was learning about her or him. I couldn't know all the answers and directions in advance, which put me on uncertain ground, but it taught me about being in the moment and trusting in my own skills and knowledge.

Working one on one, I learned the power of individual connections. Activism began to take on a broader meaning for me. It wasn't just about the end result and always being up front in public. It was about the connections formed behind the scenes, and the power of these positive interactions to influence how these people thought and talked about homosexuality. Of course, it may not have gone any further than our discussions, but the possibility was there. I believed in creating these possibilities, which slowly began to become realities, as the following scenario shows.

Scenario #2: The Sole Voice Becomes Multiple Voices

The staff are listing examples of bullying they're familiar with.

I have to do it.
I push through the fears and the tension,
raising the issue of bullying of students thought or known to be gay or lesbian.
But this time it's different
I'm no longer alone.
For the first time ever,
someone comes in as support,
showing that it's not just Greg's issue,
not just the "gay boy's" issue.
Public support? Can this really be happening?
It's so unfamiliar to me
and it feels like normality at last.
I'm spinning out now
as one staff member speaks of homophobia within his class.
The issue is now shown to have relevance to this school.
It's not something that's relevant only to secondary school, something distant.
This is so, so crucial.
Part of me is in awe at what is happening.

Another part is trying to make the most of it.
I wish I could just step aside and watch how this moment unfurls, in order to wring every drop of excitement out of it.
Another staff member recalls the abuse and torment another elementary student had faced because he had lesbian parents.
It's like, how can you argue with these situations?
They are the realities that remain hidden until staff have the courage to name them.
Stories like this broaden the focus, showing the wider implications of homophobia.
They need to be named and recorded.
One person speaking up had been like WOW, but two people, I wanted this moment to go on and on.
I seek to add just another point while the going is good.
BUT
one staff member is visibly unsettled by this.
He sits back seeking distance,
recoiling from all the talk focusing on homosexuality.
Leaning forward now, visibly annoyed and frustrated, he spits at me,
"You've made YOUR POINT!"
He'd had enough and now sought to slam the gate shut, but it was too late, much too late.
It had gone beyond Greg's speaking up,
to being an issue that others were concerned about.
It now had wider support.
And so I refute what he says.
I refuse to let his negativity dampen the moment.
With the ideas now recorded I choose to let go.
And I smile within, knowing that though the discussion has stopped, it isn't over.
This has provided me with fresh inspiration,
while other staff now know that they do have what it takes to speak up.

But back to him for a moment. What was that point that I was sup-posedly making? To him everything I was saying had no more substance than a point. The people attached to and affected by what I was saying seemed to be irrelevant. He couldn't get past the "homosexuality" to the people affected. His snapping at me was the signal that my time in the spotlight was over. It was time for the safe and comfortable issues to re-claim *their* space in the spotlight.

A sharp kick to the stomach,
a stinging slap to the face that moment.
But resonating around that was the delight of homosexuality being discussed,
the door being edged slightly ajar.
BUT
it edges even further ajar as another staff member grabs me to tell me the news.

They too broke the silence around homosexuality, describing the daily, relentless abuse a student in *their* class faced because she was thought to be a lesbian. We'd spoken about this child before, and I'd encouraged them to tell others about it, to show that this was a part of our school's reality. To know that they'd faced their fears to do this was one of those moments that has stayed with me. The connections made, the issues explored together, were now finding a public voice.

Opening my mouth, saying what is important to me opens the door to diverse possibilities. It takes me to the places where I can begin to do things, it allows me to see beyond hurdles, and it opens me to relationships with people whom I can engage with openly. It keeps me moving forward, away from negativity and feelings of doom.

SEEKING OPENINGS:
FINDING WAYS FORWARD WITH THE AID OF DOCUMENTS

Earlier I had written off the possibilities of school curriculum and policy being of any use. Now I started to question that and started to consider that there might be useful statements contained in school policy documents. These statements could provide a basis for staff discussions and could be used to support arguments in favor of lesbian and gay people.

What weighed upon me in my initial fears about raising the issues of homosexuality was the Church's institutional position. I knew that the antihomosexual teachings of the Church would be used by some people to justify prejudice against lesbians and gays. And so I felt a sense of foreboding whenever I drew close to talking about or challenging something related to the Church teachings on homosexuality.

So I looked for other openings, which I found in the all-embracing, generic statements contained in documents such as "Pastoral Care." Although documents like this often do not mention "sexuality," they nevertheless speak to acceptance of students, their background, and experiences as well as the importance of self-esteem. Such statements would certainly support action on behalf of lesbian and gay students.

Expected to be a "good" Catholic teacher, I realized that towing the "Catholic" line meant reading documents a particular way, in a way that did not recognize or see the need ever to mention gays and lesbians. What assists this process is the often nonspecific nature of these documents. Terms and phrases are often undefined or not clarified. Schools can then talk about themselves as being inclusive when their actual daily practices show that to be far from the truth.

My work as an English as a Second Language teacher and coordinator involved the critical examination of texts, curricula, and policy, and assessing how accessible and inclusive they were. Yet I had never critically examined school documents in relation to gays and lesbians. I started to do this with statements in the "Pastoral Care" document, writing down any questions that came into my head. The following is an example:

We seek to make our teaching meaningful to students and their backgrounds.

- How do we find out what is "meaningful" to the students?
- What do we mean by student "background"?
- What provision is made for staff training in this area?
- What practical actions do teachers take to show their students that their class environment is accepting of their various backgrounds?
- How do we go beyond considering only the interests of the majority and cater to those students who have been marginalized?
- What if teachers have problems relating to what is meaningful for students?

Formulating questions like these provided a means to explore the ambiguities, the gaps, and the implications of statements within documents. This meant moving beyond a surface reading of the statements, beyond the familiar and expected. I tried this approach with people I knew would be supportive and avoided those who were closed or negative.

The use of documents like "Pastoral Care" also provided fuel for another situation. I was often living in fear of "what if," so I decided to face that fear by preparing myself for worst-case scenarios. I imagined certain phrases or statements from the Bible or Church doctrine being thrown at me, with the expectation that I would know how they were supposed to be interpreted (as if there is only one possible way to read documents!). If confronted with a negative biblical or Church doctrine statement, I could counter with an all-embracing, inclusive statement from the "Pastoral Care" document.

I would also pick out particular statements and ask how they applied to different groups within the school population. For example:

We aim to accept students for who they are. How do we do this if:

- their ethnic background is different from the majority of the school population?
- they're from a single-parent family or same-sex-parent family?
- their religion is different from others'?
- they're lesbian or gay?

This variation shows an interest in equity across the board. If gays and lesbians were singled out from the list, you could ask why. This approach also allows for the opening of discussions about the similarities and differences between various forms of discrimination.

REFLECTING ON WHAT I'VE LEARNED

Look at yourself, Greg.
Walk to the edge and challenge your fears, perceptions and presumptions.

I had created a situation wherein I felt I was on my own. Getting beyond this required taking risks and confronting my fears. I was then able to connect with people and in so doing learned much about myself and how to bring about change.

For too long I had imagined there were dire consequences for speaking up. Of course there were risks, but far more damaging was the anger, disappointment, and self-betrayal that put my emotional well-being at risk. It was about not compromising myself anymore.

Whenever that inner voice piped up to caution me against speaking out, whenever I witnessed homophobia and felt hamstrung, when there seemed few avenues to challenge the heteronormative bias of the school, I began to feel the tension, to face it, to think it through, but most of all, to challenge it (to myself at least). I asked myself: How is the tension working on me? What triggers the tension? How much of the tension is self-imposed and/or based on presumption?

I began to challenge the assumptions of heterosexuality. I formed alliances with others. It didn't mean that I set out to change the whole system, that I declared my sexuality to everybody, or that I was always outspoken. I chose my moments and my audiences carefully. In these moments I have found a greater sense of freedom, energy, a sense of being at one with myself and a greater sense of self-empowerment. Each step I take makes me stronger and more determined to find ways of making school environments more inclusive of lesbian, gay, bisexual, and transgendered students.

· 19 ·

SUCCESS STORIES OF A FAT, BIRACIAL/BLACK, JEWISH, LESBIAN ASSISTANT PRINCIPAL

Karen Glasgow and Sharon Murphy

While pulling into my new school, I (Karen Glasgow) felt a mix of emotions. I was really an assistant principal here! Those old feelings of fear and anticipation started to resurface, along with the excitement. Each time I begin a new job or enter a new school, I endure similar anxiety. When they find out I'm a lesbian, will people dislike me? Will they disrespect, ignore, or embrace me? Will they give me a chance to show how great I really am? Will I know if a rejection is due to my being a lesbian, or because I am fat, Jewish, female, and biracial/black?

I taught for eighteen years in special education high schools that had both diverse student and staff populations. Special education lends itself to acceptance a bit more readily than does regular education because of the severe disabilities we have to accept and then work beyond. Though I had a few homophobic experiences with staff, students, and their parents, most of my interactions in the past were positive. However, here I was, starting a new job in a "regular" education elementary school, wondering if there would be a diverse staff here. Should I have taken the rainbow triangle off the bumper of my car? What if someone knows what it means and tells the staff before I have a chance to tell them myself?

Upon arriving at my new school, I first surveyed the staff to see who "looked" gay (any fag or dyke would do!). There were sixty teachers and twenty teacher assistants. Eight of these teachers were black, one Asian, and the rest white, with all Latino teaching assistants, except one who was black. Only one teacher was gay whom I was able to identify with some certainty. I really wanted an ally of any type, just someone who could give me support and knowledge about the school climate. June—National Gay and Lesbian Pride Month—was only two months away! I thought briefly and tentatively about how to take over the front-office bulletin board to put up a display. I

217

knew that it was essential to be honest and open in the workplace, even though at times it can be scary. Yet, through the use of the school's bulletin board and the Los Angeles Unified School District's diversity education policies, I began to introduce myself to my staff with some modicum of safety.

I have survived two years now at this school. As I reflect on those first few months, I realize how I have struggled to increase my school community's awareness and assist them in acquiring the tools to combat homophobia effectively. In this chapter we propose some strategies, with relevant stories as examples of some of the successes I have enjoyed as assistant principal.

STRATEGY 1:
BECOME FAMILIAR WITH RELEVANT DISTRICT POLICIES

I have learned that I can use the district mandates and policies already in place to support teachers in their ability to teach about homosexuality. For example, in the Los Angeles City schools, June is recognized as Gay and Lesbian Awareness Month. In our diverse district of over 650,000 students, representing ethnicities from all over the world, there has been a conscious effort in the past five years to recognize and celebrate diversity and multiculturalism. Two of our past board of education presidents are gay and have made gay and lesbian issues part of diversity recognition and training. The district's Human Relations Commission sends a packet once a year to every school, including posters, lesson plans, and resources to equip teachers with gay-awareness activities. I use the posters for the front-office bulletin board, and I give teachers any information to assist them to become queer friendly in their lesson presentations.

My district mandates that administrators at all schools coordinate cultural-diversity training and staff development every year. I coordinate monthly training sessions to discuss the month's featured group as scheduled in our district's multicultural and diversity calendar. Speaking to issues of diversity has always been easy for me. I am aware, however, that among my not-so-diverse staff there is racism, sexism, religious intolerance, homophobia, and other prejudices. This is where the challenge lies: how to deal with these issues in a setting where some people are not exactly receptive.

STRATEGY 2:
CREATE EVEN THE UNLIKELIEST OF ALLIES THROUGH HONESTY

Recently one of our teachers told a student that he looked gay because of his haircut. The child told his father what the teacher said, who in turn told the principal. The principal confronted the teacher immediately, telling her that she had acted inappropriately. He told her that he had promised the father that he would write her up and put a copy in her personnel file. I was absent that day, but upon my return my principal asked to speak to me. He wanted to know if I thought that he had handled the situation appropriately. I was encouraged to hear what he had done, considering that he is a black man in his sixties who is heterosexual, a Seventh Day Adventist, and a rather traditional person. This was his first time to deal with such a situation, but I believe that because I am out to him, he feels comfortable conferring with me and having me there for support in these situations.

Unfortunately, there is only one other gay educator at my school. We share a special bond, as we both are gay and out, and we often deliberate over how to change attitudes and awareness within our school community. There also are heterosexual teachers who embrace the same ideals that we do, but despite their sensitivity, they do not have the training to address homophobia, and to play a proactive role in homophobic interventions, effectively.

It is essential to have our own organizations for support, but it is necessary to have alliances with heterosexual supporters in order to institute reform of any kind. My experience has shown me that heterosexuals more readily accept issues of importance to gays and lesbians if those issues are presented by another heterosexual. Groups such as the Gay, Lesbian, and Straight Education Network (GLSEN) are perfect examples of how straight and gay educators are forming alliances. I recently have begun to develop strategies to identify other administrators in my district who are gay, lesbian, and queer sensitive, to begin a similar network for all of us.

STRATEGY 3: COORDINATE ANTIHOMOPHOBIA TRAINING

Working with teacher interns and their supervisors is a wonderful way Karen and I (Sharon Murphy) have made a human-educator connection to queerness for our participants. Such training instigates an important dialogue that we hope will continue throughout their careers. Always in the back of our minds, we are thinking of ways to institutionalize our work to inspire their antihomophobia evolution without the constant need for our direct involvement. Therefore, we agreed to form a working group for gay, lesbian, bisexual, and transgender (GLBT) issues in education for a university's teacher-education program.

First, we survey our future participants' attitudes and knowledge regarding queer issues in education. The survey always exposes a lack of understanding of how queer issues are related to the elementary level. The survey also reveals a use of queer language even among our most resistant respondents. Oftentimes the same respondents who say they think that homosexuality is against their religion, or that queer issues could not possibly be relevant at the elementary level, are the same ones who write remarks such as, "I hear students call each other homophobic names." When religious respondents use words like *homophobic,* it opens the door to places of agreement. These teachers desperately want *all* their students to be safe, happy, and to have an equal opportunity to learn and grow in their classroom. Therefore, we use such responses to the survey during our presentations to expose our common ground; it is not a question of *if* queer situations will arise for teacher interns and their supervisors, but, rather, will they be ready to respond appropriately when they do arise. And when they do, such an explanation tends to allay their fears of having to follow what they perceive to be a "gay agenda."

Our working group of presenters has been rather successful in the inclusion of diverse perspectives. Our group consists of (Karen and me), a Cuban immigrant, an older lesbian, and a working-class white lesbian with her heterosexual teenage daughter. We also present diverse speakers who are somehow related to schools so that participants can listen to others who come from a variety of identities, varying in age, school-related role (staff, students, parents), religious background, race/ethnicity, gender, and sexual orientation. Our presenters and speakers provide a richness and depth to our presentations that would be impossible if Karen were to work alone. Karen's variety of identities does not make her "every woman." She is not transgender nor from a working-class background, so she must struggle like everyone else to avoid her role as oppressor.

Despite our representations of a variety of identities, we do not represent all queers and their communities. It is important that we make this distinction clear to our participants. Otherwise, the participants I fear the most are those heterosexuals who say, "Well, I have a gay friend . . ." Often, such a comment reflects a stagnation in what should be their evolving understanding of homophobia. I tell these participants that as a queer person for numerous years, I am still learning more about the complexities of homophobia and our queer communities.

Our use of the training-length version of the film *It's Elementary* (Chasnoff and Cohen 1996), followed with small group discussions, has been well received by our participants. We have utilized the companion manual to the video and have facilitated small-group discussions to address some of the manual's questions. Lecture has its place in these workshops; however, our participants tend to experience the most growth in the small-group interactions. We lead a six-hour training with the teacher interns' supervisors to prepare them to lead these small-group discussions. From the supervisors' feedback after leading the discussion groups, we can gauge what progress was made. In one instance it was very powerful to witness a heterosexual Latina supervisor take a strong stance against homophobia with her interns. She suffered some harsh criticism when the interns accused her of not allowing dissent for religious reasons. Because she disallowed participants to use religious intolerance to cloud the issues of safety and equity, I was reassured that she was prepared to equip the interns with the tools necessary to address homophobia head-on in their own classrooms.

After one of our presentations, I overheard one participant say to another, "I just never really even thought about a black person being gay." Shocking as this comment seemed, it helped us realize that perhaps our most difficult challenge is to speak to the various levels from which the participants come. Raising participants' awareness of general queer issues has been criticized by some participants in their evaluations of our workshops. For example, brainstorming activities to expose people's stereotypes of homosexuality were useful for those who had limited exposure to queer communities. However, other participants wanted to talk about queerness strictly *as it relates to them as educators.*

At the end of the training we allow for a question and answer period, and we provide our resource list, which includes both scholarly and K–12 student literature sources, organizations, websites, and speaker-contact information. We are looking forward to incorporating the work of a local theatrical group consisting of adults and students who role-play queer-themed interactions and provide scripts for others to experiment with on their own.

The intellectual and emotional capacities of participants are not separated, nor is one addressed to the exclusion of the other in our presentations. Queer issues in education should be viewed as a subject worthy of academic inquiry. Workshop participants who deny the worth of spending five hours of their teacher training addressing these issues probably would be unable to pass a test of their knowledge base in this area. We do not allow our participants to dismiss this work as merely "touchy-feely," nor to demote the workshop as less important than other topics. At the same time, queer presenters and speakers who, along with our allies, share publicly their thoughts and feelings, evoke compassion and political motivation from the participants. Our most successful method has been our honesty regarding our experiences, successes, and failures. We always receive numerous compliments afterward, such as "Thank you for sharing your stories," and "Wow, that was really brave!"

STRATEGY 4: CREATE AWARENESS WITHIN YOUR COMMUNITY

I (Karen Glasgow) try to find a connection with each person I meet, as that is how I form relationships. I don't enter these relationships waving my banner of "gayness" any more than I wave my other identities. I try to get people to look at me for the woman I am and all of my endearing qualities, as well as my capabilities and skills as an administrator, and not at the package in which these come. Of course, I know I am usually tried and judged by my size, color, gender, or sexual orientation first. I bring so many issues to the table that I'm a walking buffet! A positive aspect of my membership in so many minority communities is that it affords me a connection with a lot of people who understand discrimination. These people may be suspect of a nonmember who tries to link his/her oppression to theirs. In the following instance I used the umbrella of district policy, along with a black woman's ability to relate to racism and discrimination and the fact that I too am black, as a means of teaching about homophobia.

Last year, after putting up the June Gay and Lesbian Awareness Month bulletin board, I had a black parent stop the principal and me in the parking lot in the morning to tell us how upset she was about the bulletin board. "I just don't think that children need to see that. It gives the wrong message. They may want to try *that* if they see it," she said. During this interaction there was an unspoken code transmitted from this mother to us. She was saying, without speaking aloud, "You're black and therefore you're straight. You understand what I'm saying?" I am out to my principal, and I felt that, because of this, he waited for me to respond. I said, "I'm sorry you feel that way. One poster says only 'Stop Name Calling,' and the other says 'Love Makes a Family,' with photographs of many different kinds of families, including gays and lesbians. Certainly you don't think there's anything wrong with those messages?" She said, "Well, the Bible says that's not right." I wanted to respond with, "I'm a lesbian. Are you saying I'm not right?" However, I have learned to challenge these remarks with facts or by connecting my point to something we hold in common. Remaining professional and willing to respond to homophobic situations in a way that can teach, without becoming confrontational, is one of my biggest challenges. It parallels the challenges I deal with in my everyday life as I am affected by my many identities. I answered, "Well, as you know, we do not teach religion in our public schools. That's for you to do at home. Here at school we send the message to children that name calling is not only mean, but also inappropriate behavior at our school, so it will not be tolerated. We also know that, whether or not you agree with it, some of our staff, students, parents, and administrators may be gay and lesbian, and disrespect of any kind due to any differences will not be tolerated. The district recognizes June as Gay and Lesbian Awareness Month so that our students will learn to respect and appreciate diversity and, therefore, so do we. Besides, I do a bulletin board for Black History Month also, and there are people who work at our school or have children in attendance who don't feel that's right either. My response is the same to them."

This concerned black parent had no answer to that one. I did, however, spot a glimmer of understanding.

CONCLUSION

We accept that our suggestions are reflections of certain freedoms and identities that we may not hold in common with you, the reader. Our work locations might be considered more tolerant than others. In addition, we share a unique life together by blending a variety of identities into an interracial partnership. Regardless of these coincidences, we work tirelessly to transform the work environment in an effort to connect with others, and we believe that we have achieved some success. We have found that by being out, honest, and by challenging the hearts and minds of the individuals and audiences with whom we work, we have witnessed growth. We have felt the joy and rewards of discovering unanticipated allies. We remain in educational settings because we believe that our teaching and leading allow us to best utilize our talents in working toward a more queer-positive environment for our students of today and tomorrow.

REFERENCES

Chasnoff, D., director/producer, and H. Cohen, producer. (1996). *It's elementary: Talking about gay issues in school.* San Francisco: Women's Educational Media. Film.

· 20 ·

LESBIAN MOTHER AND LESBIAN EDUCATOR:
AN INTEGRATIVE VIEW OF AFFIRMING SEXUAL DIVERSITY

Rita M. Marinoble

In the fall of 1998 I was thrilled to learn that the photo-text exhibit "Love Makes a Family: Gay, Lesbian, Bisexual, and Transgender People and Their Families" (see Kaeser, this volume) had arrived at my university campus. As a lesbian mother and an educator, I believe in communicating about the love that exists in so many families with sexual-minority parents. As I hurried to the campus Multicultural Center to experience the exhibit, my excitement was abruptly interrupted at the entryway. The center director had distributed to faculty and staff throughout the campus a flyer advertising the exhibit. One of the copies had been returned and posted, scribbled with an inflammatory comment that said, "This is disgusting! I resent our university exhibiting this crap! I work here and I get this in my mailbox?"

I felt anger and frustration toward the anonymous scribbler, wishing he or she would get to know me and my children and then reconsider this harsh judgment. This experience certainly reawakened me to the reality of how much remains to be done in affirming sexual diversity throughout our communities and institutions.

Affirming diversity has been, for me, both a personal and a professional endeavor. My profession as an educator has included many years as an elementary-school counselor. Having emerged from the struggle of my own coming-out process, I became a strong advocate for affirming sexual diversity in my school district. And then, in tandem with this rewarding professional role, I began a rich and challenging personal journey that continues to transform me—I became a mother. Over a three-year period I adopted two infant girls from Mexico. At this writing my daughters are in kindergarten and third grade. Although I have been single since adopting them, they have become aware of my sexual-minority status through some of my friendships and through various community events in which we participate as a family.

This chapter describes the many dimensions of awareness I have experienced around affirming sexual diversity in elementary schools. In integrating the two perspectives of mother and educator, I seek to frame the affirmation of sexual diversity in a way that transcends some of the usual controversy.

LESBIAN EDUCATOR: REFLECTIONS FROM OUTSIDE THE CLOSET

My earliest thoughts and writings about coming out as a lesbian educator focused on the sense of freedom and personal integration I felt (Marinoble 1990). Later, as I settled down from that emotional high point, I was able to better assess my surroundings. Only then did I perceive the challenges of affirming sexual diversity in the elementary schools where I worked.

The stories presented here are a sampling of incidents from my experiences as an elementary-school counselor from 1987 to 1994 in the San Diego City Schools. They illuminate various aspects of affirming sexual diversity in the elementary school.

Gay and Lesbian Parents

- Two women arrived for the parent-teacher conference. I was there because seven-year-old William was spending a lot of time in my counseling office. One woman introduced herself as William's mother, the other as his aunt. The conference was fairly routine, with the women agreeing to try behavior contracts and positive discipline strategies. When the women left, the teacher turned to me and said in a mocking tone, "That's not his aunt! Those two are lesbians, and that's how they hide it. She pretends to be his aunt." Due to my recent arrival at the school, William's teacher was not aware of my openness as a lesbian. After the conference I mentioned to her that I, too, am lesbian and that I felt saddened by these women's perceived need to conceal the reality of their relationship from the school.
- I strolled through the fifth-grade classroom to see the proverbial science projects. In the reports that accompanied them, students had included an "acknowledgments" section. Trevor's first sentence caught my eye and warmed my heart. He wrote, "I wish to thank my two mothers, who made this project happen." I had seen Trevor and his mothers just a few weeks before at the community's annual Lesbian and Gay Pride Parade. We had ex-

changed smiles and waves, and Trevor seemed thrilled to discover someone from his school at this event.

- A colleague of mine at a nearby elementary school phoned me for advice. Gricelda, age ten, had confided to him that her father was gay and that her friends were making jokes about it. Ted, my colleague, was concerned but felt immobilized by Gricelda's request to maintain confidentiality. She said her father didn't mind her knowing he was gay, but didn't want her talking to others about it. Although not legally bound to confidentiality due to Gricelda's age, Ted did not want to jeopardize his counseling relationship with her.

Parents with a lesbian or gay sexual orientation are present, though often invisible, in every elementary school. William and Trevor represent opposite ends of the spectrum in terms of their mother's openness and comfort levels. In the case of William, I counseled him further and continued to communicate with his mothers. I consistently normalized the women's roles as coparents of William. For example, I referred to William as "your son" in interactions with both women, and I verbally acknowledged each woman as a caring parent. Although they never fully came out to me, I did sense that I had broadened their safety zone somewhat. William, too, seemed more relaxed in his sessions with me, incorporating both women into his drawings.

In contrast to William's situation, Trevor's teacher supported the open acknowledgment of a household headed by two lesbians. As I left the classroom, I commended the fifth-grade teacher for his honoring of Trevor's family, even in this subtle way. Aside from the teacher's understanding, Trevor clearly had the benefit of being in a lesbian family where love existed in a context of openness and pride rather than deception and fear.

The case of Gricelda highlights the dilemma in which so many children of gays and lesbians find themselves. Gricelda experienced some level of openness by her gay parent, yet on another level she carried the shame and fear that apparently still plagued her father. In this instance I assisted Ted in furthering Gricelda's trust and then setting up a meeting with the father. We told him about the teasing and its effect on Gricelda. The tone of this meeting was supportive and nonjudgmental, with the issue framed in the context of the school's policy about students' treatment of one another. In a follow-up phone call I broached the subject of family diversity with Gricelda's father and mentioned to him my own sexual orientation. He confided that he was single and struggling with whether or not to date men in light of his parenting role with Gricelda. I referred him to a gay fathers support group and a family therapist.

The stories of William, Trevor, and Gricelda are examples of gays and lesbians raising families, with all the joys and struggles that accompany that endeavor. Until recently the concept of family was perceived as incompatible with a homosexual orientation. Lesbians and gays were viewed as uninterested and/or inappropriate when it came to raising children. Weston (1991) described the ideological transition of the 1980s and 1990s that has moved gays and lesbians into a much more compatible position with respect to parenthood.

Although misunderstandings still persist, there is a growing recognition of the existence of lesbian and gay families. In my work with parents such as those described here, I have found them to be at many different points in their journeys toward self-acceptance and openness. It has been helpful for me to remember that at each of those points stands a person who deserves respect and affirmation for leadership of a family.

Children with Sexual Orientation Issues

- At recess David rarely was seen playing with other third-grade boys. He hung out by the drinking fountain, occasionally chatted with one or two girls, and sometimes stopped by my office. One day another student told me that derogatory comments were being made about David. Some students were referring to him as "queer," "fagbag," and "the gay guy." When I checked with David, he said he didn't like it, but wasn't sure what to do about it.
- Crystal was twelve and in sixth grade when I met her. One afternoon she stopped by to see me, appearing fidgety and nervous. She showed me a copy of Rita Mae Brown's *Rubyfruit Jungle*. She asked me if I knew about the book and told me she had taken it from a neighbor's house and intended to return it. I replied that I did know about the book and encouraged her to return it to the owner. Crystal said she had a lot of questions about "girls like that." I told her it was okay to ask about what felt important to her, and I suggested there might be someone in her family she also could trust with such questions.

Even education professionals often deny the presence of sexual-orientation issues at the elementary school. A few years ago I submitted a manuscript to *Elementary School Guidance and Counseling*, a journal of the American School Counselor Association. I received a rejection letter, including a suggestion by the editor that confronting these issues was more appropriately a task for secondary schools. The article, later published elsewhere, called for changes in school policy, curriculum, support services, and staff development (Marinoble 1998). Experiences of students like David and Crystal contributed to such changes in my school district.

David eventually confided to me that he did not think he was "like the other guys." Although only in third grade, David seemed to be developing an internal awareness of difference that possibly pointed to an eventual identity as a gay male. I counseled with David about his worthiness of respect from other students, and I initiated remedial action toward the offending students once they were identified. David's mother expressed concern for David's future, but mostly a loving acceptance of her son regardless of the possibility that he had a homosexual orientation. This level of parental acceptance is a blessing that, sadly, many young gays and lesbians do not experience.

David's story, and others like it, mobilized me and some of my colleagues to take action regarding school district policy and staff development efforts. Fortunately, most of our district's board members were open to our concerns and were willing to weather the resistance that came from some parents and school staff. As a result, the San Diego City Schools' nondiscrimination policy was amended to include sexual orientation, and staff training about sexual diversity was mandated for all school principals and other district administrators. These changes, though not entirely eradicating cases like David's, represented significant steps toward affirming sexual diversity in every district school.

In Crystal's case I initially was unsure of her motives for asking me about the book. She may have been simply curious, or she may have begun to experience homosexual feelings that confused her. At her age Crystal was not entirely ready for the content of *Rubyfruit Jungle*, although she may have benefited from a book such as *One Teenager in Ten* (Heron 1983). I perceived a seriousness in Crystal's inquiry that compelled me to follow her case over the next few months. I learned that Crystal's older sister had come out as a lesbian and was experiencing stress at home and at school. As the case developed, I served as a sounding board for Crystal's concerns and also connected her sister with an excellent counselor at her high school.

As a result of this case, the high school counselor and I collaborated the following year to bring some books with positive lesbian/gay themes to our libraries. At the elementary school these included *Is Your Family Like Mine?* (Abramshic 1993), *Gloria Goes to Gay Pride* (Newman 1991), and *How Would You Feel If Your Dad Was Gay?* (Heron 1994). We also initiated a training session to promote curriculum development and supportive services regarding sexual-minority issues at the elementary and secondary schools in our district.

School Staff and Sexual Diversity Issues

- "We saw you on TV last night, Dr. Rita!" I heard this gleeful greeting from a group of first-graders the morning after I had been featured along with my two daughters, then ages one and four, in a news report about lesbian mothers. These young students radiated love and acceptance, oblivious to the controversy my openness stirred among the staff at the school. A few teachers stopped to acknowledge my courage; other staff avoided my gaze at a morning meeting. The next day Elaine, the principal, conferred with me about a parent who had phoned with anxiety over my suitability to be working at the school. Elaine told the parent I was an excellent counselor whom she was grateful to have at her school site.

- Three teachers solemnly entered my office after school. Harriet spoke for the group and said, "We've got a problem with a gay thing and we need your advice." They proceeded to share that each of them was teaching a sibling from a family recently enrolled at our school. The parents were divorced and shared joint custody of the children. The fifth-grader had written as part of a poetry assignment, "My dad is queer and he likes his beer, But I don't care so please don't stare." The boy had read the poem in class, setting off quite an uproar. These teachers not only asked me how to handle the situation, but also expressed their shock that a gay man would have custody of children. This was prior to my adoption of my two children. Harriet commented to me, "Look at you, you're gay but at least you have sense enough not to put that on any children!"

Historically, training programs for teachers and school administrators have failed to address sexual-diversity issues adequately. Sears (1992) presented evidence that eight out of ten preservice teachers held negative attitudes toward homosexuality. These attitudes are rarely challenged or explored in most teacher preparation programs. Teachers, administrators, and other school personnel usually approach these issues from whatever personal perspective they have developed through their life experiences.

Elaine's response to the anxious parent points to the importance of administrative support for sexual diversity in the school setting. Elaine refused to participate in the stereotyping represented by the parent's phone call. Her support as school principal greatly enhanced my continuing effectiveness as an openly lesbian school counselor.

By contrast, Harriet and her colleagues clearly held to the traditional stereotypes about sexual-minority parents. In working with these teachers, I gently challenged their assumptions and attempted to refocus them on the children's needs. I visited the fifth-grade classroom and conducted a session about the many aspects of diversity among people. I incorporated that session into a staff workshop, which I began conducting annually at the school site.

School personnel must understand that doing their best for children includes affirming sexual diversity in the school setting. Some school systems are finding new ways to address this need. For example, Hulse-bosch and Koerner (1997) described an excellent model for training elementary-school teachers about family diversity. Their family diversity workshops include presentation of critical incidents involving sexual-minority parents or students that might occur in a school setting. Teachers respond to the incidents in a small-group discussion format. These and similar training efforts offer hope for improvement in affirming sexual diversity in elementary schools.

LESBIAN MOTHER: REFLECTIONS FROM INSIDE THE HEART

For me there was never a question about whether or not I would become a parent. The only question, as I came to terms with my lesbian identity, was how I would fulfill this lifelong dream. The process led me to the adoption of two babies from Mexico, one in 1990 and the other in 1993. My daughters are now in elementary school, which gives me an alternate, and more personal, vantage point about affirming sexual diversity. We have become one of the diverse families for whom I have advocated during my life as an educator. The thoughts presented here illustrate aspects of my lesbian motherhood in relation to our family's involvement in the elementary school.

Acknowledgment and Validation

In 1994 I moved to northern California to work as a university professor in counselor education. In many ways the elementary school my children attend in Sacramento fails to acknowledge the possibility of the presence of gay or lesbian parents. Registration forms, athletic enrollment cards, and field trip approval slips usually request information in the "Father/Guardian" and "Mother/Guardian" format—a constant reminder that I am outside the norm. It would be much more validating to see "Parent" written twice on the forms, allowing for the fact that two adults of either gender might be involved in a household.

I have not had a partner since adopting my girls, so I am much less visible as a lesbian parent. As a single parent I have commonality with other single parents, but as a lesbian I find it difficult to meet other lesbian or gay parents at the school. Although blended families that have resulted from divorce/remarriage are quite accepted, I see no evidence that a family with two mothers or two fathers openly exists at our school.

Another aspect of our family diversity has resulted from the interracial adoption process. I am white and my daughters are Latina. This difference is more visible and more acknowledged at our school. The school is in a fairly diverse area that includes many Latino families. I am often complimented on my commitment to raising my children with a strong awareness of their Mexican heritage. It is notable that as a family with multiple diversities (interracial, single parent, sexual minority), not all aspects of our diversity are equally affirmed in the school environment.

Ideally, I would place an ad in the school bulletin and organize a support group for sexual-minority parents. Realistically, I do not believe this would be well received by most school staff and the majority of parents. I have found that the schools in Sacramento are, for the most part, much less progressive than the schools where I worked in San Diego in terms of affirming sexual diversity. There seems to be considerably less political activism regarding sexual-minority issues among professional educators in Sacramento.

I have approached our school principal and offered to conduct an information workshop dealing with sexual diversity issues. I was invited to put a proposal together, which I am preparing at this time. I hope to use my position as a former school counselor and a current counselor educator to raise awareness among staff and parents at our school.

Parent Participation at School

As a parent who is highly involved in my children's lives, I find myself participating in a variety of activities at the school. I am, for instance, art docent, field trip driver, and basketball coach. I am often aware of the possible effect of my lesbian identity on my participation at the school. Although my single status makes my orientation less obvious, there have been several opportunities for other parents to learn about it.

My former partner once visited us from out of state on the weekend of a family dinner at the school. I introduced her to others as my former partner. I expect that the more oblivious folks chose to interpret us as business partners, while the more savvy types got some information about me that they may or may not have found within their comfort level.

Many school families have visited us in our home. Prominently displayed in our living room is a framed poster from the 1987 Lesbian/Gay March on Washington, in which I participated. No parent has commented about it, and all have remained involved with me and my family. My younger daughter and I were briefly interviewed once on the television news coverage of a gay/lesbian festival. I have experienced no negative repercussions. I am highly respected as a contributing member of the school community. Still, I expect that my children may be questioned or teased about my sexual orientation as they move into the higher elementary grades.

It is a sad reality that sexual-minority parents must do the most important work of their lives with, at worst, deep fears about openness or, at best, an air of uncertainty about how their families will be perceived at school. Although I am very relaxed about my openness at my workplace, I am a bit more anxious about it at our elementary school. Perhaps I am simply hesitant to have my daughters' innocence shattered by the hurt that can come from the school's failure to affirm this aspect of our diversity as a family.

Children's Understanding of Their Diverse Families

When I adopted my daughters, I was open about my sexual orientation with the social worker who conducted my home study. She was happy to hear of my plans to talk with my children, in age-appropriate ways, about my lesbian identity. Although it is not always easy to decide precisely what is appropriate, I believe I must be honest with my children if I am to expect affirmation from others.

I have found the best approach is to seek every opportunity to teach my daughters about all types of diversity. They may see something on television, meet a new friend, or notice something as we go about the activities of our lives. If there is diversity evident, such as religion, ethnicity, physical challenge, socioeconomic status, or sexual orientation, I make a point of chatting with my children about it in ways that are affirming of difference. Occasionally the topic of who marries whom comes up in conversation, and I hear about their friends who say that "boys marry girls and girls marry boys." I always correct this assumption, using as examples several of the lesbian or gay couples with whom we are acquainted.

I have spoken directly with my older daughter, who is eight at this writing, about what the words *gay* and *lesbian* mean in terms of caring relationship between people. I have used the example of a relationship I had with a woman for a time, which, although it did not evolve to a serious partnership, was a positive experience for my girls. I also have explained to her that many people do not understand or approve of gays or lesbians, mostly because they are different, and sometimes difference frightens people.

These discussions seem most appropriate, given my children's ages. As time goes on, the discussions will mature, with the guiding principle being open, honest communication that affirms the worth of our family and each person in it. Such communication is no different from what is needed in any healthy family and, by extension, in any school that wishes to support children and families.

MOTHER AND EDUCATOR: SEEKING A LENS THAT TRANSCENDS

Affirming sexual diversity in elementary schools amounts to nothing less than a paradigm shift in the school culture. Those engaged in paradigm shifts often must navigate the turbulent waters of resistance and uncertainty. I have found myself in these waters as both mother and educator. Often I have pondered a way to somehow get past the turbulence and enter calmer seas. As I reflect upon the intersection of my experiences as mother and educator, I find three facets of a lens that might help transcend some of the controversy around affirming sexual diversity in elementary schools.

One facet involves hopefulness, which lies at the heart of both parenting and schooling. Educators and parents, when they are functioning responsibly, are motivated by hope for the futures of children. Hope is a powerful and essential virtue, one that looks beyond sexual orientation or any other type of diversity. If elementary schools emphasize the hopefulness of their mission and celebrate the hopefulness of all the families they serve, affirming sexual diversity might be much easier. The focus would be on shared hopes for children rather than on personal differences among parents, staff, or students.

Another facet of the lens involves survival, a very basic goal of humans and their institutions. As an educator in elementary schools, I wanted to give all my students skills for survival. As a parent, I want to teach my children how to survive. Beyond the physical elements, survival entails social and emotional aspects. If elementary schools attend to the social and emotional survival of all their students and families, affirming sexual diversity could become an integral part of that effort. The focus would be on teaching children to value themselves and others in their similarities as well as their differences. This valuing is an important survival skill, not just for individuals, but for the global community as well.

The third facet of the lens involves generativity, a process that is found in both schools and families. At their best, parents and educators desire to leave the world a better place by the knowledge and experiences they impart to children. Like hopefulness and survival, generativity may be viewed as a common thread that unites, rather than separates, people in schools. If schools and families look deeply at the kind of world they wish to pass on to their children, affirming sexual diversity might be less controversial. The focus, I hope, would be on creating a terrain of peaceful coexistence rather than a battleground of differences.

Paradigm shifts take time and effort, and school cultures often are embedded with norms that tenaciously resist change. The challenges of affirming sexual diversity in elementary schools are complex and formidable. I have suggested here that by focusing a lens that attends to hopefulness, survival, and generativity, elementary schools might better respond to those challenges.

As I look through this lens myself, with the eyes of a lesbian who is both mother and educator, I see my own children and the children of others. They are different in many ways, but similar in their humanity and their promise. We must keep them all in focus and teach them well. They are the future.

REFERENCES

Abramshic, L. (1993). *Is your family like mine?* Brooklyn: Open Heart/Open Mind.
Brown, R. M. (1983). *Rubyfruit jungle.* New York: Bantam Books.
Heron, A. (1983). *One teenager in ten: Writings by gay and lesbian youth.* Los Angeles: Alyson.
———. (1994). *How would you feel if your dad was gay?* Los Angeles: Alyson.
Hulsebosch, P., and M. E. Koerner. (1997). You can't be for children and against their families: Family diversity workshops for elementary school teachers. In *Overcoming heterosexism and homophobia: Strategies that work,* ed. J. T. Sears and W. W. Williams. New York: Columbia University Press.
Marinoble, R. (1990). My closet door swings wide: The coming out victories of a professional educator. *Empathy* 2: 6–8.
———. (1998). Homosexuality: A blind spot in the school mirror. *Professional School Counseling* 1(3): 4–7.
Newman, L. (1991). *Gloria goes to gay pride.* Los Angeles: Alyson.
Sears, J. T. (1992). Educators, homosexuality, and homosexual students: Are personal feelings related to professional beliefs? In *Coming out of the classroom closet: Gay and lesbian students, teachers and curricula,* ed. K. M. Harbeck. Binghamton, N.Y.: Harrington Park Press.
Weston, K. (1991). *Families we choose: Lesbians, gays, kinship.* New York: Columbia University Press.

· 21 ·

WHEN *QUEER* AND *TEACHER* MEET

Kate Evans

When I decided I wanted to do a study of queer people who were in the process of becoming certified teachers, I set up an appointment to speak to a supportive teacher education program administrator about how to put out a call for participants. As we talked, he said, "I can see how one of the difficult things will be how to recruit participants." He paused, the word *recruit* hanging in the air. He then joked, "Well, I guess we'd better use a word other then *recruit*," and we both laughed.

The administrator's recognition of how a stereotype about queer people was surfaced in his language creates an interesting point of tension. Researchers often talk about "recruiting" participants, so why was this term potentially problematic in my case, the case of a lesbian researcher? Why might the term *recruiting* sprout a negative connotation when *lesbian* bumps up against *educational researcher*? As Ellen Degeneres parodied in the coming-out episode of her television show, queer people are historically portrayed as deviants who desire to convert as many "normal" people as they can into the "lifestyle" (working to receive multiple notches on their bedposts, or in the case of Ellen, multiple toaster ovens).

In this chapter I explore how historically imbued stereotypes about sexual minorities (such as their desire to "recruit" people) surface in language, and how they provide particular sites of tension for those who are becoming teachers. My hope is that those who work with preservice teachers—be they university faculty, administrators, or mentor teachers—will consider the ways in which their spoken and written curricula might unintentionally evoke these negative discourses. "Speaking correctly" is not my goal; instead I am suggesting a reflective stance in which the multiple effects of language are considered as crucial to attend to in educational endeavors.

An Automatic Barrier

I spoke with three preservice teachers: Ruth and Audre, both self-identified lesbians, and Jonas, a self-identified queer man.[1] Ruth and Jonas attended one teacher education program, and Audre another, both in Washington State. Our conversations took place during a time in which lesbian and gay issues were grabbing headlines. Voters had recently defeated a state initiative that would require employers not to discriminate against employees based on sexual orientation. And in one of the state's largest urban school districts, a controversy was heating up about books in elementary schools that depicted gay families (such as *Daddy's Roommate* and *Heather Has Two Mommies*).

When I first talked to Ruth, she told me that she was out in every aspect of her life—except education. "I can't really pinpoint what the barrier is. But it's an automatic barrier," she said. She was not out to anyone at the university, though she was not at all closeted with her family, or with her close friends who were not connected to the university.

In contrast Jonas told me he was out in his teacher education program, and he expressed interest in attempting to be out as a teacher, but he struggled with what that might look like. And Audre said that when she entered her teacher education program, "I don't think I thought about [being a lesbian and a teacher]. Because I already thought that [teaching] is what I'm going to do, and I'm not going to let my sexuality get in the way of it. Because it's not that big of a deal." Later on in her program, however, Audre found that attempting to set aside her sexuality as not a "big deal" was in conflict with the ways that (homo)sexuality circulates in schools.

Tokens and Confessions at the University

In his first quarter of course work Jonas said the professor in his multicultural education class told the students that they would be addressing gay issues. The professor indicated that she stated this at the outset so that there would be "no surprises" in that "some people don't feel comfortable with [homosexuality]." In response Jonas raised his hand and said, "Excuse me! I just want to say something here right now. *Heterosexuals* really make me nervous. . . . I can deal with it—some of my family—I admit it, most of my family—are heterosexuals. Some of my best friends are heterosexuals. But I just don't know why you people have to talk about it all the time. I have to look at you in the news, I have to look at you in the movies, I have to look at you in the newspapers. It's sickening, okay? Sex, sex, sex, sex, sex.

Hetero sex. . . . So I'm just going to put that out there right now. I'm not going to be happy when we're talking about that stuff."

Jonas reported that most of the students in the class laughed in response to his fake tirade. He characterized his move as a "preemptive strike," a kind of strategic way to out himself in order to call attention to heteronormative statements that express an "opinion" about homosexuals. He emphasized how a well-meaning professor's comments can privilege a heteronormative lens.

Jonas's humorous rant in his multicultural education class highlighted social structures of heteronormativity by playing on the discourses of confession ("I admit it"), tokenism ("Some of my best friends are. . ."), and deviancy ("It's sickening"). He also surfaced the stereotype that being gay means having an agenda ("I don't know why you people have to talk about it all the time") and that gayness is conflated with rampant, uncontrolled sexuality ("Sex, sex, sex, sex, sex").

Jonas's willingness to take the risk of using his identity in an attempt to undercut societal prejudices fits his confrontational and witty personality. Ruth, on the other hand, had a calmer demeanor. She was concerned about how her coming out might label her, might reduce her to a rigid conception based upon a group in which she happened to belong. Ruth often invoked the notion of the "label" as she struggled with the idea of coming out to, or merely discussing anything related to gay issues with, her colleagues, university professors, and mentor teacher.

For example, in one of Ruth's classes the professor showed the film *It's Elementary*. Ruth said that initially, when she learned of her instructor's plans, she was "so excited to see the video. It was like the best day of class. 'Yeah!'" But then when the day came to view the video, Ruth said she felt that "it was almost embarrassing, or I felt like the hot seat. Or I felt like if I speak up I'll be, you know, labeled then. I love to learn about it. I love to have other people learn about it. But for some reason I didn't contribute to the conversation. I just felt, I don't know . . . I felt like I would come out then if I started talking about it."

Merely talking about gay issues might potentially target Ruth as a lesbian. In effect, the "agenda" stereotype silenced her: "It gets a little hard . . . when people are talking about gay issues, . . . [I] don't want to comment too many times, because then people are going to go, 'Well, why do you have such a beef with this?'"

The notion of gays having an agenda was explicitly tied to Jonas by an administrator in his program. The administrator called into question the fact that Jonas's resume included work he had done at a queer youth center. The resume was intended to emphasize any work at all he had done with youth, but the administrator said, according to Jonas, that "when people looked at my resume they might think that I had an agenda. And that, you know, the most important thing that we want to communicate is that we have this commitment to youth and education and not to our own agendas. . . . So he basically made the recommendation that I take it off my [resume]. . . . I basically felt coerced into doing it and I did [remove it]. . . . And I felt really uncomfortable with that, actually."

Even though Jonas had been accepted into his teacher education program as an out gay man, it appears that when his queer identity moved from his position as university student to his position as teacher (and perhaps representative of the university), it formally came into question. Even though Jonas's resume did not say that he was queer, the mere association with the queer community was read as an agenda ("We need to have a commitment to youth, not to our own agendas"). As a result of this interaction, Jonas felt "very distant from the program. It definitely put a hostility there."

Jonas's reflections on his interaction with the administrator speak to the interactive nature of identity negotiation in a public sphere. Jonas considered his work with queer youth as appropriate for a public resume, but the administrator framed it as a personal agenda. Here the construction of *public* and *private* highlights the fact that the delineation between the two is not a given. They are constantly renegotiated, often initiated and controlled by whoever has the most power (Fraser 1995). There are no clean lines between *public* and *private*. Whoever determines what should be public or private is likely to be drawing on the power of conventionalized norms.

LABELS AND DANGER IN THE FIELD

Audre also spoke about the conundrum of agendas and labeling. Referring to the classroom where she was student-teaching, if a child or her mentor teacher said something in the classroom that Audre perceived as homophobic or heteronormative, she wanted to speak up. But she feared being labeled: "When that comes up, I get so scared. And I feel like if I were straight, I wouldn't be so scared. I just feel like it's on my forehead. 'Lezzie.'" Audre spoke to how the label of *lesbian* can overshadow other aspects of herself that she values, such as her kindness, her compassion, and even her political affiliations, such as her feminism: "I feel like I have less validity when I'm talking about feminism because they'll just write me off as this lesbian."

By saying that heterosexual women might have more "validity" when speaking about feminist concerns, Audre emphasizes how heterosexuality is not marked out as difference; instead, heterosexuality, even though highly visible in schools (through wedding rings, heterosexual family pictures on people's desks, "boys'" and "girls'" bathrooms, and assumptions of heterosexuality in the curriculum), is so naturalized that it is paradoxically invisible. This naturalization is why *gay teacher* is "controversial," whereas *heterosexual teacher* is not.

Ruth also talked about the neutral presentation of heterosexuality when she mentioned that her mentor teacher, Missy, "talks about her husband all the time [in class]. [The students] all know him. They call him George. . . . I want the kids to know me, but how much can I tell them . . . about my experiences?" Unlike her mentor teacher's experiences, which are marked as the norm, Ruth's experiences are read as potentially disruptive. For Missy heterosexuality was so naturalized that when she asked Ruth if she had a boyfriend and Ruth said no, Missy assumed that Ruth was single and asked her if she would like to be "set up" with one of George's friends. Missy often encouraged Ruth to socialize with her and George, perhaps as a way to attempt to bond with Ruth. Missy seemed unaware, however, that her approach to inviting Ruth positioned her within a heterosexual framework, which further distanced Ruth.

One particular conversation with Missy stood out in Ruth's mind. Referring to one of their students—who was "effeminate," and who Missy believed might grow up to be gay—Missy told Ruth that she really liked the boy a lot, but that her husband "can't stand to be around him because he's so effeminate." Thus Missy seemed to treat Ruth as a heterosexual insider, someone who might wink and nod in understanding someone's homophobia.

Needless to say, Ruth felt that these interactions required a kind of censoring of herself that took a certain amount of emotional work. Ruth appeared to be willing to exact this emotional toll while student-teaching. However, she considered what such inner work might mean for the future:

> I think when I am a teacher, I can't imagine keeping this up. I can't imagine. I mean, it just wouldn't be a good thing. . . . I have to be more guarded. And—and I'm not used to it. . . . I feel like I have two lives. One is my school life—and one is my life, regular life—outside life, my work life, my home life, my friends, my family. That's what really identifies [me]. And then I basically just step outside myself and go to school. I don't really feel like I'm being honest. Or I'm not really attached to school because I don't identify myself with it. It's just something I'm doing.

QUEER + CHILDREN = DANGER

The tensions, conflicts, and ambiguities of negotiating queer and teacher identities gained in intensity when the participants talked about queer teachers in relationship to their students. Ruth said, "I guess it's, um, the association with kids. . . . I was out [when I worked] at the publishing company, and that was totally fine. . . . Definitely a difference, though. I don't know if I'm quite sure how to pinpoint it."

Ruth, Audre, and Jonas talked about how coming out or staying closeted was not always their personal choice. In part this is because of the complex overlapping between gender and sexuality issues (as with the "effeminate" boy presumed to be gay). Ruth was conscious of feeling "like a big dyke" with her short hair, tall stature, and style of wearing pants and boots in contrast to most of the other women teachers who wore more "feminine" clothing. When Jonas saw a videotape of himself teaching, he became self-conscious about his voice intonations and body movements, which he felt made him appear "faggy." As a result, he dueled internally: "I just had to say to myself, 'There's nothing wrong with being faggy.'" Audre also felt the sting of gender values in relationship to her lesbianism: "One time this kindergartner was sitting on my lap and he saw the hair on my leg and he stood up and was like, 'You have hair on your legs!' And then he looked at my shirt and he jumped up out of my lap and said, 'Oh, you have a man's shirt on! You're a man! You're a man!' I was like—it kind of shook me up. . . . Right before I started student-teaching, I shaved my legs. I don't let my armpits show, and I'm trying to conform."

This concern about physically conforming speaks to the ways in which the teacher education program attempted to control the ways that *queer* and *teacher* might meet, especially when working with children. Even Jonas, who was so spontaneously out at the university, made a distinction between being out, or even being perceived as queer, around children: "Within the context of the faculty, I will be out, no questions asked. . . . I believe the only way we're going to change things is by being out, ultimately. Among my peer group, there's no question. Within the context of, you know, the students—[they] are the only real issue."

As these preservice teachers were (consciously or unconsciously) aware, the mixing of adults with young people surfaces some of the harmful stereotypes that position homosexuality as deviant and homosexuals as a danger to children. Homosexuals are read as being out to "recruit," particularly in a school venue where the most vulnerable of all—the children—reside.

The conflation of *homosexuality* and *danger* became evident when, at one point, Jonas called himself a "safe fag." Because Jonas is committed to disrupting norms, he prefers the more defiant word *fag* over the more staid phrase *gay man*. However, with the adjective *safe*, he forefronted the fact that he has been in a relationship with his boyfriend Rob for ten years. Thus, with *safe fag*, Jonas employed two discourses: one of people who are in established, long-term relationships as somehow safe and stable (who wouldn't sexually harm children), and another of homosexual deviance.

Jonas, then, is "safe unsafe." By coinciding these two discourses, Jonas attempts to create a space for himself in the realm of the heteronormative world of education, while honoring his more personal/political motive of disrupting norms. It's worth noting here that because we cannot step outside of language as we speak, one effect of enlisting stereotypes can be to reinscribe them, while another can be to disrupt them.

In talking about the issue of queer teachers in relationship to students, the three preservice teachers also reflected on themselves as students. They noted that they had never had an out lesbian or gay teacher. However, they recalled teachers who were rumored to be queer, or who got outed in the context of a scandal.

Ruth believed that if she had had an out gay teacher, "it would have given me a frame of reference. I would have known how I responded, or how other people responded. I would have some experience with it. I've never seen it, never known it. I don't know what it would look like. . . . What does a gay teacher—what's that look like? You know? How does that work? . . . I mean because I've never seen it."

Jonas, too, felt that having had a queer teacher would serve as a point of reference: "to have seen a queer teacher function and operate with their students and how the other students, how my peers reacted with that person. . . . It would have been really interesting."

To have had an out, queer teacher working with children with full social, public acknowledgment that the teacher was *not* harming the students might have provided the participants with some fodder against the "danger to children" and agenda discourses. Without that frame of reference they believed they did not have as much of an opportunity to challenge the popularly circulating discourses of homosexuals as sexual deviants who harm children.

Because of these popularly circulating notions of homosexuality-as-deviant, Ruth, Audre, and Jonas feared that coming out (intentionally or not) might create disconnection, dislike, and even anger or fear between them and the students and parents. Ruth said: "My biggest fear is that somebody's going to think negatively about me. And not want me to teach their kids. . . . It'd just break my heart if somebody . . . didn't think I could teach their kids. Or was scared to have their kids around me." Jonas worried that coming out to his students might "interfere with some of their educations . . . I really want to be able to forge healthy relationships with all the kids. And I mean, you know, I want to present myself as a person that's likable to everyone . . . or acceptable to everyone, anyway. . . . That's the one thing that I'm trying to find, is, like, a way that they'll—that they can understand. When I present it to them, it's only going to be presented as a really positive thing."

All three expressed the importance of presenting gayness in a positive light, as an effort to engage a counterdiscourse to the circulating discourses of homosexuality as deviant and dangerous to children. They all expressed hopes to be out one day, queer teachers. Audre believed that if she taught at a liberal, private school she might be able to come out, but her ultimate dream was to be an out lesbian teacher at a public school. Ruth said: "If I was an out teacher . . . maybe they could look back and say, okay, Ms. Rogers was cool. She was an okay person. And she was gay." Perhaps Jonas's sentiments about coming out to students can best be summed up by these words: "I don't want my sexuality to be a barrier. I want it to be a bridge. Because in so many ways it has been a bridge to the world."

BRIDGING THE GAP

The metaphor of the bridge emphasizes how bringing together *queer* and *teacher* is a complicated endeavor. It is public *and* private, in an arena in which public and private are shifting, changing tensions. Because preservice teachers—and, indeed, all learners—enter an arena to engage in the highly interactive processes of learning and teaching, it is worthwhile examining the ways in which our practices might be inscribing *public* and *private* in multiple ways. We can also examine the ways in which we might be promoting rigidity and stereotypes as opposed to looser scripts that allow for less oppressive ways of being (Appiah 1996).

How might we do this? By *being an ally*, and by *representing gayness and critiquing heteronormativity*. While I discuss these following recommendations, I hope they are taken less as "solutions" and more as springboards for ongoing discussion about heteronormativity in educational arenas.

Being an ally. Generally it is much riskier personally and professionally for a queer person to speak out (or come out) than for a straight person to "come out" as gay friendly. Straight people need to educate themselves about how to be an ally because "abstract good will does not make one an ally; allies actively seek out and acquire . . . knowledge" (Narayan 1988, 37). Teacher education program personnel can get familiar with queer issues in education by reading from the growing body of available literature and becoming active in organizations such as GLSEN (the Gay, Lesbian, and Straight Education Network) and PFLAG (Parents and Friends of Lesbians and Gays).

Professors, administrators, and mentor teachers can explicitly present themselves as allies by talking with students and colleagues about these resources. And university administrators can place student teachers only in schools that include sexual orientation in their antidiscrimination policies. If university allies discover local districts without such policies, they can work toward change by speaking at school board meetings and talking with their professional contacts.

Allies can be mindful of not assuming everyone is heterosexual. This is not easy. However, even small verbal cues—such as the use of "partner" instead of "husband/wife"—can signal ally status. Straight allies can also reflect on how they might be implicitly (a wedding band) or explicitly ("my wife") representing their own heterosexual status. This does not mean that such representations are necessarily detrimental, but an ally is conscious of the potential effects of these moves and engages others in discussion about them.

For instance, after sharing a story in which she mentions her male spouse, a professor could then ask her education students how they feel about the fact that she just "came out" to them as heterosexual. She could generate a discussion about why, and to what effects, teachers share their "personal" lives with students and colleagues. Such a discussion prompts a critique of heteronormativity, which I expand upon next.

Representing gayness and critiquing heteronormativity. Including materials about queer issues in teacher education courses is a good start, but it's not enough. Being inclusive is not synonymous with being aware of the ways in which difference is framed. For instance, if an education professor shows *It's Elementary* with the implicit message that "today is gay day," the fact that heterosexuality structures the remaining class sessions goes unstated. Including queer-related articles, films, and guest speakers in the curriculum is important. But so is the critical work of analyzing unspoken assumptions, as in the professor's discussion of "coming out" as heterosexual.

Another way to highlight heteronormativity is to ask preservice teachers to observe in classrooms how "compulsory heterosexuality and homosexual repression" are being produced (Pinar 1994). For instance, do straight teachers mention their spouses in the classroom and in the faculty lounge? Do school memoranda publicly announce a wedding or a new baby of heterosexually married faculty? What family configurations are depicted in school books, songs, and posters? Do teachers assume that girls have "little boyfriends" and vice versa? Discussions about these issues are likely to help educators consider how heteronormativity structures conversations, pedagogies, and institutions.

Projects such as this book can encourage us all to critique dominant discourses. That way we can work on expanding discursive space (Fraser 1997) in which differences have more room to speak. This work is especially significant in educational arenas, for "education always involves a dialogue about who we are" (Bingham 1998, 25).

NOTES

I would like to thank Charles Bingham, Pam Grossman, Diana Hess, Susan Janko, Donna Kerr, Susanne Tobin, and most especially the participants in this study for their feedback, encouragement, and inspiration.

1. I am using the terms that they used for their sexual identity. All names are pseudonyms. Some nonessential details have been changed in order to protect the participants' anonymity.

REFERENCES

Appiah, K. A. (1996). Race, culture, and identity: Misunderstood connections. In *Color conscious: The political morality of race,* ed. K. A. Appiah and A. Gutmann. Princeton, N.J.: Princeton University Press.

Bingham, C. (1998). The poetic theorizing of Langston Hughes: Curriculum and the education of identity. *Journal of Thought* 33(4): 15–26.

Fraser, N. (1995). Politics, culture, and the public sphere: Toward a postmodern conception. In *Social postmodernism: Beyond identity politics,* ed. L. Nicholson and S. Seidman. Cambridge, Mass.: Cambridge University Press.

———. (1997). *Justice interruptus: Critical reflections on the "postsocialist" condition.* New York: Routledge.

Narayan, U. (1988). Working together across difference: Some considerations on emotions and political practice. *Hypatia* 3(2): 30–47.

Pinar, W. (1994). *Autobiography, politics, and sexuality: Essays in curriculum theory, 1972–1992.* New York: P. Lang.

· 22 ·

CONFRONTING HOMOPHOBIA IN A MULTICULTURAL EDUCATION COURSE

Margaret Mulhern and Gregory Martinez

For many teacher educators, inclusion of sexual diversity issues in multicultural education courses has been relatively recent. Armed with few resources except their personal experiences and a sense of social justice, they forge ahead, encouraging their students to embrace another marginalized group. Yet this time the journey is different. The introduction of sexual orientation—immediately laden with morality, religious intolerance, ignorance, and lack of experience—creates unexpected challenges.

Here we share our journey of teaching about sexual diversity issues to undergraduate elementary preservice teachers for over two and a half years. We include both the fear and ignorance we faced (within ourselves and our students) as well as the successful strategies we have used. Margaret taught a cultural diversity course every semester; Greg taught the same course one semester and participated in Margaret's class during other semesters when sexual diversity was the topic of discussion.

As heterosexual partners, we had regular opportunities to reflect on our growing knowledge of homosexuality and to discuss how the topic could best be approached with preservice teachers. Those conversations are recreated in this chapter in the form of a dialogue. We view such dialogue as an essential tool for teacher educators, since it fosters an ongoing shared reflection in which issues are pushed forward while the disappointments and successes of our daily work are processed.

GM: Living in Idaho has provided me an excellent opportunity to observe the social and political forces that have informed the state throughout the eighties and nineties. While being one of the comparatively liberal cities in Idaho, Boise still has little cultural diversity.

As a result, the cultural diversity of students in teacher education classes is limited and Anglo women are in the majority. However, I don't want to negate other kinds of diversity among the students, because it is always helpful to engage in dialogue about sexual orientation and racism from differing viewpoints afforded by age, family structure, and socioeconomic background, especially when diverse racial viewpoints are not available. Different religious perspectives are represented, including a conservative religious element that plays out in class, especially in discussions of sexual diversity. For example, the Mormon church has a strong influence, with its members constituting about one quarter of Boise's population.

MM: It's true that students from Idaho are less diverse than those students I have taught in larger cities. While they are open to discussing diversity issues, it is still a struggle to help them see that we all harbor stereotypes and prejudices learned from our families and society. For instance, some students were reluctant to acknowledge these influences when we discussed ethnic and racial differences, believing that discrimination is something to be studied in history class and is a nonissue in Idaho.

GM: Yes, but an important point can be made about their lack of experience with diversity. If we engage them in critical dialogue, they seem to be willing to shift their viewpoints more easily than people who have developed strong prejudices based on previous experiences. I've found that when students have strong opinions that are not experience based, the possibilities for change are better than one might reasonably expect them to be in such a conservative classroom setting.

MM: One reason I wanted to address sexual orientation for the first time in my teaching was that I thought it would more clearly demonstrate how subtle conditioning influences our beliefs. However, I was nervous about introducing sexual diversity for several reasons. I was not tenured, and being new to the university and to the state of Idaho, I didn't know the context well and I wondered if there would be any repercussions. When I brought up the topic in class, I faced an unexpected obstacle—my own homophobia. I quickly asserted my own heterosexuality, not only to clarify to students that I could not represent the perspectives of gay men and lesbians, but also because I was afraid they would think I was a lesbian who was promoting "an agenda." I was uncomfortable thinking that my students might guess I was a lesbian if I did not tell them otherwise. I had to face the fact that my own homophobia was as hidden to me as white racism was hidden to me and my Anglo students.

GM: I remember you were both surprised and upset when you acknowledged your homophobic feelings. As we talked, we began to recognize the pervasiveness of societal homophobia, and in looking into the research, we found that even those who are gay, lesbian, bisexual, or gay allies have internalized at least some homophobia (Walters and Hayes 1998). The fact that both of us have good friends who are gay and lesbian didn't erase all of our fears, even though it was those relationships and knowledge of the difficulties our friends had faced in coming out that motivated us to address the topic in class.

MM: My feelings surprised me, but I thought it was important that I admitted them. I also began to recognize how little I knew about the experiences of gay and lesbian youth. Despite twenty-three years of formal schooling, I could not recall a teacher even mentioning sexual diversity issues—hardly a common occurrence in our schools (Pohan and Bailey 1997). So I was both shocked and angered by statistics such as the 30 percent suicide rate of gay and lesbian teens and high rates of homelessness and alcohol and drug abuse (Hetrick and Martin 1988). But knowledge of the consequences of homophobia strengthened my resolve to address the topic, despite my ignorance. I strongly felt future teachers needed to be better educated so the discrimination that can lead to destructive behavior would not continue.

GM: So what transpired in the class when you raised these issues?

MM: That first semester we had one of the most heartfelt and open dialogues in the course. In retrospect I think this was possible because I explained to my students that I was a learner as well and felt as uncomfortable as many of them did talking about homosexuality. Bell hooks (1994) writes about the need for teachers to be vulnerable if they want their students to take risks. This allows us to move beyond the position of "all-knowing, silent interrogators" (21). I realized I was less willing to position myself as a learner about topics I know well and about which I have strong opinions.

During our discussion a variety of perspectives were expressed. Some students shared how their opinions about people with a homosexual orientation had changed once they personally interacted with them, a point supported in the research (Nelson and Krieger 1997, Waldo and Kemp 1997). Other students voiced strong opposition to the "lifestyle," since their religion viewed homosexuality as a sin and unnatural. I found it difficult to respond to their comments without coming across as putting down their religious beliefs. This dilemma has remained the most difficult aspect of teaching about this topic for me. What were some dilemmas that you had to face the following semester?

GM: I definitely had some fears going into those lessons, my own lack of experience with gay and lesbian issues being the main one. Like you, I was nervous about how to approach this topic. Even though students read "A Rose for Charlie" (Carnes 1995), the story of the murder of a young gay man in Maine, I knew this was not enough to explore the issues. I began by asking how students felt about what they had read. The literature did help some students gain a new perspective on why this issue needed to be taught in schools. But I also found it difficult to temper emotions that arose when some students perceived others as hostile toward them, due to their opposition of homosexuality. Some students said that they couldn't openly express their beliefs, and this troubled me because until then the class had had an atmosphere of open expression.

MM: I recall discussing that issue with you, and it came up again in my class the following semester.

GM: Going into that first lesson, I knew that valuing students' experiences and perspectives would be crucial, but I also wanted to talk about the "banking" concept of education (Freire 1970), and the negative impact this practice can have on one's ability to be critical. I wanted the students to reflect on their own childhood education, a strong societal influence, and begin to identify the educational impact of excluding certain issues from the curriculum. Through this process I felt that some could gain an initial understanding of why this issue might be difficult to discuss. In other words, I hoped they could see that it is more difficult to talk about subjects that had never been discussed openly before. I wanted them to see that what has traditionally been unspoken has to be spoken before change can occur.

Upon further reflection I became more convinced it was students' lack of experience that limited their ability to feel comfortable discussing homosexuality. This was reinforced on two occasions. The first was reading student journals, in which only a fifth of the class mentioned the sexual orientation lesson and how it had affected them, while a majority wrote about specific racial issues we had discussed. The second occasion was seeing the documentary *It's Elementary: Talking about Gay Issues in School* (Chasnoff and Cohen 1996) the following semester. It became evident to me that I had a lot to learn about presenting these issues in a way that would enhance students' understandings. The openness of the discussion about gay and lesbian issues demonstrated by teachers and students in the video was not representative of the discussion in my class.

MM: We were both grappling with how to present sexual diversity that first year, and it was not until I saw the documentary that I felt I had something substantive to share with my students. Viewing the film, I was impressed not only by the schools and teachers who were teaching queerly, but also by the children. I hadn't realized the amount of negative information and stereotypes they had already absorbed at young ages, primarily from the media. Yet the children were willing to listen to each other and to challenge their teachers and classmates to stop name-calling.

GM: The video modeled the possibilities of classroom instruction I needed to share with our students, and it helped bring my fears to light. I remember I had just read David Sedaris's piece "I Like Guys"(1997) and felt it had so much to offer our students as an inside look through the eyes of a gay child, yet I held back, fearing it might offend. *It's Elementary* allowed me to see how these controversial topics could be introduced to young children and how a piece like Sedaris's could be used with preservice teachers.

Although I was excited about using the documentary, I couldn't help but notice that the filmmakers were documenting practices in New York City, San Francisco, and Madison, Wisconsin, rather than conservative places like Idaho. So a big question was "Can it work anywhere?" Having watched students view the documentary and respond to it since that time, I believe the answer is yes. Most important, I think it helps preservice teachers to focus on the issue of sexual orientation rather than sex, which I noticed was an obstacle for some before watching it. There might have been fewer comments about sex in previous classes if I had shown the documentary. For example, one student had gone as far as suggesting that if we were going to be open to any person's sexual orientation, then we would also have to become more tolerant of pedophiles because they are simply expressing a particular sexual orientation. Thoughts of sexual acts provoke images that some students found difficult to overlook.

MM: The documentary convinced me about the need to address sexual orientation in elementary classrooms and made a difference in my ability to understand what it means to teach queerly. I was able to spend three class periods on the topic, whereas I had allotted it only one class period in previous semesters. Yet a small group of students were strongly opposed to the acceptance and celebration of homosexuality portrayed in sections of the documentary. They explained that their religious views conflicted with the acceptance of homosexuality; however, they were willing to confront stereotypes and name-calling, because it fit their understanding of teaching for social justice. This view was again revealed in some of the responses students anonymously provided me at the end of the unit.

GM: Yes, there were some reservations, but it was heartening that most of the student responses documented their awareness of the need to teach elementary students about sexual orientation issues. Out of the twenty-one responses we received, sixteen students were willing to address the topic, three were still unsure where they stood, and two said they would not teach it to elementary students. Comments from those who supported teaching about gay and lesbian issues included: "I feel that it is appropriate, especially the way we saw it done on the video. Students of gay parents need to see themselves in the classrooms. I would be willing to discuss this as early as first grade." "Any grade is 'old' enough because even five-year-olds are calling each other 'gay' and 'faggot.' I wouldn't teach explicit sex roles and functions, but leave it at a basic humanitarian level." Five students were willing to address stereotypes and name-calling only. For example, one student who expressed her religious objections to homosexuality wrote, "I think the issue should be addressed. It has stretched my beliefs to know that I will teach about stereotypes, but I can't teach acceptance of gay/lesbian lifestyles." The strongest negative comment was: "I would not feel comfortable talking about homosexuality in my classroom with my students because it is something I am totally against. I would feel that if I would talk about this in my class, then I would be promoting it."

MM: It was gratifying to find out that over half of the students had changed their ideas about addressing sexual orientation issues with kids because of the diversity class. But some doubts about my handling of the discussion lingered because a few students commented that I was not considerate of views that differed from my own. These comments concerned me because I had stressed the importance of listening to each other and thinking about the issues; I had also stated that I wasn't expecting everyone to agree with my perspective.

But inside, something didn't feel right. On the one hand, I felt I wasn't practicing what I preached, since I was having a hard time accepting their perspectives and valuing their religious "culture." On the other hand, I supported our college of education statement on the dispositions necessary to be a teacher, which included the acceptance and appreciation of diversity. Certainly a few students were not willing to move beyond tolerance. If I accepted their beliefs, I felt that I was betraying myself as well as the gay and lesbian community. I remember spending a lot of time trying to sort out whether it was possible to disagree with homosexuality and accept a person with a homosexual orientation. It didn't seem possible to me. I asked myself what my role was as a teacher educator. Was it enough to get students to think about the issues? Was it possible to do more? Was I imposing my beliefs on my students? These questions echo again and again as I teach cultural diversity courses.

GM: I believe that gets right to the heart of the issue. By engaging in dialogue with students and reading their reflections, we have seen some who fundamentally disagree with homosexuality and yet take a firm stand against oppression. For students who are having a difficult time getting there, a personal struggle occurs as they reflect on their own complicity in creating an oppressive world for gays and lesbians. It is a necessary step in their growth toward action. It is important for us as educators to remember that this is not a stance against religious beliefs (as some students feel it is), but instead, against any forces that lead us to negate an individual's humanity. It is an issue of social justice.

I can see why you struggled with the fact that some students felt their views were rejected, but you did establish a climate wherein all positions could be expressed. You created the pedagogical space necessary for students to share openly, and you asked their opinions about the unit when it was over. You never know what will transpire when you engage in critical pedagogy.

MM: That's true. I listened to what they had said and changed my approach the following semester. I decided to show selected clips of the *It's Elementary* documentary to allow more time for discussion and a guest speaker, which students had requested. I invited Sarah, the lesbian mother of a six-year-old boy, to speak to my class. Sarah had offered to come to the class when two colleagues and I presented a session on "Sexual Orientation Issues in Teacher Education" as part of the university's Human Rights Week Celebration. Prior to the session I spoke with my colleagues about possible reactions from the conservative community. We were surprised not only by the full-house turnout (approximately sixty people), but by the overwhelmingly positive reaction to the session. It turned into a wonderful dialogue about various issues, including: how a high school teacher could respond to a student's threat to "beat up" another student "because he was gay"; problems teens had faced in high schools where teachers were not openly gay and where no support groups existed; how a major corporation was addressing sexual orientation among employees; children's literature with gay themes; and other topics. We received much thanks for putting on the session.

I share this experience because it had a significant impact on my motivation to continue teaching about sexual diversity. It also pointed out to me that Idahoans were not all as closed-minded as I had initially perceived them. The high school honors students from a small Idaho town who attended the session were willing to challenge their teacher's homophobia, pointing out that it operated similarly to racism. I had renewed hope for change in schools.

That semester I approached the sexual orientation lessons with new confidence. Sarah shared with us her concerns and experiences raising a young child with two mothers. She had chosen to place her son in a small private school where she could be open about being a lesbian and her son's family would be accepted. Since the preservice teachers had already embraced the idea that all students should be accepted and represented at school, this point was significant to them.

GM: Sarah also related her experience of being a guest speaker in a nearby high school in 1991. The presentation was well received by the students; however, due to parent protests following it, the teacher who had invited her was suspended from the school. Because of the negative reactions and media coverage, for the first time Sarah feared for her own, her son's, and her partner's lives.

MM: The reaction to Sarah's presentation was intense, but I'd like to think that we have made progress since the early 1990s. Still, I know there exists a great fear on the part of preservice teachers who feel they will have to confront conservative parents and administrators if they teach about sexual diversity. I hope that by educating our students they will become advocates for their students. I believe the presence of more children of gay and lesbian couples will force schools to be more open to this issue.

In my own classroom Sarah's visit helped me to realize how critical it was to bring in gay and lesbian speakers. This strategy has been found to be effective in positively changing students' attitudes toward homosexuality (Nelson and Krieger 1997). Sarah helped students, some of whom did not know an openly gay person, to see how similar her concerns were to those of other parents. The following semester I invited three additional speakers, one a teacher, as a panel. This class session was opened to other members of the college of education, under the sponsorship of the Equity Committee. I viewed this as a major step forward for the college, since one administrator was initially hesitant to approve the session, fearing that we would be "promoting" homosexuality. Approval of the panel and the administrator's attendance speak to the slowly growing tolerance for gays and lesbians in Idaho.

GM: As slow as change is, I agree with you that we are moving forward. Though some of our students still find it difficult to resolve conflicts with their religious beliefs, the idea that they may need to address sexual orientation in elementary schools as a social justice issue is developing momentum. I know it is important for us to view the resistance we have seen from students and administrators as a driving force to stay on the path of educating preservice teachers about sexual diversity. Even with persistent resistance we have had some success in showing students that transformation is important, especially in terms of how their actions will play out in their future classrooms, and that it can only come about through deep critical reflection and action.

As heterosexuals, we see and feel the marginalization and oppression of gay men and lesbians in our own lives, even though it is not directed toward us. The perpetuation of stereotypes and rigid gender roles, as well as the ongoing violence, repression, and discrimination toward homosexuals, leaves a deep scar on all of us. We "pay the price" of living in a homophobic society (Blumenfeld 1992).

As teacher educators, we feel responsible for educating preservice elementary teachers about how they can help children understand the damaging effects of homophobia and the positive contributions of gays and lesbians. Thus, the decision to include sexual orientation in our multicultural education courses was easy.

However, as this chapter details, teaching queerly required more than a conviction. Confronted with a lack of knowledge and remnants of the homophobia we had grown up with, we had to peel back layers of fear and discomfort and educate ourselves. Reading personal testimonials, literature, and research helped reduce our ignorance and allowed us to empathize further with gays and lesbians. Access to *It's Elementary* opened our eyes to the need to speak the unspoken in elementary classrooms and had a profound impact on our ability to share with our students a vision of possibility. We learned to listen carefully to the voices of our students, to acknowledge their attitudes, and to accept that we would not be able to change all of them. The factors contributing to homophobia are complex and cannot necessarily be resolved in one semester. We also found it vital to debrief and reflect together on our exciting but often challenging attempt to teach queerly.

By far the most effective strategy for increasing our own and our students' understanding was inviting gays and lesbians to the class who could share their experiences as students, parents, and teachers. These interactions helped break the silence and misinformation that create distance between heterosexuals and homosexuals. Success in bridging this distance has reinforced our commitment to confronting homophobia in our multicultural education courses.

REFERENCES

Blumenfeld, W. J. (1992). *Homophobia: How we all pay the price*. Boston: Beacon Press.

Carnes, J. (1995). *Us and them: A history of intolerance in America*. Montgomery, Ala.: Teaching Tolerance.

Chasnoff, D., director/producer, and D. Cohen, producer. (1996). *It's elementary: Talking about gay issues in school*. San Francisco: Women's Educational Media. Film.

Freire, P. (1970). *Pedagogy of the oppressed*. New York: Continuum.

Hetrick, E. S., and A. D. Martin. (1988). The stigmatization of the gay and lesbian adolescent. *Journal of Homosexuality* 15: 19–34.

hooks, b. (1994). *Teaching to transgress: Education as the practice of freedom*. New York: Routledge.

Nelson, E. S., and S. L. Krieger. (1997). Changes in attitudes toward homosexuality in college students: Implementation of a gay men and lesbian peer panel. *Journal of Homosexuality* 32(2): 63–81.

Pohan, C. A., and N. J. Bailey. (1997). Opening the closet: Multiculturalism that is fully inclusive. *Multicultural Education* 5(1): 12–17.

Sedaris, D. (1997). *Naked*. Boston: Little, Brown.

Waldo, C. R., and J. L. Kemp. (1997). Should I come out to my students? An empirical investigation. *Journal of Homosexuality* 34(2): 79–94.

Walters, A. S., and D. M. Hayes. (1998). Homophobia within schools: Challenging the culturally sanctioned dismissal of gay students and colleagues. *Journal of Homosexuality* 35(2): 1–23.

AFTERWORD

Glorianne M. Leck

CONTEXT FOR THESE REMARKS

I dedicate my reading and the perspective of this Afterword to my friend Jama Smith.[1] Jama's circumstances are a symbolic afterword to a long silence about children, sexuality, and schools.

Many of the consequences we see in the lives of racialized, gendered, and sexualized minorities are the results of dogmas that have disallowed teachers, parents, and schools from participating in an open dialogue about children, sexuality, and diversity. The outstanding feature of this book is that it intends to focus our attention on the context and inhibitions of the elementary school. These writers look at the underlying presumptions that are made about children and their social positioning.

Among these researchers, scholars, and artists are those who recognize themselves as "queer." "Queer"-identified people are "beings in the margins" who question and challenge heteronormativity. Being able to look at the world from a "queer" perspective is one of the gifts that can be received from this barrier-breaking anthology, *Queering Elementary Education*.

As I read these chapters, I found myself intrigued and invigorated by the new perspectives and challenges posed by these authors. I want to believe that the "Afterword" I am constructing about this important new anthology may, in fact, foretell of an "Afterword" to a long history of sexual silences in elementary schools.

In my everyday work with teachers and those who aspire to become teachers, I, a queer-identified person, have struggled with the barriers to conversations about children and human sexualities. In and among those challenging and challenged conversations I have argued that "limited public discourse" on social/sexual matters in K–12 schools ought to be exposed for what it is—shortsightedness and arrogance by those who hold positions of privilege and power.

It is unacceptable to deprive children of credible information about their sexuality, about human and social diversity, and about the abuse of power within families, within schools, and within religious group relationships. Such damage can hardly be said to be offset or balanced by the meager compensations of a public social, psychological, medical, and criminological system. Underfunded, entrenched, and often equally dogmatic, public service workers have been expected to deal with the fallout of ignorance and prejudice. In similar straits, the public school has been locked out of an open dialogue or strong-armed into serving up concepts that preserve "intact heterosexist families" and "sweeping religious freedoms."

As I was reading these chapters, I was also going about my own day-to-day dealings with four particular and wonderful young people and the horrible consequences of their history with their "family's parochial/heterosexual values." One of these young people (to whom I dedicated this writing) is twenty-five years old and living/dying with/of AIDS, which he contracted at age seventeen when he ran away from a foster home and sought love and acceptance in sexual intimacies.

Each of the other three is under the age of eighteen and struggling with the violence of adult men in their "homes." The "adult" men in these "homes" cannot tolerate the younger person's social/sexual behaviors. Each of these younger people have run away from their physically and emotionally abusive situations. Two have sought help from their religious leaders, and all four have sought help from social service professionals. All have been returned to their abusive families by social service agencies and clergy who lacked the resources, the personnel, and/or an advocacy perspective. All have returned to their hell with no new coping skills, no greater sense of protective "care," and with very little, if any, new information. Certainly none have learned anything about dealing with the marginalization of their sexual socialization.

These young people have spoken of their need in their *early* lives to be taught that it was okay to be who they were and what they were. All have indicated that there were questions they wanted to ask, but were prohibited from asking at school. What if some of their teachers had taken the time to interrupt the heterosexist discourse, the abusive name-calling by the peer group, or in some way to have broken through the isolation these young children were feeling?

What if the teachers of the young people with whom I am associated had examined the examples that they used in their selection of music or more carefully considered the wording of a math story problem? How might we re-examine the way we approach the teaching of science? What information are we selecting out and putting in with our choice of literature? Some of the authors in this book help us look at these questions.

Schools have maintained, by social custom and with reinforcement from the law, the promotion of the heterosexual family as predominant, and therefore as the essence of normal. From having been presumed to be "normal," heterosexual behavior has gained status as the right, good, and ideal lifestyle. Lesbian, gay, transgender, bisexual, queer, and questioning youth have rarely been able to fend off the damage of those enforcements, those reinforcements, the silences, and the taunts by the "authorized" heterosexual dogma.

REFLECTIONS ON QUEER THEORY: A NOTE TO THE READERS

Queer theory sometimes stands people off by both its discourse and its demand that we think through and pay attention to new words and difficult deconstructions of meaning. It would be very unfortunate to avoid reading queer theory because it is strange (queer). Queer theory offers a perspective that challenges its reader to reconsider what we have come to know and easily access as "identity" discourse. Popular research, for the most part, has not challenged the heterosexual "we" and the homosexual "they," the patriarchal "he" and the feminist "she."

Until we examine lesbian, gay, and sexual-minority issues as byproducts of oppression by a deeper social, linguistic construction, we are doomed to work within a contest of war by identity groups and types. Queer theorists can actually provide us with different ways of seeing our lives and the worlds within which we operate. It seems to me that it would be a mistake to enter the conversation about schools and sexual politics not knowing that there is much more to it than a polarization over "moral" issues, human rights concerns, identity types, and issues of safety for our children. Readers of this book are encouraged to work with the authors in attempting to overcome some of the "antidifferent" socialization that can prevent one's understanding of her or his own socialization and related social/sexual arrangements.

OPENINGS FOR OUR WORK

The articles in this book are arranged in just such a way that they offer us some very astute "queer" observations while, almost simultaneously, providing us with very practical suggestions. We can learn about moving, challenging, and comforting those living in the interfaces of polarized sexual politics in schools. That is an incredible accomplishment.

We have been invited to look into the face of childhood, parenting, and teaching, and into the terrors, the safe spaces, and the comforts that can free, redress, and/or coconstruct sexual/social interactions. This book moves us forward into new opportunities for dialogue that can dramatically, dynamically, and subtly open vital new possibilities for more reflective and just practices of schooling.

IMPLICATIONS FOR RESEARCH

This anthology poses and invites research questions about the extent to which modern societies have cemented our ideas of child development around the behaviors that have been self-promoted and assumed to be "normal." Related concerns can certainly be raised about whether and how we can extract ourselves from such entrenched beliefs. These author/scholar/thinkers have asked us to undo and examine (deconstruct) the assumptions we have been taught about polarization and the processes of "normalization" of sexual identities.

Presumed heterosexuality, when put forth as the norm for social and sexual behavior and of social and sexual identity, is an artifact of oppression that truly invites these authors and other researchers to do a scholarly "queering." Claiming a position as "queer" is taking advantage of and creating social benefits of being positioned as "other." When we see ourselves as, and when we are seen as, "queer," we can choose to suspend ourselves from full immersion in the presumed consensus of social "reality."

We are motivated by these readings to examine the supposed "Truth" that we see being placed before young children. We are asked to challenge the presumption that all people are heterosexually predispositioned. A path has been opened for the exploration of toys, music, games, and classroom examples of how we learn that we are teaching that there are "right" and "wrong" sexual, racial, and cultural beings.

Much of the literature and research on lesbian, gay, bisexual, transgender, questioning, and queer youth has been testimonial to the fallout from oppression by heterosexualized silences. What has not been as vigorously explored are the underlying patterns, commonalities of, and promotions of the social exclusion of those who are different from the concept of "normal" or the construct of "good." I would suggest that enough has not been done to speak of the risks and costs of extinction of unique and diverse individuals, and of certain cultural characteristics within our human symbiosis.

Perhaps we are, as a human group, just beginning to see how dominant human groups use and abuse resources and power to destroy "other" species, individuals, and environments that serve as contrasts to the enforced and privileged ideal types. Individuals have long pondered, and artists and writers have shared their perspectives on, war and domination by political and religious groups and tyrants. Consideration of patriarchal dominance and the subjugation of women and children is beginning to hit home. There is an ongoing struggle to examine and reconsider the motives for the preservation of contructions of "race." We are beginning to speak out on the deliberate persecution of nonheterosexuals and people who are differently abled. In light of these reconsiderations of power and oppression it may be time that we reconsider what constitutes "appropriate" adult control over the spiritual and intellectual lives of children.

As we study constructions of power, we can see the often defensive, reactionary, and diverse responses of those who are in positions of power. We soon discover that privilege positions individuals as the "good," the "normal," the "God blessed," and the "deserving" progeny. As we further our studies of human social constructions and the promotion of competition between and among biological species, geographical localities, "races," genders, classes, religions, and ethnicities, we are more likely to become aware of interconnections among the resisting groups. Shared resistance by oppressed groups may open greater dialogue about, among other things, the motives for privatization of schooling and the justifications being presented for the use of child labor in mobile corporate manufacturing.

Researchers need to continue to look at the redirection and reinvestment by particular groups in efforts to preserve their privacy through their power and privilege. The study of how heterosexual norms are privileged in school discourse is a fertile ground for greater understanding of the distribution, use, and abuse of power and privilege.

WORKING ON THE UNDERLYING ASSUMPTIONS

In the instance of this assembly of articles, the authors collectively assist us in challenging the overriding presumption and use of institutionalized dualistic (oppositional) logic. Dualistic thinking has long served as the ideal or as the supposed best framework for European-based linguistic and social organization. As such, teaching children to think in terms of reverse-valued opposites has been a mainstay of teaching.

Children who come to equate differences with opposites are bound to feel a need to side with one or the other of the features. We need to follow this opening into understanding with our recognition that deep structure must be analyzed before we misappropriate our time treating the symptoms (outcomes) of a detrimental way of organizing our thinking. I can't begin to say how important it is that we examine the way we teach children how to learn.

Sears, along with many of the other contributors, makes clear the importance of not constructing and defining *queer* within the dualistic rendering of "normal" and "abnormal" notions of sexual/social development. Authors here make a strong case for looking at lesbian and gay oppression as a way of moving to "queer" discourse. These authors take us to sites, which when approached by educators and parents who are well intentioned but who have not actively deconstructed the sexual indoctrinations of their own childhoods, are likely to disclose grand episodes of social injustice and great opportunities for improved practice.

Just as canaries are kept in coal mines to foretell disasters, children's lives in schools tell us of the risks, injustices, and calamities within our cultural confines. Elementary schools and the educational practices used on children provide the texts in which these authors have located occasions and practices that reveal existing and impending tragedies. We learn through these readings to reconsider the acts through which children are taught and the organizational structures that surround the teacher and the student. We are asked to challenge ourselves to critically assess embedded meanings as they construct even our simplest classroom examples.

NOTES

Through the work of the authors of this book an important dialogue has begun. I would like to thank the many courageous teachers, parents, and youth who identify as lesbian, gay, bisexual, transgender, questioning, and/or queer who have come forward to make this dialogue possible. Additionally, I want to thank the writers who, like Jonathan G. Silin in his important book *Sex, Death, and the Education of Children: Our Passion for Ignorance in the Age of AIDS* (New York: Teachers College Press, 1995), have broken the silence.

1. Jama is a young, beautiful dancer and articulate spokesman for the needs of youth who have been racialized and sexualized into minority status and political oppressions. He carries the vivid consequences of the privatization of "heterosexual family values," and inadequate response from social service programs.

ANNOTATED BIBLIOGRAPHY OF RESOURCES

William J. Letts IV, with assistance from Betsy Cahill, Kate Evans, Rita Kissen, Rita Marinoble, and Rachel Theilheimer

CHILDREN'S BOOKS INVOLVING GAY/LESBIAN CONTENT

Alden, J. (1992). *A boy's best friend*. Los Angeles: Alyson. This is a book about a young asthmatic boy who wants only a dog for his birthday, and the tale that ensues.

Kennedy, J. (1998). *Lucy goes to the country*. Los Angeles: Alyson. The tale of a cat who travels to the countryside for a weekend with her two "Big Guys."

Newman, L. (1991a). *Belinda's bouquet*. Boston: Alyson. The story of a girl who comes to terms with the beauty of her own body, thanks to the advice of a friend's lesbian mom.

———. (1991b). *Gloria goes to gay pride*. Boston: Alyson. Tells of Gloria's fun-filled adventures with her two moms at Gay Pride Day.

Valentine, J. (1991). *The duke who outlawed jellybeans and other stories*. Boston: Alyson. Five original fairy tales about kids with gay and lesbian parents.

———. (1992). *The day they put a tax on rainbows and other stories*. Los Angeles: Alyson. Three more fairy tales featuring the adventures of more kids with lesbian and gay parents.

Vigna, J. (1995). *My two uncles*. Morton Grove, Ill.: Albert Whitman. When her grandfather refuses to invite her uncle's partner to a family celebration, a confused young girl talks with her father to try to understand the grandfather's biased attitudes.

Woodson, J. (1995). *From the notebooks of Melanin Sun*. New York: Scholastic. Thirteen-year-old Melanin has to decide what to do when his mother informs him that she's gay.

CHILDREN'S BOOKS ABOUT HIV/AIDS

Alexander, E., S. Rudin, and P. Sejkora. (1996). *My dad has HIV.* Minneapolis: Fairview Press. Seven-year-old Lindsey's journey of coming to understand what HIV is, told in a clear, first-person narrative.

Atkins, J. (1999). *A name on the quilt: A story of remembrance.* New York: Atheneum Books. A story of how Lauren and her family choose to remember Uncle Ron.

Fassler, D., and K. McQueen. (1990). *What's a virus anyway? The kids' book about AIDS.* Burlington, Vt.: Waterfront Books. Explains viruses, and specifically HIV, from a kid's perspective.

Forbes, A. (1996). *When someone you know has AIDS.* New York: PowerKids Press. This is one of several books for young children dealing with various aspects of HIV infection and AIDS. Other books from the AIDS Awareness Library, all by Anna Forbes, include: *What you can do about AIDS*; *Heroes against AIDS*; *Where did AIDS come from?*; *Kids with AIDS*; *Living in a world with AIDS*; and *Myths and facts about AIDS.*

Jordan, M. K. (1989). *Losing Uncle Tim.* Morton Grove, Ill.: Albert Whitman. The story of a young boy coming to terms with his uncle's having AIDS, and eventually his uncle's death from it.

Newman, L. (1995). *Too far away to touch.* New York: Clarion Books. How Zoe learns about death, and also about love, from an uncle who has AIDS.

Schwartz, L. (1997). *AIDS: First facts for kids.* Santa Barbara, Calif.: Learning Works. Aimed at students in grades 4–6, this book explores more than thirty questions that kids might have about HIV and AIDS.

Wiener, L. S., A. Best, and P. A. Pizzo, ed. (1994). *Be a friend: Children who live with HIV speak.* Morton Grove, Ill.: Albert Whitman. Through words and pictures, children living with HIV and AIDS describe their lives.

Wolf, B. (1997). *HIV positive.* New York: Dutton Children's Books. Chronicles the life of Sara, a twenty-nine-year-old mother of two, who is HIV positive and develops AIDS.

CHILDREN'S BOOKS ABOUT SEXUALITY AND SEXUAL HEALTH

Harris, R. H. (1994). *It's perfectly normal: Changing bodies, growing up, sex, and sexual health.* Cambridge, Mass.: Candlewick Press. Provides accurate, unbiased answers to virtually every question—from conception to puberty to AIDS to birth control—that young people might ask about their bodies and sexual health.

CHILDREN'S BOOKS ABOUT GENDER AND (NONTRADITIONAL) GENDER SOCIALIZATION

Caple, K. (1994). *The wimp.* Boston: Houghton Mifflin. Describes how Arnold, the class wimp, eventually stands up for himself.
De Paola, T. (1979). *Oliver Button is a sissy.* New York: Harcourt, Brace, Janovich. Despite the name-calling and slurs, Oliver fools them all by excelling at his own special talent.

CHILDREN'S BOOKS ABOUT DIVERSE TYPES OF FAMILIES

Abramshic, L. (1993). *Is your family like mine?* Brooklyn: Open Heart/Open Mind. Examines a variety of constructions of families.
Bösche, S. (1983). *Jenny lives with Eric and Martin.* London: Gay Men's Press. This is a story about a five-year-old girl who lives with her father and his boyfriend and how they spend their weekend.
Brown, F. (1991). *The generous Jefferson Bartleby Jones.* Los Angeles: Alyson. The story of a boy who is lucky to have two dads.
Elwin, R., and M. Paulse. (1990). *Asha's mums.* Toronto: Women's Press. A young girl has to educate her teacher about her life with two mothers.
Greenberg, K. E. (1996). *Zack's story: Growing up with same sex parents.* Minneapolis: Lerner. This is the story of Zack growing up in a family with his mother and her partner Margie.
Heron, A., and M. Maran. (1991). *How would you feel if your dad was gay?* Boston: Alyson. A "lifeline" for kids who come from families headed by gay men and lesbians.
Jenness, A. (1990). *Families: A celebration of diversity, commitment, and love.* Boston: Houghton Mifflin. Seventeen children and their parents discuss the challenges and joys of family life.
Newman, L. (1989). *Heather has two mommies.* Northhampton, Mass.: In Other Words. The story of Heather, starting before her birth, and her life with her two mommies.
Skutch, R. (1995). *Who's in a family?* Berkeley, Calif.: Tricycle Press. Examines a variety of configurations of families, all with one thing in common—they contain the people you love the most!

Valentine, J. (1993). *The daddy machine.* Los Angeles: Alyson. Two kids with lesbian mothers dream about what it would be like to have a daddy—so they create a "daddy machine"!

————. (1994). *One dad, two dads, brown dad, blue dads!* Boston: Alyson. Looks at similarities and differences between dads, tackling stereotypes about gay parenthood.

Willhoite, M. (1990). *Daddy's roommate.* Los Angeles: Alyson. A story about Nick's life with his dad and his dad's lover, Frank.

————. (1996). *Daddy's wedding.* Los Angeles: Alyson. Nick is best man at the wedding of his father to his longtime partner Frank.

CHAPTER BOOKS

Bauer, M. D., ed. (1994). *Am I blue? Coming out from the silence.* New York: HarperCollins. Short stories by noted authors about growing up lesbian or gay, or with lesbian or gay parents.

Chase, C., ed. (1998). *Queer 13: Lesbian and gay writers recall seventh grade.* Philadelphia: William Morrow. These original essays take us back to the homerooms and hallways of our youth, from obsessive crushes to pummelings after school.

Garden, N. (1982). *Annie on my mind.* New York: Farrar, Straus, and Giroux. Liz puts aside her feelings for Annie after the disaster at school, but eventually she allows her love to win out over the ignorance of others.

Greene, B. (1992). *The drowning of Stephan Jones.* New York: Bantam Doubleday Dell Books for Young Readers. Carla, drawn in as a silent partner in her boyfriend's campaign of hate against a gay couple, must decide whose side she's on and what she stands for.

Homes, A. M. (1989). *Jack.* New York: Vintage Books. This story, of a teenager who wants nothing more than to be normal, details Jack's struggle to deal with having a gay father.

Salat, C. (1993). *Living in secret.* New York: Bantam Books. A fictional chapter book that describes how a young girl runs away to live with her mother and her mom's female partner "in secret."

Singer, B., ed. (1994). *Growing up gay/Growing up lesbian.* New York: New Press. A literary anthology with nearly fifty coming-of-age stories ranging from Radclyffe Hall and Walt Whitman to Dorothy Allison and James Baldwin.

Van Dijk, L. (1995). *Damned strong love: The true story of Willi G. and Stefan K.: A novel.* New York: Henry Holt. A fictionalized true story of a teen imprisoned by the Nazis during World War II because he wrote a love letter to his boyfriend.

BOOKS ABOUT GAY, LESBIAN, BISEXUAL, AND QUEER YOUTH

Bernstein, R., and S. Silberman. (1996). *Generation Q.* Boston: Alyson. A cacophony of queer voices all born post-Stonewall speak to the diversity of youth experiences and identities.

Besner, H. F., and C. I. Spungin. (1995). *Gay and lesbian students: Understanding their needs.* Washington, D.C.: Taylor and Francis. Deals with issues of homosexuality and education, especially as they relate to gay and lesbian students.

Brimmer, L. D. (1995). *Being different: Lambda youths speak out.* Danbury, Conn.: Franklin Watts. Interviews with lesbian, gay, and bisexual youths about teenage homosexuality.

Cantwell, M. A. (1996). *Homosexuality: The secret a child dare not tell.* San Rafael, Calif.: Rafael Press. Sheds light on the feelings and insights that gay people experienced as children.

DeCrescenzo, T., ed. (1994). *Helping gay and lesbian youth: New policies, new programs, new practice.* Binghamton: Haworth Press. A book for educators and social service providers, this volume offers rich insights into the problems attendant on growing up different.

Harris, M. B. (1997). *School experiences of gay and lesbian youth: The invisible minority.* New York: Haworth Press. Chapters look at the ways in which the school-based lives of lesbian, gay, and bisexual youths are fraught with dangers, denials, and silences.

Herdt, G., and A. Boxer. (1996). *Children of horizons: How gay and lesbian teens are leading a new way out of the closet.* Boston: Beacon Press. This book explores the life experiences and debunks myths about lesbian and gay teens.

Hunter, S., ed. (1998). *Lesbian, gay, and bisexual youth and adults.* Thousand Oaks, Calif.: Sage. A helpful overview of issues facing queer youth across the human life span.

Irvine, J., ed. (1994). *Sexual cultures and the construction of adolescent identity.* Philadelphia: Temple University Press. This edited volume examines a range of identity issues that arise in a variety of venues, from theories and cultures to texts and conversations.

Kay, P., A. Estapa, and A. Dessetta, ed. (1996). *Out with it: Gay and straight teens write about homosexuality.* New York: Youth Communications. An excellent resource for educators searching for teen perspectives to use in classroom instruction. Includes teacher resource section.

Mallon, G. P. (1998). *We don't exactly get the welcome wagon: The experiences of gay and lesbian adolescents in the child welfare system.* New York: Columbia University Press. This volume consists of narratives of the marginality of gay and lesbian youths trying to find the "right fit" as they navigate the child welfare experience.

Mastoon, A. (1997). *The shared heart.* New York: Morrow. Forty black-and-white photographs accompanied by narratives bring a personal dimension to queer youth.

Owens, R. E., Jr. (1998). *Queer kids: The challenges and promises for lesbian, gay, and bisexual youth.* Binghamton, N.Y.: Harrington Park Press. Helps the average straight (or queer) adult see the world from a queer kid's point of view.

Pallotta-Chiarolli, M., ed. (1998). *Girls' talk: Young women speak their hearts and minds.* Sydney: Finch. Girls and young women speak out on a variety of topics, including bodies, health, love, sex, prejudice, and discrimination.

Reed, R. (1997). *Growing up gay: The sorrows and joys of gay and lesbian adolescence.* Illustrated with beautiful photographs, this book follows the lives of two gay teens, Amy and Jamie, showing the challenges and triumphs they experience.

Renafedi, G., ed. (1994). *Death by denial.* Boston: Alyson. A collection of empirical studies about suicide among queer youth edited by an authority on the topic.

Ryan, C., and D. Futterman. (1998). *Lesbian and gay youth: Care and counseling.* New York: Columbia University Press. A comprehensive guide to the bodily and mental health of LGBT youth.

Savin-Williams, R. C. (1990). *Gay and lesbian youth: Expressions of identity.* New York: Hemisphere. Reports about a longitudinal study of the experiences that gay and lesbian youth had growing up.

———. (1998). *". . . And then I became gay": Young men's stories.* New York: Routledge. Examines the personal narratives of gay and bisexual men, describing childhood memories, feelings, and attractions.

Schneider, M. S., ed. (1997). *Pride and prejudice: Working with lesbian, gay, and bisexual youth.* Toronto: Central Toronto Youth Services. A comprehensive resource for educators and other professionals who work with adolescents of all kinds.

Sears, J. T. (1991). *Growing up gay in the south.* New York: Haworth Press. A sociological narrative of thirty-six young adults who live in the nation's most conservative region.

Unks, G., ed. (1995). *The gay teen: Educational practice and theory for lesbian, gay, and bisexual adolescents.* New York: Routledge. Written by and for educators, these essays explore gay, lesbian, and bisexual adolescent sexuality from both practical and theoretical perspectives.

BOOKS ABOUT TEACHERS AND SCHOOLS

Harbeck, K. M., ed. (1992). *Coming out of the classroom closet: Gay and lesbian students, teachers and curricula.* Binghamton, N.Y.: Harrington Park Press. A collection of essays that examine a range of issues, such as homophobia, textbooks, curricula, and personal development, that relate to being gay and lesbian in school.

Harbeck, K. (1997). *A matter of justice and compassion.* Boston: Amethyst. A noted educator and legal scholar explores how to address the needs of lesbian, gay, and bisexual youth.

Herek, G., ed. (1998). *Stigma and sexual orientation.* Thousand Oaks, Calif.: Sage. These essays explore the nature of prejudice against lesbians, gay men, and bisexuals, and discuss educational interventions.

Jennings, K., ed. (1994). *One teacher in ten: Gay and lesbian educators tell their stories.* Boston: Alyson. Teachers talk about the difficulties and the joys of being gay and lesbian educators.

Khayatt, D. (1992). *Lesbian teachers: An invisible presence.* Albany: State University of New York Press.

Kissen, R. (1996). *The last closet: The real lives of lesbian and gay teachers.* Portsmouth, N.H.: Heinemann. Stories from educators often caught between their desire for authenticity and their need for safety.

Lipkin, A. (1999). *Understanding homosexuality: Staff development and student development.* Boulder, Colo.: Westview Press. A synoptic book on homosexuality for educators written by a veteran gay teacher.

Woog, D. (1995). *School's out: The impact of gay and lesbian issues on America's Schools.* Los Angeles: Alyson. Interviews with gay and straight educators, students, and parents reveal the myriad of ways in which lesbian and gay issues are already present in our schools.

BOOKS ABOUT CURRICULA, SEXUALITIES, AND SCHOOLS

Beckett, L., ed. (1998). *Everyone is special: A handbook for teachers on sexuality education.* Sandgate, Australia: Association of Women Educators. A collection of essays, aimed specifically at teachers, that examine voice, visibility, and inclusion as they relate to issues of sexuality in schools.

Epstein, D., ed. (1994). *Challenging lesbian and gay inequalities in education.* Buckingham: Open University Press. Demonstrates the implication of sexuality in all aspects of education from a variety of viewpoints.

Epstein, D., and R. Johnson. (1998). *Schooling sexualities.* Buckingham: Open University Press. This book examines the connections and contradictions between nations and schools, and intersections of issues dealing with sexualities and schooling.

Laskey, L., and C. Beavis, ed. (1996). *Schooling and sexualities: Teaching for a positive sexuality.* Geelong, Australia: Deakin Centre for Education and Change. These essays examine the social construction of sexuality, teaching about sexuality, teaching against homophobia, and violence, harassment, and abuse.

Sears, J. T., ed. (1992). *Sexuality and the curriculum.* New York: Teachers College Press. Thirteen essayists challenge assumptions about sexuality education with implications for curriculum develoment and teacher education.

Sears, J. T., and W. Williams, eds. (1997). *Overcoming heterosexism and homophobia: Strategies that work!* New York: Columbia University Press. GLSEN-award-winning anthology of the theory and practice of reducing prejudices within specific populations and locations, including elementary schools.

Silin, J. G. (1995). *Sex, death, and the education of children: Our passion for ignorance in the age of AIDS.* New York: Teachers College Press. This groundbreaking book interrogates how we culture ignorance in children and imagines different ways to interact with and respond to children.

Trudell, B. (1993). *Doing sex education.* New York: Routledge. This well-written ethnography examines the perils of teaching about sexuality in a ninth-grade classroom.

Walling, D., ed. (1996). *Open lives, safe schools: Addressing gay and lesbian issues in education.* Bloomington, Ind.: Phi Delta Kappa Educational Foundation. Offers a comprehensive overview of gay and lesbian issues, such as curricular matters and the needs of youth, parents, and families, in public schools in the United States.

RESOURCES FOR AND ABOUT FAMILIES

Alternative Family Magazine is an international publication for lesbian and gay parents and their children. Contact them at P. O. Box 7179, Van Nuys, CA 91409, 818-909-0314, <http://www.altfammag.com>.

COLAGE: Children of Lesbians and Gays Everywhere can be reached at 2300 Market Street, Box 165, San Francisco, CA 94114, 415–861–KIDS, <http://www.colage.org>.

Family Diversity Projects is a nonprofit educational organization that creates exhibits and books and distributes exhibits nationwide. The four exhibits they have produced are: *Love makes a family: Lesbian, gay, bisexual, and transgender people and their families; Of many colors: Portraits of multiracial families; In our family: Portraits of all kinds of families;* and *Nothing to hide: Mental illness in the family.* There are also books for *Love makes a family* and *Of many colors,* published by the University of Massachusetts Press. Contact them at P. O. Box 1209, Amherst, MA 01004–1209, e-mail at famphoto@aol.com, <http://www.familydiv.org>.

Family Pride Coalition (formerly Gay and Lesbian Parents Coalition International) provides information, support, and advocacy, and publishes a newsletter. Reach them at P. O. Box 34337, San Diego, CA 92163, 619-296-0199, <http://www.familypride.org>.

Family Q, a resource for families headed by gays and lesbians, can be accessed at <http://www.studio8prod.com/familtq>.

Human Rights Campaign is a political organization fighting for equal rights for lesbians and gays. Contact them at 1001 14th St., NW, Suite 200, Washington, DC 20005, 202-368-4160, <http://www.hrc.org>.

Lesbian and Gay Parents Association, 6705 California St. #1, San Francisco, CA 94121. 415-387-9886.

Lewin, E. (1993). *Lesbian mothers: Accounts of gender in American culture.* Ithaca, N.Y.: Cornell University Press. Lesbian mothers tell in their own words their stories about relationships, children, child–care arrangements, and custody, among other topics.

My Child Is Gay! Now What Do I Do? addresses parents' questions and concerns with sensitivity and honesty. <http://www.pe.net/~bidstrup/parents.htm>.

Parents, Families and Friends of Lesbians and Gays (P-FLAG), with numerous local chapters, offers speakers, publications, and support groups. Contact them at 1101 14th St., NW, Suite 1030, Washington, DC 20005, 202-638-4200, <http://www.pflag.org>.

Queer Resources Directory contains tons of information, including sites on queer youth, health, history, and much more. <http://www.qrd.org/QRD/www>.

Rafkin, L., ed. (1990). *Different mothers: Sons and daughters of lesbians talk about their lives.* Pittsburgh: Cleis Press. Case studies of children and their lesbian mothers.

RESOURCES FOR LESBIAN AND GAY YOUTH

AllTogether.com: A Place to Explore Sexuality and Coming Out offers diverse voices to introduce a wide range of audiences to the GLBT community. <http://alltogether.com>.

Bass, E., and K. Kaufman. (1996). *Free your mind: The book for lesbian, gay, and bisexual youth and their allies.* New York: HarperCollins. Alive with the voices of more than fifty young people, this book speaks to the basic aspects of the lives of LGB youth.

The Cool Page for Queer Teens! Includes all kinds of tips and information, including a special section for transgender youth. <http://www.pe.net/~bidstrup/cool.htm>.

Getting Real, a website from Australia, is aimed at same-sex-attracted young people, their parents, peers, and schools. Find them at <http://gettingreal.org/>.

Glenbard East Echo.(1987). *Voices of conflict.* New York: Adama Books. Teenagers speak for themselves about a variety of personal issues, including queer issues.

Gray, M. (1999). *In your face.* New York: Haworth Press. A compendium of real-life accounts penned by fifteen lesbian and gay youth.

The Indianapolis Youth Group operates the National Gay/Lesbian/Bisexual Youth Hotline, 7:00–11:45 p.m. EST at 1-800-347-TEEN.

Oasis, the world's only monthly webzine for LGBT and questioning youth, has poetry, fiction, feature stories, and columns, as well as extensive links to resources. Join in at <http://www.oasismag.com>.

OutProud! The National Coalition for Gay, Lesbian, Bisexual, and Transgender Youth provides advocacy, support, and resources to LGBT youth and schools and agencies that work with them. 369-B Third St., Suite 362, San Rafael, CA 94901-3581, 415-499-0993, <info@outproud.org, http://www.outproud.org>.

The TransBoy Resource Network (TBoRN) has a comprehensive new website for female-to-male transgendered, transsexual, genderqueer, and questioning youth. This much-needed resource for trans youth answers frequently asked questions and has a host of resources and links to resources. Reach them at <http://www.geocities.com/West Hollywood/Park/6484>.

YOUTH runs a listserv for LGBT and questioning youth ages thirteen to seventeen to talk to each other on issues such as coming out, relationships, friends, parents, school, and other youth issues. Subscribe to YOUTH 13-17 by sending a message to <listproc@critpath.org>. In the body of the message include "subscribe youth 13–17 YourName" without the quotation marks. Visit their website at <http://youth-guard.org/youth/>.

RESOURCES FOR SOCIAL JUSTICE

The Association for Supervision and Curriculum Development Network on Gay and Lesbian Issues for teachers and curriculum directors. Contact ASCD at 1703 N. Beauregard Street, Alexandria, VA 22311-1714, e-mail to <info@ascd.org>, or visit them on the Web at <http://www.ascd.org>.

American Educational Research Association's Lesbian and Gay Studies Special Interest Group provides a forum for researchers and scholars exploring queer issues and education. Contact AERA at 1230 17th Street, NW, Washington, DC 20036-3078, or visit them on the Web at <http://aera.net>.

Deaf Queer Resource Center offers a variety of resources, references, and links. <http//www.deafqueer.org>.

Gay and Lesbian Alliance against Defamation (GLAAD) analyzes mass media and textbooks for antigay bias and advocates for the fair treatment of sexual minorities in the media. <http://www. glaad.org>.

Gay, Lesbian, and Straight Education Network is an organization of educators, parents, students, and other concerned citizens working to end homophobia and promote the valuing and respect of all students in K–12 schools. Contact them at 122 West 26th Street, Suite 1100, New York, NY 10001, 212-727-0135, <glsen@glsen.org>, <http://www.glsen.org/respect>.

The Governor's Commission on Gay and Lesbian Youth (GCGLY) in Massachusetts provides speakers and printed text to help develop a plan for passing gay and lesbian students rights bills in your state or locality, and to help communicate with your local media. GCGLY, State House, Room 111, Boston, MA 02133, 617-727-3600 (ext. 312).

The Hetrick-Martin Institute, a New York–based social service agency, is a leader in providing services for gay youth and publishes *You are not alone: The national lesbian, gay, and bisexual youth directory*. Contact them at 2 Astor Place, New York, NY 10003, 212-674-2400.

Lambda Legal Defense and Education Fund provides support and legal advice for people experiencing sexual-orientation-based discrimination or harassment. 120 Wall St., Suite 1500, New York, NY 10005, 212-809-8585, <http://www.lambdalegal.org>.

National Center for Lesbian Rights can be contacted at 870 Market Street, Suite 570, San Francisco, CA 94102, 415-392-NCLR.

National Education Association has a Gay and Lesbian Caucus under their division of Human and Civil Rights. Contact the NEA at 1201 16th St., NW, Washington, DC 20036-3290, 202-822-7700, or the Caucus at PO Box 3559, York, PA 17402-0559, 717-848-3354.

Public Education Regarding Sexual Orientation Nationally (PERSON) is a listserv that disseminates information about a wide range of issues related to education and sexual orientation, <http://www.youth.org/loco/PERSONProject/>.

Queer Asian Pacific Resources contains references, links, and other information, <http://www.geocities.com/WestHollywood/Heights/5010/resources.html>.

The Rainbow Classroom Network of Ontario, Canada, has as its goals to inform, support, and mobilize people working to create safe and equitable learning environments in schools for gay, lesbian, bisexual, and transgender students, parents, and staff, <http://www.dezines.com/rainbow>.

Rethinking Schools, an activist, urban educational journal published by Milwaukee-area educators, focuses on local and national issues of equity, reform, and social justice. Contact them at 1001 East Keefe Avenue, Milwaukee, WI 53212, 414-964-9646, FAX 414-964-7220, rethink@execpc.com.

The Safe Schools Resource Guide, from the Safe Schools Coalition of Washington State, is an incredibly extensive website with recommendations and strategies, agencies and organizations, and other important resources in a variety of media. A *must* for those associated with schools! Visit them at <http://members. tripod.com/~claytoly/ssp_home>.

School shouldn't hurt: Lifting the burden from gay, lesbian, bisexual, and transgender youth is a report of the Rhode Island Task Force on Gay, Lesbian, Bisexual, and Transgender Youth, 1996, that can be downloaded from the Web. It identifies a number of problems that GLBT youth face in schools and recommends a variety of solutions, <http://members.tripod.com/~twood/safeschools.html>.

SCHOOLS is an e-mail list connecting people working for queer-friendly secondary and elementary schools in the United States. Subscription info is at <http://www.youth-guard.org/schools>.

Teaching Tolerance, from the Southern Poverty Law Center, examines issues of social justice in education. It is mailed free to educators twice a year. Contact them at 400 Washington Avenue, Montgomery, AL 36104, FAX 334-264-3121.

Transgender Resources has information, resources, and links, plus a special section for parents of transgender children. Reach them at <http://www.transgender.org/info/rsrc.html>.

VIDEOS

Both my moms' names are Judy. (1994). Children ages seven to eleven candidly discuss their families, teasing, and classroom silence. Eleven minutes. Available from Lesbian and Gay Parents Association, 6705 California St. #1, San Francisco, CA 94121, 415-387-9886.

Different and the same. A series of nine videos that explore issues of discrimination and prejudice using puppets. Although they do not deal directly with gay and lesbian inclusion, they do draw out themes of social justice as it deals with name-calling and family differences. Available from Family Communications, GPN, PO Box 80669, Lincoln, NE 68501-0669, 800-228-4630.

I know who I am. . . . Do you? A ten-minute documentary featuring black and Latino gay and lesbian youth, detailing their struggles and successes. Produced by Skyline Community, Louis Perego.

It's elementary: Talking about gay issues in school (1996), by Debra Chasnoff and Helen Cohen. Intended for teachers and parents of elementary-aged children, this film details ways in which to educate kids about gay and lesbian issues in school. Women's Educational Media, 2180 Bryant St., Suite 203, San Francisco, CA 94110, 415-641-4616.

Safe schools: Making schools safe for gay and lesbian students. (1997). Targeted to a range of audiences—from administrators and teachers to parents and community members—this twenty-eight-minute video provides an introduction to Massachusetts's Safe Schools Program for Gay and Lesbian Students, in effect since 1993. For more information, or to order the video, contact the Safe Schools Program at 617-388-3300 (ext. 409).

Teaching respect for all. (1996). A comprehensive training video from GLSEN dealing with antigay bias in schools. Produced by Gay, Lesbian, and Straight Education Network, 122 West 26th Street, Suite 1100, New York, NY 10001, 212-727-0135, <glsen@glsen.org, www.glsen.org/respect>.

INDEX

activism: effect of gay/lesbian teachers on that of students, 88–89, 91; by gay/lesbian teachers for gay/lesbian students, 207–16

administrators. *See* school administrators

adoption, by gay/lesbian parents, 167, 168–69, 197, 231–33

Adventures in Time and Place (Banks et al.), 156

agendas, gays/lesbians having, 239–40, 243

AIDS, 258; children of gay/lesbian parents dealing with, 72, 74–75; homophobia and, 16; novel on, 137–49; songs on, 117; teaching about, 18

Amherst, Massachusetts, "Love Makes a Family" shown in, 179–80

Anna Day and the O-Ring (Wickens) (book), 11, 45, 154

Anti-Bias Curriculum, 46

antihomophobic training programs, 219–21, 229–31

artificial insemination: children of lesbian parents understanding, 73; by lesbian parents, 168, 171; teacher dealing with, 171–72

Asha's Mums (Elwin and Paulsee) (book), 11–12, 185

Asian American queer males, 61–70; Asian American communities and, 67–69; changing reading practices and, 69; critical reading strategy and, 64–67; cultural-difference reading strategy and, 62–64; gay/lesbian communities and, 67–69; mainstream society and, 62–67; reading for different citations and, 67–69

assistant principal. *See* lesbian assistant principal

Beecher, Catherine, 29

biology, sexual orientation and, 6–7, 42

biology lesson, sex education in, 19. *See also* science education, heteronormative nature of

black males, in middle schools, 49–59; female teachers and demasculinization of, 54–55; interracial dating and, 52; programs assisting, 55, 57; sexuality and code of masculinized conduct for, 49–54, 56, 57–58; sissies among, 54, 56, 57; transgressive sexualities among, 53–54, 56–57

blacks, as children of gay/lesbian parents, 167, 170

Boston Area Gay and Lesbian Schoolworkers, 84

Both of My Moms' Names Are Judy (Lesbian and Gay Parents Association) (video), 42, 188

Bryant, Anita, 9, 84

Cambridge, Massachusetts, "Love Makes a Family" shown in, 177–78

277

49–54, 56, 57–58; perversity and desire in teaching and, 30–34; regulation of, 32–34; unsaid in discourses on, 30, 31
Shepard, Matthew, 41
silence on gay/lesbian issues, 189, 257–58; homophobia and, 152–53; oppression and, 260–61; on sexuality, 30, 31; by teachers, 17, 18, 20, 130–31, 138, 188–89, 258. *See also* social studies curriculum, silence on gay/lesbian issues in
"Sing About Us" (Pirtle) (song), 121–22
single-parent families, gay/lesbian families designated as, 43
sissy boys: middle-school black males as, 54, 56, 57; teachers and, 8
social studies curriculum, sex education in, 19, 20
social studies curriculum, silence on gay/lesbian issues in, 151–61; implicit *versus* explicit social studies and, 154–55; lack of teacher knowledge on gay/lesbian issues and, 156–58; waiting rather than creating opportunities for gay/lesbian issues and, 155–56
Someone You Know (Pallotta-Chiarolli) (book), 74
songs, 111–24; for adults explaining homosexuality to children, 115–17; on AIDS, 117; for children, 118–22; on discrimination, 117–18; on gay/lesbian couples, 117–18; on gay/lesbian families, 115–16, 117, 118, 119–22; on gender identity, 117; gender roles in, 114–15; messages conveyed by, 122–23; multicultural, 111, 112; for older students and adults, 117–18
South Park, 146
staff meetings, activist teacher raising gay/lesbian issues in, 207–10

Stonewall, in early childhood classroom, 39
straight thinking, interrupting in English classroom, 137–49. *See also* heterosexuality
suicide, gay/lesbian teenagers and, 41, 152, 178, 179, 249
survival, sexual diversity affirmation and, 234

teacher education programs, 237–46; gay/lesbian teachers as danger to students and, 242–44; gays/lesbians having agenda as issue and, 239–40, 243; heteronormativity and, 238–39, 241, 244, 245–46; homophobia in multicultural course in, 247–55; labeling and, 240–41; language as issue and, 237–46; openness as issue and, 238–40, 241, 242–44; straight teachers in as allies and, 244–45; students' lack of experience with diversity and, 247–48, 250
teachers: activism on behalf of gay/lesbian students by, 207–16; alliances with gay/lesbian teachers and, 169, 219; antihomophobic training programs for, 229–31; artificial insemination handled by, 171–72; censorship of gay/lesbian issues in curriculum by, 17, 18, 20; children learning about homosexuality from, 43–44; children of gay/lesbian parents and, 78, 79, 165–66, 183–84, 186–89, 191; children's sense of identity and, 42; communication with families on gay/lesbian issues in classroom by, 46; gay games played by children and, 44; gay/lesbian children and, 207–16, 228–29, 230; gay/lesbian issues handled by, 197, 198, 199, 201–2, 203, 251–52; gay/lesbian parents and, 8, 43–44,

ABOUT THE CONTRIBUTORS

Kathy Bickmore is assistant professor in curriculum and sociology/equity studies at the Ontario Institute for Studies in Education, University of Toronto, having earned her Ph.D. from Stanford. Her research and teaching emphasize conflict resolution and democratic processes in schools, as well as feminist/equity efforts and controversial matters in the politics and practice of curriculum.

Originally from Savannah, Georgia, **Perry Brass** has published eleven books, including novels, short stories, poetry, and nonfiction. His latest, *How to Survive Your Own Gay Life*, deals extensively with surviving antigay violence and the healing, embracing gay tribe. For more information visit him at *www.perrybrass.com*.

Betsy Cahill is coordinator of early childhood education at New Mexico State University. She is coauthor, with Rachel Theilheimer, of a January 1999 *Young Children* article, "Can Tommy and Sam Get Married? Questions about Gender, Sexuality, and Young Children."

Kevin P. Colleary is a doctoral student at the Harvard Graduate School of Education, where he is completing his dissertation on New York City elementary teachers' incorporation of lesbian/gay content into the curriculum.

Formerly an elementary and English as a second language teacher/coordinator, **Greg Curran** is a Ph.D. student at the University of Melbourne, Australia. His research focuses on teachers who seek to be more inclusive of homosexuality in their teaching. He can be reached at gcurran@iname.com.

Barbara Danish was the director of the Writing Center at New York University for eleven years and now teaches in the Art and Design Education Department at Pratt Institute. She is the author of a children's book, *The Dragon and the Doctor* (1996).

James Earl Davis is an associate professor in the School of Education at the University of Delaware. His current research focuses on African American males' construction of masculinity and the effects of college racial and gender environments on students.

Kate Evans has written on prejudice for *JCT: Journal of Curriculum Theorizing* (Winter 1998) and has coauthored a writing book, *Composing the Natural Way* (with Gabriele Rico and Janelle Melvin, in press, Mayfield Press).

Karen Glasgow balances her life between her profession as an assistant principal, her Ph.D. program studying Urban Transformational Leadership at Claremont Graduate University, and her relationship with coauthor Sharon. She cooks Jewish soul food, too.

Pat Hulsebosch is associate professor of elementary education and director of the doctoral program in curriculum and social inquiry at National Louis University. She teaches cultural foundations courses and practicum seminars and has presented and published on the generative potential of parent-teacher partnerships. She has two adult children, and she and her partner of fifteen years are parents of a five-year-old.

A former high school history teacher, **Kevin Jennings** is the founder and executive director of GLSEN, the Gay, Lesbian, and Straight Education Network. Through its ninety-plus local chapters, GLSEN is leading the fight against antigay bias in K–12 schools. Kevin is also the author of three books, including the 1998 Lambda Literary Award winning *Telling Tales out of School.*

Gigi Kaeser is a writer and photographer who, with Peggy Gillespie, chronicled the lives of familes headed by gays and lesbians in the acclaimed photo/text exhibit *Love Makes a Family.*

James R. King is a professor of childhood/language arts/reading at the University of South Florida in Tampa, where he teaches in literacy and qualitative research. He has taught in classrooms ranging from first grade to graduate school. His studies with faculty at Western Michigan and West Virginia universities resulted in two graduate degrees in reading and literacy. Currently, he is researching in queer theory in education and the construction of error and accuracy in writing/reading pedagogy.

Rita M. Kissen is an associate professor in the Department of Teacher Education at the University of Southern Maine. She is the author of *The Last Closet* (1996) as well as a number of articles about teaching for diversity. She is a cofounder and past president of the Portland, Maine, chapter of Parents and Friends of Lesbians and Gays (P-FLAG), and of the southern Maine chapter of the Gay, Lesbian, and Straight Education Network.

Mari E. Koerner is associate dean of the College of Education at Roosevelt University in Chicago, where she is also professor in teacher education. Her research interests include diversity issues and the roles of cooperating teachers in student teaching.

Kevin K. Kumashiro is a doctoral candidate in educational policy studies at the University of Wisconsin–Madison. A former mathematics and English teacher, he is currently researching pedagogies and policies that challenge multiple forms of oppression.

Glorianne M. Leck is a professor of education at Youngstown State University. She moves her life and her work through shifting identities as Susan Savastuk's life partner, as a community activist, a queer, a lesbian, a crone, and as a scholar.

A former science teacher, **Will Letts** is a doctoral candidate in science education, with a minor in science and gender studies, at the University of Delaware. He is also on the faculty of education at Charles Sturt University, Bathurst, Australia, where he teaches courses in science methods to preservice teachers. His areas of research interest include the sociocultural context of science education, queer theory and education, and science teachers' understandings of how issues of cultural diversity relate to their practice. His current research involves elaborating a queer critique of the natural sciences. Reach him at wletts@csu.edu.au.

Rita M. Marinoble is associate professor of counselor education at California State University, Sacramento, where she prepares graduate students for careers in elementary and secondary schools. Previously, she spent fourteen years as a school counselor with the San Diego Unified School District. She is the single parent of two daughters, ages six and nine, adopted from Mexico.

Gregory Martinez is adjunct instructor in teacher education and director of the TRIO Student Support Program at Boise State University. He has earned two master's degrees in education, one in reading and one in curriculum and instruction with an emphasis in bilingual/ESL.

Wayne Martino lectures in the School of Education at Murdoch University in Perth, Western Australia. His research interests involve exploring the links between masculinities and learning, with a particular focus on sexualities. He has published two textbooks, *Gendered Fictions* (Chalkface Press) and *From the Margins: Exploring Ethnicity, Gender, and Aboriginality* (Fremantle Arts Centre Press). Currently he is working on a book for Open University Press with Maria Pallotta-Chiarolli entitled *Schooling Masculinities*.

Margaret Mulhern is an assistant professor of elementary and specialized studies at Boise State University. She received her doctorate from the University of Illinois at Chicago in 1994. Her areas of specialization include multicultural education, bilingual/ESL education, and literacy.

Sharon Murphy is the director of education for Women in Nontraditional Employment Roles (WINTER). She is also a doctoral student at

Claremont Graduate University and San Diego State University exploring critical theory/pedagogy.

Maria Pallotta-Chiarolli lectures in the School of Health Sciences, Deakin University, Melbourne. Her areas of research, writing, and social activism are gender, cultural diversity, sexuality, and HIV/AIDS. She is the author of the AIDS biography *Someone You Know* (Wakefield Press) and *Tapestry* (Random House), about the lives of five generations of women in her family. She is the editor of *Girls Talk: Young Women Speak Their Hearts and Minds* (Finch), a collection of writings and visual pieces about growing up female in Australia.

Eric Rofes teaches in the Department of Education at Bowdoin College and has published nine books, including *Socrates, Plato, and Guys Like Me: Confessions of a Gay Schoolteacher*. He received his doctorate in social and cultural studies in education from the University of California at Berkeley.

Daniel P. Ryan is the director of Baker Demonstration School, a prekindergarten through eighth grade laboratory school at National Louis University. He received his doctorate from Teachers College in educational administration with his dissertation on gay- and lesbian-headed families and school personnel. He and his partner are parents of a four-year-old Guatemalan daughter.

Mara Sapon-Shevin is professor of education in the teaching and leadership department of Syracuse University. She specializes in areas of inclusion, social justice, and diversity. Her most recent book is *Because We Can Change the World: A Practical Guide to Building Cooperative, Inclusive Classroom Communities* (Allyn and Bacon).

Jenifer Jasinski Schneider is an assistant professor of literacy at the University of South Florida, where she teaches writing theory and pedagogy. Her current research centers on writing, process drama, and reconceptualizing the writing processes.

James T. Sears, Ph.D. is an independent scholar living near Charleston, South Carolina, on one of the sea islands, and in cyberspace at www.jtsears.com. The author or editor of eleven books, he has lectured at universities throughout the United States and is a 1995 Southeast Asian Fulbright Senior Research Scholar. Sears serves on the editorial boards of several journals, including *Review of Educational Research, The Journal of Homosexuality, The International Journal of Qualitative Studies in Education*, and the *Journal of Sexual Identity*.

Rachel Theilheimer, Ed.D., assistant professor at Manhattan Community College, coauthored (with Betsy Cahill) "A Messy Closet in the Early Childhood Classroom," a manuscript under consideration for a chapter in a book about reconceptualizing early education.

Lisa Weems is a doctoral candidate in the Cultural Studies of Education Program at Ohio State University. She works with both preservice and in-service teachers in the areas of history of education and qualitative research methodology. Prior to OSU she served as a counselor/advocate with a pregnancy-prevention program for early adolescents.